164418

Mark Twain on tł

D1606074

DATE DUE

"Full-Dressed Tourist," from *The Innocents Abroad* (Hartford, CT: American Publishing Company, 1869).

Mark Twain on the Move

A Travel Reader

Edited and with an Introduction by
Alan Gribben and Jeffrey Alan Melton

THE UNIVERSITY OF ALABAMA PRESS
Tuscaloosa

<Designer?>
Typeface: Caslon

∞

The paper on which this book is printed meets the minimum requirements of American National Standard for Information Sciences-Permanence of Paper for Printed Library Materials, ANSI Z39.48-1984.

Library of Congress Cataloging-in-Publication Data

Twain, Mark, 1835–1910.
 Mark Twain on the move : a travel reader / edited and with an introduction by Alan Gribben and Jeffrey Alan Melton.
  p. cm. — (Studies in American literary realism and naturalism)
 Includes index.
 ISBN 978-0-8173-1640-2 (cloth : alk. paper) — ISBN 978-0-8173-5521-0 (pbk. : alk. paper) — ISBN 978-0-8173-8123-3 (electronic) 1. Twain, Mark, 1835-1910—Travel 2. Europe—Description and travel. 3. Middle East—Description and travel. 4. West (U.S.)—Description and travel. 5. Hawaii—Description and travel. I. Gribben, Alan. II. Melton, Jeffrey Alan, 1962– III. Title.
 PS1302.G7 2009
 818′.409—dc22

TWA   2008014742

Contents

List of Illustrations   ix

Introduction   xi

Note on the Texts   xxi

1.   *The Innocents Abroad* (1869)   1

2.   *Roughing It* (1872)   67

3.   *A Tramp Abroad* (1880)   111

4.   *Life on the Mississippi* (1883)   169

5.   *Following the Equator* (1897)   201

Selected Readings   221

Index   225

Illustrations

Frontispiece   ii

1. "The Pilgrim's Vision" from *The Innocents Abroad*   xxiv

2. "The Miner's Dream" from *Roughing It*   66

3. "The Caravan" from *A Tramp Abroad*   110

4. "The Tower" from *A Tramp Abroad*   116

5. "Leaving Heilbronn" from *A Tramp Abroad*   118

6. "My Picture of the Matterhorn" from *A Tramp Abroad*   163

7. "The 'Baton Rouge'" from *Life on the Mississippi*   168

8. "Cab Substitute" from *Following the Equator*   200

Introduction

Travel books became a crucial forum for nineteenth-century Americans to discover the beckoning world. Even literary figures who principally distinguished themselves in other genres—including Washington Irving, Margaret Fuller, Julia Ward Howe, William Dean Howells, and Henry James—became partly dependent on the income from this genre. Behind every strolling tourist with a travel book in hand sat countless other less adventurous readers who merely traveled vicariously. As Benjamin Moran observed in 1859, "This would seem to be the age of *travel literature,* judging from the many narratives now published, and the general excellence of such works. No nation has given more good books of this class to the world since 1820 than the United States, considered with regard to styles or information."[1] Harold Smith estimates that nearly two thousand travel books were published in the United States before 1900, excluding those describing areas within the continental forty-eight states. Virtually all major newspapers and periodicals in the latter nineteenth century featured travel sections.

Travel literature, by its nature a composite literary form, combines elements of autobiography, journalism, history, geography, anthropology, political science, and fiction (among other possible categories) into smorgasbord narratives. More than anything else, travel writing exhibits a strong sense of *self* and *place.*[2] A first-person narrator within this convention ventures into unknown realms and ostensibly learns from these experiences. Readers follow a personal journey that is physical, intellectual, and emotional all at once. The presence of a self-conscious narrator separates the travel book from the guidebook, or from works purely of history or journalism. Of course, this self has to go to some new place in order to distinguish travel from memoir. It is this movement that provides narrative tension and interest as a self-absorbed traveler interacts with unfamiliar surroundings.

Travel writing both fueled a cultural transformation and followed it as well. Readers clamored for travel books not only to revel in foreign vistas but also to prepare for their own conquests. These narratives additionally afforded the benefit of conferring aesthetic standards and cultural identity for anxious new generations of Americans. One inevitable consequence of the popularity of the travel genre was its yielding to predictable formulas, especially in the hands of numerous inferior writers. Its structure grew repetitive as more and more authors trod the same ground, weighing down the literary turf and creating ruts all too easy to recognize. Nonetheless, the most capable practitioners of the field left behind a vital and provocative record of how Americans saw the international community and themselves.

The twin assignments of instructing and entertaining charged the writers to enable their readers to learn something of value while enjoying that process. Authors needed to balance factual material with less heavy fare. Many pages of these books were typically larded with heights, weights, distances, populations, temperatures, and expenses—anything from the average yearly rainfall in Rome to the number of cats in Constantinople. In this regard travel books endeavored to appear "realistic" in reporting exactly and objectively what the writer had witnessed. Yet this side of the narrative had to be counterbalanced with admiration for natural beauty and fine art, often expressed in terms of romantic rapture. Readers desired the most fulfilling and uplifting rhetoric possible; the genre hardly encouraged understatement. Mere physical descriptions of any wonder, from Lake Tahoe to St. Peter's Cathedral to the Sphinx, required emotional and spiritual reactions as well.

The travel book was (and remains) a highly subjective narrative form wholly based on cultural baggage and individual circumstance. This subjectivity, however, gave the genre a vibrancy and lasting appeal. It also ensured that travel readers could count on acquiring books that introduced them to international cultures while simultaneously affirming their own national pride. That complacency may have reflected a disagreeable chauvinism, but it also signaled the fact of political and cultural ascendancy. As one prominent author emphatically and unapologetically declared:

"We always took care to make it understood that we were Americans—
Americans!"[3]

That particular spokesman was Mark Twain. In June 1867 an enthusi-
astic group of well-to-do Americans boarded the steamship *Quaker City*
and left the New York City harbor, beginning a five-month voyage around
the Mediterranean Sea. This much-publicized Holy Land tour incongru-
ously took aboard an itinerant journalist, humorous lecturer, and author
of a book of comical sketches, Mark Twain, who had neither the means
nor the respectability to associate in normal society with his shipmates.
The fact of the matter was that despite manifold improvements in speed
and accommodations, in the second half of the nineteenth century the diversions and pleasures of extended "travel" remained luxuries that the majority of Americans still could not afford. To be sure, ordinary people in
that day definitely made "trips," even traversing the oceans and penetrat-
ing the vast American continent, but this was generally for the purpose
of relocating—to be closer to relatives, to follow job prospects, to explore
the lure of a better life in the West. Only the truly affluent could enjoy the
privilege of lengthy "travel," either domestic or foreign, for the purposes
of seeing new sights, meeting ethnic people, shopping for unusual goods,
sampling exotic cuisines, and savoring the contrast of cultures.

There was, nevertheless, one expedient by which a professional writer
could afford distant journeys aboard the increasingly efficient and ex-
panding railway lines and steamship fleets: by recording his or her adventures in journals, then sending off travel correspondence for publication
in newspapers and magazines, eventually compiling the letters chapter-
by-chapter into books, and subsequently joining the lecture circuit to pro-
mote these publications. Availing himself of this tried-and-true formula,
a dauntless literary comedian whose name was gaining recognition had
already found it possible to visit the Hawaiian Islands and would now
manage to investigate Europe and the Holy Land; later Twain would rely
upon the same methods to return to Europe several times, make a celebrated visit back to his hometown and river landmarks of his youth, and
eventually circumvent the globe on a grand finale tour that made headlines wherever he went.

Twain's correspondence from Europe and the Middle East, written in
the course of the *Quaker City* voyage, would announce a transformation

in the history of American tourism and travel writing. This alteration in American identity was recorded by an American innocent destined to grow into his nation's most beloved international traveler and its most popular public face to the world. All five of Twain's travel narratives—*The Innocents Abroad* (1869), *Roughing It* (1872), *A Tramp Abroad* (1880), *Life on the Mississippi* (1883), and *Following the Equator* (1897)—evinced quintessentially "American" qualities.

His first and best-selling travel book debunked the Old World and elements of the Holy Land that had been slavishly and redundantly eulogized by preceding generations of writers. After a little more than a decade he would go back to European scenes as a less brash and thoroughly self-indulgent man of leisure. Between these two books he delved into the heart of American mythology about Wild West desperadoes and mining camps, and later found his way back to the symbolic center of the country, the Mississippi River. Human folly continued to be his endless subject, whether amid desert canyons or crumbling castles. His final travel narrative provided a bookend for the first three decades of American mass tourism and marked a huge shift in tone and subject. Understanding that the days of innocence were gone forever, Twain acknowledged complicity in European and American imperialism. He closed that work with a simple statement: "Human pride is not worth while; there is always something lying in wait to take the wind out of it."[4]

None of his journeys was ever particularly easy, and ill-humor could understandably have been excused in any traveler. From the Clemens brothers' jouncing ride across rutted prairies and sandy wastelands in an overland stage coach in 1861 to Twain's pivotal voyage on the *Quaker City* in 1867 to his later crossings of the Atlantic for business and recreational purposes, the very act of travel itself in that era was predictably uncomfortable and often risky. Sailing for New York City on the *San Francisco* in 1866, he watched apprehensively as eight of his fellow passengers succumbed to cholera. Only a few months after Twain revisited the scene of his piloting days in 1882 to gather material for the book that would become *Life on the Mississippi,* the steamboat from which he had recently disembarked, the *Gold Dust,* exploded, killing one of the pilots whom he had interviewed and seriously injuring the other one. In fact, steamboat fires, explosions, and sinkings were so unexceptional that one can scarcely glance over a nineteenth-century newspaper without encountering headlines about some disaster on an interior waterway of the United States. Clemens's younger brother Henry, scalded when the *Pennsylvania* blew up and burned in 1858, was one of the many thousands of fatalities resulting from steamboat catastrophes. In view of all the times that Samuel Clemens piloted steamers up and down the vast Mississippi River, it is nothing short of a miracle that he survived to become a famous author and live into his mid-seventies.

And if steamboats were a dangerous form of travel, railroads were only slightly less hazardous. Charles Dickens, among many possible examples, was badly shaken up when a train on which he was riding left the tracks in England. As for ocean voyages, shipwrecks in those days of undependable lighthouses and shipboard fires were such common occurrences as to make their tolls resemble a form of inescapable fate. War correspondent and novelist Stephen Crane's grueling ordeal in an open boat following the sinking of his ship, the *Commodore,* off Florida in 1897 would weaken his health and hasten his early death. The *Titanic* disaster, which occurred two years after Twain's passing, was only notable for its toll, not its unusualness.

The more routine rigors of travel were themselves incessant and unpleasant to extremes. The basic task of finding palatable drinking water, let alone safe and tasty foodstuffs, was something never to be taken for granted. Toilet facilities were often too primitive to describe. Again and again in his writings Twain complains about the lice and bedbugs that infested his hotel beds. Steamboats shivered and clanged from the noisy engines; train coaches were hot and stuffy in the summer unless the passengers were willing to open the windows and brave the smoke, soot, and cinders that blew in; in the winter a single stove at one end inefficiently under-heated or overheated each train coach; ocean steamers pitched and rolled mercilessly. It took a strong stomach and a sturdy constitution to travel in the nineteenth century, along with, quite frankly, considerable courage. Mark Twain, like his fellow professional travel correspondents, took most of these perils and discomforts in stride, overlooking them in favor of scenic sights and humorous incidents—and the occasional moment of monumental revelation. He pioneered as well as encouraged the legions of travelers and tourists who would follow him in the succeeding century.

The loneliness of travel Twain was always willing to stave off by soliciting companionship. Travel partners often became comic foils to his opinions and experiences and allowed him the chance to create fictionalized conflicts along with moments of genuine enjoyment. "Mr. Brown" served these purposes usefully in Twain's letters from Hawaii to the *Sacramento Union,* appeared briefly in the letters written during the *Quaker City* cruise, and became "Mr. Billings" in a few chapters of *Roughing It.* "Harris," partly inspired by the Reverend Joseph H. Twichell, went with Twain as a vaguely appointed "agent" in *A Tramp Abroad.* James R. Osgood, an obliging publisher, is alluded to as "Rogers" in *Life on the Mississippi.* And of course Twain's wife Olivia and daughter Clara are real-life companions in *Following the Equator,* and bear their own identities. Behind these stratagems lay a truth that every traveler soon learns about the emptiness of solo journeys. As Twain wrote in a maxim he posted above chapter 48 of *Following the Equator,* "To get the full value of a joy you must have somebody to divide it with."

While his ability to work with and against conventional formulas served Twain well, it was his masterful blend of self and place that demonstrated his gifts. Travel writing proved to be a perfect fit for his keen skills at observation, and the genre permitted him the freedom to hold forth on nearly any subject that struck his fancy. Richard Bridgman's *Traveling in Mark Twain* insightfully points out how this type of authorship enabled Twain to tap into his native talent: "All that the form demanded Twain had in abundance: curiosity, a reactive intelligence, and stamina."[5] Larzer Ziff concurs, calling travel narratives "a perfect vehicle for Twain's imagination."[6] His body of travel writing had no peer in its tremendous versatility or its power of implication. Twain's portraits of his native country and prominent parts of the international community were instrumental in transporting travelogues from the days of quaint line etchings to an age of instantly evocative photographs.

Because his contemporary audience primarily associated him with descriptive writing on the road—a fact that often surprises twenty-first-century readers—Twain was more readily recognized in his day as a travel writer and comic lecturer than as the author of novels, short stories, and essays, many of them serious in nature. "Say!—Mark!—is he dead?" someone shouted out repeatedly from a lecture audience in Melbourne, Australia in 1895, alluding to Twain's joshing interrogation of a European tour guide in *The Innocents Abroad.*[7] In yelling this tribute the fan notably drew on Twain's earliest travel book rather than on *Tom Sawyer* or *Huckleberry Finn*. From the date of his return from the Sandwich Islands in 1866 and his subsequent decision to offer a series of clever platform performances based on his travel letters, Twain's inimitable "takes" on his visits to foreign climes became a staple of his public persona. His full-length foreign travel narratives, sometimes previewed in the form of serialized newspaper and magazine "letters"—*The Innocents Abroad, A Tramp Abroad*, and *Following the Equator*—held a deep and abiding attraction for English-speaking people everywhere. To these travelogues could also be added those portions of *Roughing It* and *Life on the Mississippi* that depicted the arduous nature of travel in the Far West and the vocational challenges confronting a pilot, prospector, or journalist in the Mississippi Valley and in Nevada and California.

The name "Mark Twain" became so thoroughly and indelibly linked with adventurous travel that the author occasionally capitalized on this expectation in titling and plotting fictional books such as *Tom Sawyer Abroad* (1894), in which a balloon and its bewildered passengers drift across entire oceans and continents. Similarly, Twain's two most famous titles show this tendency for the momentum of his travels to carry over into his fiction: Tom Sawyer and his mischievous comrades row out to Jackson's Island in *The Adventures of Tom Sawyer* (1876), and that same island then serves as the jumping-off point for a much longer and more complicated down-river journey undertaken by a fleeing boy and a runaway slave in *Adventures of Huckleberry Finn* (1885). *The Gilded Age: A Tale of To-day* (1873), co-written with Charles Dudley Warner, contains several chapters depicting river steamboating and other chapters portraying American towns, cities, and states. The young hero of *The Prince and the Pauper* (1881), his identity mistaken, unwillingly takes a dangerous tour of his nation. Twelve of the liveliest chapters in *A Connecticut Yankee in King Arthur's Court* (1889) chronicle the foot travels of the incognito King and the Yankee through medieval England during which they witness disturbing social injustices. "It was not a dull excursion for me," remarks the Yankee in chapter 31. "I made various acquaintanceships, and in my quality of stranger was able to ask as many questions as I wanted to."[8]

Over the years, however, Twain's narratives took ever more fantastic trips through time and historical settings in works like *A Connec-*

ticut Yankee and in the manuscripts known as *The Mysterious Stranger,* along with accounts of nightmarish voyages in "The Enchanted Sea-Wilderness," "An Adventure in Remote Seas," and "Three Thousand Years among the Microbes." *Extract from Captain Stormfield's Visit* (1909) recounts a celestial journey accomplished at meteoric speed. One might say that Twain's habits of travel became ingrained in his literary patterns, and that eventually mere earthly destinations grew too confining for his progressively unfettered imagination.

Discerning readers in Twain's day readily recognized his talents. The *Cleveland Leader* applauded *The Innocents Abroad* because of Twain's "straight-forward, matter-of-fact way of recording his impressions that is a great relief after the straining, high-pitched carols of most European voyagers. He makes no profession to the rhapsodies which most travellers bestow upon everything that smacks of the antique, and he tells in plain, honest terms what he really saw and felt."[9] *The Spectator* greeted *A Tramp Abroad* as a one-of-a-kind achievement: "There is little in modern literature with which it can be compared outside the previous works of Mark Twain himself. He is the greatest writer living of travels containing an odd mixture of sober truth, droll exaggeration, and occasional buffoonery, all mixed up together in the most incongruous way imaginable."[10] Another reviewer of *A Tramp Abroad* wrote similarly: "For a thoroughly genial travelling companion, one who knows how to combine instruction with amusement, who notices everything that is worth observing, and records his observation in a way that cannot fail to interest, who is never prosy, but in whose lively chatter there is some good suggestion, commend us to Mark Twain."[11] Even when Twain's subject matter was confined to his own country, as in *Life on the Mississippi, The Critic* declared that "this quiet fun, infinitely more original and enjoyable than broad farce, gives the book a humorous flavor; but the actual information . . . is of literary value quite apart from any of the fun."[12]

All the same, during the intervening century since Twain's death in 1910 his travel books have been vastly eclipsed in stature and readership by his novels, short stories, and essays. Indeed, periods have occurred when neither *A Tramp Abroad* nor *Following the Equator* was even in print. Few high school or college students nowadays have heard of the titles of Mark Twain's travel works, let alone absorbed their contents, whereas no such oblivion has ever been the fate of *The Adventures of Tom Sawyer, Adventures of Huckleberry Finn,* or, for that matter, *The Prince and the Pauper, A Connecticut Yankee in King Arthur's Court, The Tragedy of Pudd'nhead Wilson,* or *The Mysterious Stranger,* not to mention a perennial favorite, "The Celebrated Jumping Frog of Calaveras County." Twain's travel narratives—along with his image as a man almost continually roving—have for all intents and purposes slipped out of the public's consciousness. This is a pity, because embedded in the tales of his journeys, whether whimsical or serious in tone, are nuggets of wit and acuity that rival anything in his fiction or other prose. He saw the world with an unrelenting skepticism and keenness that have clearly affected successful modern travel writers like Paul Theroux and Bill Bryson. People who peruse Twain's travel books never see the world quite the same—or as trustingly—again.

In the infrequent instances when a couple of excerpts from his books of travel have been granted inclusion in literary anthologies or college textbooks, the pieces chosen typically repeat the same familiar selections—"Jim Baker's Blue-Jay Yarn," "Lost in the Snow," "Buck Fanshaw's Funeral," "Jim Blaine and His Grandfather's Ram," and a few others. Superb in their own ways, they nevertheless more effectively represent the traditions of tall tales, animal fables, comic monologues, social histories, or autobiography than Twain's marvelous skills at capturing atmosphere and place.[13] Presumably selected because of their self-contained structures, those stories and sketches hardly convey the restless movement that stamped so much of Mark Twain's life and literature. Has anyone ever counted the incredible number of Twain's lifetime addresses? It is a question worth pondering. These dozens of removes hint at the wanderlust that so often took him away from his houses and apartments and villas. Even in the summers of his most domesticated family years, he left Hartford and camped out, as it were, on the high elevation of East Hill outside Elmira where he could look down on the gleaming Chemung River and imagine that he was once again a roaming pilot or a travel correspondent.

By contrast with nearly all of the earlier collections that have sampled Twain's travel works,[14] the present volume more authentically introduces this neglected Mark Twain, a man en route, out of his comfortable element, on the road, on the seas, on trains, matching his travel skills against the inconveniences and hazards of living away from home and earning the thrills and diversions that the unfamiliar can bring. These writings deliver an undiluted Twain, the author as he was known and loved in his own day, vintage glimpses of Mark Twain on the move.

Notes

1. Benjamin Moran, "Contributions Towards a History of American Literature," *Trubner's Bibliographic Guide to American Literature,* ed. Nicholas Trubner (London: Trubner, 1859): lvi.

2. For more extended discussions of travel books, see William W. Stowe, *Going Abroad: European Travel in Nineteenth-Century Culture* (Princeton: Princeton UP, 1994), pp. 3–15, and Jeffrey Alan Melton, *Mark Twain, Travel Books, and Tourism* (Tuscaloosa: U of Alabama P, 2002), pp. 16–58.

3. Mark Twain, *The Innocents Abroad,* ed. Shelley Fisher Fishkin et al. (New York: Oxford UP, 1996), p. 645.

4. Mark Twain, *Following the Equator,* ed. Shelley Fisher Fishkin et al. (New York: Oxford UP, 1996), p. 712.

5. Richard Bridgman, *Traveling in Mark Twain* (Berkeley: U of California P, 1987), p. 30.

6. Larzer Ziff, *Return Passages: Great American Travel Writing, 1780–1910* (New Haven, CT: Yale UP, 2000), p. 174.

7. Miriam Jones Shillingsburg, *At Home Abroad: Mark Twain in Australasia* (Jackson: UP of Mississippi, 1988), p. 65. Twain reports the line, as we have given it, in Chapter 16 of *Following the Equator,* p. 167.

8. Mark Twain, *A Connecticut Yankee in King Arthur's Court,* ed. Bernard L. Stein (Berkeley: U of California P, 1979), p. 349.

9. *Mark Twain: The Contemporary Reviews,* ed. Louis J. Budd (Cambridge: Cambridge UP, 1999), p. 64.

10. *Mark Twain: The Contemporary Reviews,* p. 191.

11. From *The Congregationalist,* reprinted in *Mark Twain: The Contemporary Reviews,* p. 193.

12. *Mark Twain: The Contemporary Reviews,* p. 254.

13. See, for example, Joseph Csicsila's compilation of the most popular selections in college classroom textbooks in *Canons by Consensus: Critical Trends and American Literature Anthologies* (Tuscaloosa: U of Alabama P, 2004), pp. 87–106.

14. Two rare exceptions have been *The Travels of Mark Twain,* ed. Charles Neider (New York: Coward-McCann, 1961), and *Mark Twain on Travel,* ed. Terry Mort (Guilford, CT: Lyons Press, 2005), both of which reprint Twain's actual "travel" writings but arrange them geographically.

Note on the Texts

The process of winnowing Mark Twain's travel works down to the contents of a single volume proved tremendously frustrating because we were obliged to eliminate so many superb passages. Twain himself summarized our thoughts about that necessarily brutal editorial process when, in *The Innocents Abroad,* he neatly expressed his feelings about crossing a desolate desert landscape: "Fun—but of a mild type."

The excerpts collected here follow the texts of the first American editions of Twain's five travel books. There are problems with this, of course, mainly owing to the typesetters' errors. However, for *Mark Twain on the Move* we decided to make emendations only when essential to understanding the meaning of a sentence, and we have retained the original punctuation even when it is inconsistent or outdated according to current standards. Likewise, we allowed spellings ("trowsers," "mattrasses"), place names ("Wäggis"), and capitalizations ("4 P.M.") to stand as they initially appeared. We restricted ourselves to silent corrections of the most obvious misprints, such as a single instance of "Baedecker" rather than "Baedeker." Our sole concern was whether any particular sentence could be comprehended by the general reader.

The chapters chosen for inclusion are frequently abbreviated at their beginning or their end, but each of the selected extracts is presented without any internal deletions. We have supplied bracketed headings ("[Venice]") to orient the reader as to Twain's geographical locations.

Mark Twain on the Move

1. "The Pilgrim's Vision," frontispiece from *The Innocents Abroad* (Hartford, CT: American Publishing Company, 1869)

I

The Innocents Abroad (1869)

"Isn't it a most attractive scheme?" Mark Twain wrote to the editors of the *San Francisco Daily Alta California* on March 2, 1867. "Five months of utter freedom from care and anxiety of every kind, and in company with a set of people who will go only to enjoy themselves, and will never mention a word about business during the whole voyage." He was referring to the *Quaker City*'s "Pleasure Excursion to Europe and the Holy Land"— America's first luxury cruise. The editors of the *Alta* agreed to pay Twain's passage in exchange for travel letters documenting the auspicious journey back to the Old World. Thus began the chain of events that would result in Twain's first and best-selling book and set him upon a lucrative thirty-year travel-writing career. *The Innocents Abroad* launched Mark Twain as a man who could evoke an American perspective of the world and situated him as the humorous mouthpiece for this nonchalant point of view.

The excursionists began their tour on June 8, 1867, embarking on an itinerary Twain called "a brave conception" and a "picnic on a gigantic scale." The trip's ambitious program offered a five-month tour around the Mediterranean Sea, with additional options for excursions into southern Europe, Asia Minor, the Holy Land, and Egypt. Much of America followed the trip via his letters, along with correspondence from other tourists on board, so by the time the *Quaker City* returned to New York on November 19, the journey had been well-recorded in newspapers across the nation. The positive reception of Twain's letters allowed him to return a rising star. That popularity might have been short lived had it not been for the ultimate release of his full travel book in July 1869 by the American Publishing Company out of Hartford, Connecticut. It was *The Innocents Abroad* that recorded the *Quaker City* Pleasure Excursion for posterity. Even though he likened the tour to a funeral without a corpse, Twain was certain that the tourists nonetheless impressed upon the people of the Old World that there was a new force to be reckoned with: "The people stared at us every where, and we stared at them," he wrote. "We generally made them feel rather small, too, before we got done with them, because we bore down on them with America's greatness until we crushed them."

Twain manifests this air of insolent nationalism throughout the tour, snubbing many grandiose pretensions of Old World culture. He shows readers that the Old World, if viewed honestly through definitively American eyes, falls far short of overblown expectations. A natural and logical theme of any travel book derives from the inevitable differences between expectations and realities, and Twain employs the disappointments as a touchstone throughout the tour.

Twain's preface claims that his purpose is "to suggest to the reader how *he* would be likely to see Europe and the East if he looked at them with his own eyes instead of the eyes of those who traveled in those countries before him. I make small pretense of showing anyone how he *ought* to look at objects of interest beyond the sea." Statements of humility were common in nineteenth-century travel writing, but Twain's vow to see with his "own eyes" stands as an assertive statement of nationality in the bustling aftermath of the American Civil War. He metaphorically grants his readers the dignity of seeing the older world without pretension, without supplication, and with plenty of comedy. The balance of the narrative fulfills this promise. That consistency of independent thought illustrates Twain's re-invention of the American self as an appraising participant in a new world order. In places there is reverence or even sentiment—in Athens and Jerusalem, for instance—but it was the irreverence that most captivated readers and generations of critics. They responded to Twain's engaged reactions to the Old World grace and history, ornaments and shams.

While waiting to board the *Quaker City*, Twain wrote to his mother: "All I do know or feel, is, that I am wild with impatience to move, move— *Move!* Half a dozen times I have wished I had sailed long ago in some ship that wasn't going to keep me chained here to chafe for lagging ages while she got ready to go." Frustrated by problems with the departure of the *Quaker City* Pleasure Excursion, Twain's remarks also signaled his growing eagerness to get on with his life. In his early thirties, unsettled personally and professionally, Twain was indeed eager to "move." Little could he have guessed then that he would eventually travel to the four corners of the globe and achieve a literary and cultural status far removed from the Missouri village of his youth. The voyage recounted in *The Innocents Abroad* gave him the opportunity to claim a singularly prominent place in the world.

The following passages capture tourism and tourists like no other American travel narrative. The wit, charm, cynicism, bombast, and insight that stamped his literary career are here in full force.

From THE INNOCENTS ABROAD

[Paris, Chapter 12]

We have come five hundred miles by rail through the heart of France. What a bewitching land it is!—What a garden! Surely the leagues of bright green lawns are swept and brushed and watered every day and their grasses trimmed by the barber. Surely the hedges are shaped and measured and their symmetry preserved by the most architectural of gardeners. Surely the long straight rows of stately poplars that divide the beautiful landscape like the squares of a checker-board are set with line and plummet, and their uniform height determined with a spirit level. Surely the straight, smooth, pure white turnpikes are jack-planed and sandpapered every day. How else are these marvels of symmetry, cleanliness and order attained? It is wonderful. There are no unsightly stone walls, and never a fence of any kind. There is no dirt, no decay, no rubbish any where—nothing that even hints at untidiness—nothing that ever suggests neglect. All is orderly and beautiful—every thing is charming to the eye.

We had such glimpses of the Rhone gliding along between its grassy banks; of cosy cottages buried in flowers and shrubbery; of quaint old red-tiled villages with mossy mediæval cathedrals looming out of their midst; of wooded hills with ivy-grown towers and turrets of feudal castles projecting above the foliage; such glimpses of Paradise, it seemed to us, such visions of fabled fairy-land!

We knew, then, what the poet meant, when he sang of— "—thy corn-fields green, and sunny vines, /O pleasant land of France!"

And it *is* a pleasant land. No word describes it so felicitously as that one. They say there is no word for "home" in the French language. Well, considering that they have the article itself in such an attractive aspect, they ought to manage to get along without the word. Let us not waste too much pity on "homeless" France. I have observed that Frenchmen abroad seldom wholly give up the idea of going back to France some time or other. I am not surprised at it now.

We are not infatuated with these French railway cars, though. We took first class passage, not because we wished to attract attention by doing a thing which is uncommon in Europe, but because we could make our journey quicker by so doing. It is hard to make railroading pleasant, in any country. It is too tedious. Stage-coaching is infinitely more delightful. Once I crossed the plains and deserts and mountains of the West, in a stage-coach, from the Missouri line to California, and since then all my pleasure trips must be measured to that rare holiday frolic. Two thousand miles of ceaseless rush and rattle and clatter, by night and by day, and never a weary moment, never a lapse of interest! The first seven hundred miles a level continent, its grassy carpet greener and softer and smoother than any sea, and figured with designs fitted to its magnitude—the shadows of the clouds. Here were no scenes but summer scenes, and no disposition inspired by them but to lie at full length on the mail sacks, in the grateful breeze, and dreamily smoke the pipe of peace—what other, where all was repose and contentment? In cool mornings, before the sun was fairly up, it was worth a lifetime of city toiling and moiling, to perch in the foretop with the driver and see the six mustangs scamper under the sharp snapping of a whip that never touched them; to scan the blue distances of a world that knew no lords but us; to cleave the wind with uncovered head and feel the sluggish pulses rousing to the spirit of a speed that pretended to the resistless rush of a typhoon! Then thirteen hundred miles of desert solitudes; of limitless panoramas of bewildering perspective; of mimic cities, of pinnacled cathedrals, of massive fortresses, counterfeited in the eternal rocks and splendid with the crimson and gold of the setting sun; of dizzy altitudes among fog-wreathed peaks and never-melting snows, where thunders and lightnings and tempests warred magnificently at our feet and the storm-clouds above swung their shredded banners in our very faces!

But I forgot. I am in elegant France, now, and not skurrying through the great South Pass and the Wind River Mountains, among antelopes and buffaloes, and painted Indians on the war path. It is not meet that I should make too disparaging comparisons between hum-drum travel on a railway and that royal summer flight across a continent in a stage-coach. I meant in the beginning, to say that railway journeying is tedious and tiresome, and so it is—though at the time, I was thinking particularly of a dismal fifty-hour pilgrimage between New York and St. Louis. Of course our trip through France was not really tedious, because all its scenes and experiences were new and strange; but as Dan says, it had its "discrepancies."

The cars are built in compartments that hold eight persons each. Each compartment is partially subdivided, and so there are two tolerably distinct parties of four in it. Four face the other four. The seats and backs are thickly padded and cushioned and are very comfortable; you can smoke, if you wish; there are no bothersome peddlers; you are saved the infliction of a multitude of disagreeable fellow-passengers. So far, so well. But then the conductor locks you in when the train starts; there is no water to drink, in the car; there is no heating apparatus for night travel; if a drunken rowdy should get in, you could not remove a matter of twenty seats from him, or enter another car; but above all, if you are worn out and must sleep, you must sit up and do it in naps, with cramped legs and in a torturing misery that leaves you withered and lifeless the next day—for behold they have not that culmination of all charity and human kindness, a sleeping car, in all France. I prefer the American system. It has not so many grievous "discrepancies."

In France, all is clockwork, all is order. They make no mistakes. Every third man wears a uniform, and whether he be a Marshal of the Empire or a brakeman, he is ready and perfectly willing to answer all your questions with tireless politeness, ready to tell you which car to take, yea, and ready to go and put you into it to make sure that you shall not go astray. You can not pass into the waiting-room of the depot till you have secured your ticket, and you can not pass from its only exit till the train is at its threshold to receive you. Once on board, the train will not start till your ticket has been examined—till every passenger's ticket has been inspected. This is chiefly for your own good. If by any possibility you have managed to take the wrong train, you will be handed over to a polite official who will take you whither you belong, and bestow you with many an affable bow. Your ticket will be inspected every now and then along the route, and when it is time to change cars you will know it. You are in the hands of officials who zealously study your welfare and your interest, instead of turning their talents to the invention of new methods of discommoding and snubbing you, as is very often the main employment of that exceedingly self-satisfied monarch, the railroad conductor of America.

But the happiest regulation in French railway government, is—thirty minutes to dinner! No five-minute boltings of flabby rolls, muddy coffee, questionable eggs, gutta-percha beef, and pies whose conception and execution are a dark and bloody mystery to all save the cook that created them! No; we sat calmly down—it was in old Dijon, which is so easy to spell and so impossible to pronounce, except when you civilize it and call it Demijohn—and poured out rich Burgundian wines and munched calmly through a long table d'hote bill of fare, snail-patties, delicious fruits and all, then paid the trifle it cost and stepped happily aboard the train again, without once cursing the railroad company. A rare experience, and one to be treasured forever.

They say they do not have accidents on these French roads, and I think it must be true. If I remember rightly, we passed high above wagon roads, or through tunnels under them, but never crossed them on their own level. About every quarter of a mile, it seemed to me, a man came out and held up a club till the train went by, to signify that every thing was safe ahead. Switches were changed a mile in advance, by pulling a wire rope that passed along the ground by the rail, from station to station. Signals for the day and signals for the night gave constant and timely notice of the position of switches.

No, they have no railroad accidents to speak of in France. But why? Because when one occurs, *somebody* has to hang for it! They go on the principle that it is better that one innocent man should suffer than five hundred. Not hang, may be, but be punished at least with such vigor of emphasis as to make negligence a thing to be shuddered at by railroad officials for many a day thereafter. "No blame attached to the officers"—that lying and disaster-breeding verdict so common to our soft-hearted juries, is seldom rendered in France. If the trouble occurred in the conductor's department, that officer must suffer if his subordinate can not be proven guilty; if in the engineer's department and the case be similar, the engineer must answer.

The Old Travelers—those delightful parrots who have "been here before," and know more about the country than Louis Napoleon knows now or ever will know,—tell us these things, and we believe them because they are pleasant things to believe, and because they are plausible and savor of the rigid subjection to law and order which we behold about us every where.

But we love the Old Travelers. We love to hear them prate, and drivel and lie. We can tell them the moment we see them. They always throw out a few feelers; they never cast themselves adrift till they have sounded every individual and know that he has not traveled. Then they open their throttle-valves, and how they do brag, and sneer, and swell, and soar, and blaspheme the sacred name of Truth! Their central idea, their grand aim, is to subjugate you, keep you down, make you feel insignificant and humble in the blaze of their cosmopolitan glory! They will not let you know any thing. They sneer at your most inoffensive suggestions; they laugh unfeelingly at your treasured dreams of foreign lands; they brand the statements of your traveled aunts and uncles as the stupidest absurdities; they deride your most trusted authors and demolish the fair images they have set up for your willing worship with the pitiless ferocity of the fanatic iconoclast! But still I love the Old Travelers. I love them for their witless platitudes; for their supernatural ability to bore; for their delightful asinine vanity; for their luxuriant fertility of imagination; for their startling, their brilliant, their overwhelming mendacity!

By Lyons and the Saone (where we saw the lady of Lyons and thought little of her comeliness;) by Villa Franca, Tonnere, venerable Sens, Melun, Fontainebleau, and scores of other beautiful cities, we swept, always noting the absence of hog-wallows, broken fences, cowlots, unpainted houses and mud, and always noting, as well, the presence of cleanliness, grace, taste in adorning and beautifying, even to the disposition of a tree or the turning of a hedge, the marvel of roads in perfect repair, void of ruts and guiltless of even an inequality of surface—we bowled along, hour after hour, that brilliant summer day, and as nightfall approached we entered a wilderness of odorous flowers and shrubbery, sped through it, and then, excited, delighted, and half persuaded that we were only the sport of a beautiful dream, lo, we stood in magnificent Paris!

What excellent order they kept about that vast depot! There was no frantic crowding and jostling, no shouting and swearing, and no swaggering intrusion of services by rowdy hackmen. These latter gentry stood outside—stood quietly by their long line of vehicles and said never a word. A kind of hackman-general seemed to have the whole matter of transportation in his hands. He politely received the passengers and ushered them to the kind of conveyance they wanted, and told the driver where to deliver them. There was no "talking back," no dissatisfaction about overcharging, no grumbling about any thing. In a little while we were speeding through the streets of Paris, and delightfully recognizing certain names and places with which books had long ago made us familiar. It was like meeting an old friend when we read "*Rue de Rivoli*" on the street corner; we knew the genuine vast palace of the Louvre as well as we knew its picture; when we passed by the Column of July we needed no one to tell us what it was or to remind us that on its site once stood the grim Bastile, that grave of human hopes and happiness, that dismal prison-house within whose dungeons so many young faces put on the wrinkles of age, so many proud spirits grew humble, so many brave hearts broke.

We secured rooms at the hotel, or rather, we had three beds put into one room, so that we might be together, and then we went out to a restaurant, just after lamp-lighting, and ate a comfortable, satisfactory, lingering dinner. It was a pleasure to eat where every thing was so tidy, the food so well cooked, the waiters so polite, and the coming and departing company so moustached, so frisky, so affable, so fearfully and wonderfully Frenchy! All the surroundings were gay and enlivening. Two hundred people sat at little tables on the sidewalk, sipping wine and coffee; the streets were thronged with light vehicles and with joyous pleasure seekers; there was music in the air, life and action all about us, and a conflagration of gaslight every where!

After dinner we felt like seeing such Parisian specialties as we might see without distressing exertion, and so we sauntered through the brilliant streets and looked at the dainty trifles in variety stores and jewelry shops. Occasionally, merely for the pleasure of being cruel, we put unoffending Frenchmen on the rack with questions framed in the incomprehensible jargon of their native language, and while they writhed, we impaled them, we peppered them, we scarified them, with their own vile verbs and participles.

We noticed that in the jewelry stores they had some of the articles marked "gold," and some labeled "imitation." We wondered at this extravagance of honesty, and inquired into the matter. We were informed that inasmuch as most people are not able to tell false gold from the genuine article, the government compels jewelers to have their gold work assayed and stamped officially according to its fineness, and their imitation work duly labeled with the sign of its falsity. They told us the jewelers would not dare to violate this law, and that whatever a stranger bought in one of their stores might be depended upon as being strictly what it was represented to be.—Verily, a wonderful land is France!

Then we hunted for a barber-shop. From earliest infancy it had been a cherished ambition of mine to be shaved some day in a palatial barber-shop of Paris. I wished to recline at full length in a cushioned invalid chair, with pictures about me, and sumptuous furniture; with frescoed walls and gilded arches above me, and vistas of Corinthian columns stretching far before me; with perfumes of Araby to intoxicate my senses, and the slumbrous drone of distant noises to soothe me to sleep. At the end of an hour I would wake up regretfully and find my face as smooth and as soft as an infant's. Departing, I would lift my hands above that barber's head and say, "Heaven bless you, my son!"

So we searched high and low, for a matter of two hours, but never a barber-shop could we see. We saw only wig-making establishments, with shocks of dead and repulsive hair bound upon the heads of painted waxen brigands who stared out from glass boxes upon the passer-by, with their stony eyes, and scared him with the ghostly white of their countenances. We shunned these signs for a time, but finally we concluded that the wig-makers must of necessity be the barbers as well, since we could find no single legitimate representative of the fraternity. We entered and asked, and found that it was even so.

I said I wanted to be shaved. The barber inquired where my room was. I said, never mind where my room was, I wanted to be shaved—there, on the spot. The doctor said he would be shaved also. Then there was an excitement among those two barbers! There was a wild consultation, and afterwards a hurrying to and fro and a feverish gathering up of razors from obscure places and a ransacking for soap. Next they took us into a little mean, shabby back room; they got two ordinary sitting-room chairs and placed us in them with our coats on. My old, old dream of bliss vanished into thin air!

I sat bolt upright, silent, sad, and solemn. One of the wig-making villains lathered my face for ten terrible minutes and finished by plastering a mass of suds into my mouth. I expelled the nasty stuff with a strong English expletive and said, "Foreigner, beware!" Then this outlaw strapped his razor on his boot, hovered over me ominously for six fearful seconds, and then swooped down upon me like the genius of destruction. The first rake of his razor loosened the very hide from my face and lifted me out of the chair. I stormed and raved, and the other boys enjoyed it. Their beards are not strong and thick. Let us draw the curtain over this harrowing scene. Suffice it that I submitted, and went through with the cruel infliction of a shave by a French barber; tears of exquisite agony coursed down my cheeks, now and then, but I survived. Then the incipient assassin held a basin of water under my chin and slopped its contents over my face, and into my bosom, and down the back of my neck, with a mean pretense of washing away the soap and blood. He dried my features with a towel and was going to comb my hair; but I asked to be excused. I said, with withering irony, that it was sufficient to be skinned—I declined to be scalped.

I went away from there with my handkerchief about my face, and never, never, never desired to dream of palatial Parisian barber-shops any more. The truth is, as I believe I have since found out, that they have no barber shops worthy of the name, in Paris—and no barbers, either, for that matter. The impostor who does duty as a barber, brings his pans and napkins and implements of torture to your residence and deliberately skins you in your private apartments. Ah, I have suffered, suffered, suffered, here in Paris, but never mind—the time is coming when I shall have a dark and bloody revenge. Some day a Parisian barber will come to my room to skin me, and from that day forth, that barber will never be heard of more.

At eleven o'clock we alighted upon a sign which manifestly referred to billiards. Joy! We had played billiards in the Azores with balls that were not round, and on an ancient table that was very little smoother than a brick pavement—one of those wretched old things with dead cushions, and with patches in the faded cloth and invisible obstructions that made the balls describe the most astonishing and unsuspected angles and perform feats in the way of unlooked-for and almost impossible "scratches," that were perfectly bewildering. We had played at Gibraltar with balls the size of a walnut, on a table like a public square—and in both instances we achieved far more aggravation than amusement. We expected to fare better here, but we were mistaken. The cushions were a good deal higher than the balls, and as the balls had a fashion of always stopping under the cushions, we accomplished very little in the way of caroms. The cushions were hard and unelastic, and the cues were so crooked that in making a shot you had to allow for the curve or you would infallibly put the "English" on the wrong side of the ball. Dan was to mark while the doctor and I played. At the end of an hour neither of us had made a count, and so Dan was tired of keeping tally with nothing to tally, and we were heated and angry and disgusted. We paid the heavy bill—about six cents—and said we would call around some time when we had a week to spend, and finish the game.

We adjourned to one of those pretty cafés and took supper and tested the wines of the country, as we had been instructed to do, and found them harmless and unexciting. They might have been exciting, however, if we had chosen to drink a sufficiency of them.

To close our first day in Paris cheerfully and pleasantly we now sought our grand room in the Grand Hotel du Louvre and climbed into our sumptuous bed to read and smoke—but alas! "It was pitiful, /In a whole city-full, /Gas we had none." No gas to read by—nothing but dismal candles. It was a shame. We tried to map out excursions for the morrow; we puzzled over French "guides to Paris;" we talked disjointedly, in a vain endeavor to make head or tail of the wild chaos of the day's sights and experiences; we subsided to indolent smoking; we gaped and yawned, and stretched—then feebly wondered if we were really and truly in renowned Paris, and drifted drowsily away into that vast mysterious void which men call sleep.

[Paris, Chapter 14]

We went to see the Cathedral of Notre Dame.—We had heard of it before. It surprises me, sometimes, to think how much we *do* know, and how intelligent we are. We recognized the brown old Gothic pile in a moment; it was like the pictures. We stood at a little distance and changed from one point of observation to another, and gazed long at its lofty square towers and its rich front, clustered thick with stony, mutilated saints who had been looking calmly down from their perches for ages. The Patriarch of Jerusalem stood under them in the old days of chivalry and romance, and preached the third Crusade, more than six hundred years ago; and since that day they have stood there and looked quietly down upon the most thrilling scenes, the grandest pageants, the most extraordinary spectacles that have grieved or delighted Paris. These battered and broken-nosed old fellows saw many and many a cavalcade of mail-clad knights come marching home from Holy Land; they heard the bells above them toll the signal for the St. Bartholomew's Massacre, and they saw the slaughter that followed; later, they saw the Reign of Terror, the carnage of the Revolution, the overthrow of a king, the coronation of two Napoleons, the christening of the young prince that lords it over a regiment of servants in the Tuileries to-day—and they may possibly continue to stand there until they see the Napoleon dynasty swept away and the banners of a great Republic floating above its ruins. I wish these old parties could speak. They could tell a tale worth the listening to.

They say that a pagan temple stood where Notre Dame now stands, in the old Roman days, eighteen or twenty centuries ago—remains of it are still preserved in Paris; and that a Christian church took its place about A.D. 300; another took the place of that in A.D. 500; and that the foundations of the present Cathedral were laid about A.D. 1100. The ground ought to be measurably sacred by this time, one would think. One portion of this noble old edifice is suggestive of the quaint fashions of ancient times. It was built by Jean Sans-Peur, Duke of Burgundy, to set his conscience at rest—he had assassinated the Duke of Orleans. Alas! those good old times are gone, when a murderer could wipe the stain from his name and soothe his troubles to sleep simply by getting out his bricks and mortar and building an addition to a church.

The portals of the great western front are bisected by square pillars. They took the central one away, in 1852, on the occasion of thanksgivings for the reinstitution of the Presidential power—but precious soon they had occasion to reconsider that motion and put it back again! And they did.

We loitered through the grand aisles for an hour or two, staring up at the rich stained glass windows embellished with blue and yellow and crimson saints and martyrs, and trying to admire the numberless great pictures in the chapels, and then we were admitted to the sacristy and shown the magnificent robes which the Pope wore when he crowned Napoleon I.; a wagon-load of solid gold and silver utensils used in the great public processions and ceremonies of the church; some nails of the true cross, a fragment of the cross itself, a part of the crown of thorns. We had already seen a large piece of the true cross in a church in the Azores, but no nails. They showed us likewise the bloody robe which that Archbishop of Paris wore who exposed his sacred person and braved the wrath of the insurgents of 1848, to mount the barricades and hold aloft the olive branch of peace in the hope of stopping the slaughter. His noble effort cost him his life. He was shot dead. They showed us a cast of his face, taken after death, the bullet that killed him, and the two vertebræ in which it lodged. These people have a somewhat singular taste in the matter of relics. Ferguson told us that the silver cross which the good Archbishop wore at his girdle was seized and thrown into the Seine, where it lay embedded in the mud for fifteen years, and then an angel appeared to a priest and told him where to dive for it; he *did* dive for it and got it, and now it is there on exhibition at Notre Dame, to be inspected by any body who feels an interest in inanimate objects of miraculous intervention.

Next we went to visit the Morgue, that horrible receptacle for the dead who die mysteriously and leave the manner of their taking off a dismal secret. We stood before a grating and looked through into a room which was hung all about with the clothing of dead men; coarse blouses, water-soaked; the delicate garments of women and children; patrician vestments, hacked and stabbed and stained with red; a hat that was crushed and bloody. On a slanting stone lay a drowned man, naked, swollen, purple; clasping the fragment of a broken bush with a grip which death had so petrified that human strength could not unloose it—mute witness of the last despairing effort to save the life that was doomed beyond all help. A stream of water trickled ceaselessly over the hideous face. We knew that the body and the clothing were there for identification by friends, but still we wondered if any body could love that repulsive object or grieve for its loss. We grew meditative and wondered if, some forty years ago, when the mother of that ghastly thing was dandling it upon her knee, and kissing it and petting it and displaying it with satisfied pride to the passers-by, a prophetic vision of this dread ending ever flitted through her brain. I half feared that the mother, or the wife or a brother of the dead man might come while we stood there, but nothing of the kind occurred. Men and women came, and some looked eagerly in and pressed their faces against the bars; others glanced carelessly at the body and turned away with a disappointed look—people, I thought, who live upon strong excitements, and who attend the exhibitions of the Morgue regularly, just as other people go to see theatrical spectacles every night. When one of these looked in and passed on, I could not help thinking—"Now this don't afford you any satisfaction—a party with his head shot off is what *you* need."

One night we went to the celebrated *Jardin Mabille,* but only staid a little while. We wanted to see some of this kind of Paris life, however, and therefore, the next night we went to a similar place of entertainment in a great garden in the suburb of Asniéres. We went to the railroad depot, toward evening, and Ferguson got tickets for a second-class carriage. Such a perfect jam of people I have not often seen—but there was no noise, no disorder, no rowdyism. Some of the women and young girls that entered the train we knew to be of the *demi-monde,* but others we were not at all sure about.

The girls and women in our carriage behaved themselves modestly and becomingly, all the way out, except that they smoked. When we arrived at the garden in Asniéres, we paid a franc or two admission, and entered a place which had flower-beds in it, and grass plats, and long, curving rows of ornamental shrubbery, with here and there a secluded bower convenient for eating ice-cream in. We moved along the sinuous gravel walks, with the great concourse of girls and young men, and suddenly a domed and filigreed white temple, starred over and over and over again with brilliant gas-jets, burst upon us like a fallen sun. Near by was a large, handsome house with its ample front illuminated in the same way, and above its roof floated the Star Spangled Banner of America.

"Well!" I said. "How is this?" It nearly took my breath away.

Ferguson said an American—a New Yorker—kept the place, and was carrying on quite a stirring opposition to the *Jardin-Mabille.*

Crowds, composed of both sexes and nearly all ages, were frisking about the garden or sitting in the open air in front of the flag-staff and the temple, drinking wine and coffee, or smoking. The dancing had not begun, yet. Ferguson said there was to be an exhibition. The famous Blondin was going to perform on a tight-rope in another part of the garden. We went thither. Here the light was dim, and the masses of people were pretty closely packed together. And now I made a mistake which any donkey might make, but a sensible man never. I committed an error which I find myself repeating every day of my life.—Standing right before a young lady, I said—"Dan, just look at this girl, how beautiful she is!"

"I thank you more for the evident sincerity of the compliment, sir, than for the extraordinary publicity you have given to it!" This in good, pure English.

We took a walk, but my spirits were very, very sadly dampened. I did not feel right comfortable for some time afterward. Why *will* people be so stupid as to suppose themselves the only foreigners among a crowd of ten thousand persons?

But Blondin came out shortly. He appeared on a stretched cable, far away above the sea of tossing hats and handkerchiefs, and in the glare of the hundreds of rockets that whizzed heavenward by him he looked like a wee insect. He balanced his pole and walked the length of his rope— two or three hundred feet; he came back and got a man and carried him across; he returned to the centre and danced a jig; next he performed some gymnastic and balancing feats too perilous to afford a pleasant spectacle; and he finished by fastening to his person a thousand Roman candles, Catherine wheels, serpents and rockets of all manner of brilliant colors, setting them on fire all at once and walking and waltzing across his rope again in a blinding blaze of glory that lit up the garden and the people's faces like a great conflagration at midnight.

The dance had begun, and we adjourned to the temple. Within it was a drinking saloon; and all around it was a broad circular platform for the dancers. I backed up against the wall of the temple, and waited. Twenty sets formed, the music struck up, and then—I placed my hands before my face for very shame. But I looked through my fingers. They were dancing the renowned "*Can-can.*" A handsome girl in the set before me tripped forward lightly to meet the opposite gentleman—tripped back again, grasped her dresses vigorously on both sides with her hands, raised them pretty high, danced an extraordinary jig that had more activity and expo- sure about it than any jig I ever saw before, and then, drawing her clothes still higher, she advanced gaily to the center and launched a vicious kick full at her *vis-a-vis* that must infallibly have removed his nose if he had been seven feet high. It was a mercy he was only six.

That is the *can-can.* The idea of it is to dance as wildly, as noisily, as fu- riously as you can; expose yourself as much as possible if you are a woman; and kick as high as you can, no matter which sex you belong to. There is no word of exaggeration in this. Any of the staid, respectable, aged people who were there that night can testify to the truth of that statement. There were a good many such people present. I suppose French morality is not of that straight-laced description which is shocked at trifles.

I moved aside and took a general view of the *can-can*. Shouts, laughter, furious music, a bewildering chaos of darting and intermingling forms, stormy jerking and snatching of gay dresses, bobbing heads, flying arms, lightning-flashes of white-stockinged calves and dainty slippers in the air, and then a grand final rush, riot, a terrific hubbub and a wild stampede! Heavens! Nothing like it has been seen on earth since trembling Tam O'Shanter saw the devil and the witches at their orgies that stormy night in "Alloway's auld haunted kirk."

We visited the Louvre, at a time when we had no silk purchases in view, and looked at its miles of paintings by the old masters. Some of them were beautiful, but at the same time they carried such evidences about them of the cringing spirit of those great men that we found small pleasure in examining them. Their nauseous adulation of princely patrons was more prominent to me and chained my attention more surely than the charms of color and expression which are claimed to be in the pictures. Gratitude for kindnesses is well, but it seems to me that some of those artists carried it so far that it ceased to be gratitude, and became worship. If there is a plausible excuse for the worship of men, then by all means let us forgive Rubens and his brethren.

But I will drop the subject, lest I say something about the old masters that might as well be left unsaid.

Of course we drove in the *Bois de Boulogne,* that limitless park, with its forests, its lakes, its cascades, and its broad avenues. There were thousands upon thousands of vehicles abroad, and the scene was full of life and gayety. There were very common hacks, with father and mother and all the children in them; conspicuous little open carriages with celebrated ladies of questionable reputation in them; there were Dukes and Duchesses abroad, with gorgeous footmen perched behind, and equally gorgeous outriders perched on each of the six horses; there were blue and silver, and green and gold, and pink and black, and all sorts and descriptions of stunning and startling liveries out, and I almost yearned to be a flunkey myself, for the sake of the fine clothes.

But presently the Emperor came along and he out-shone them all. He was preceded by a body guard of gentlemen on horseback in showy uniforms, his carriage-horses (there appeared to be somewhere in the remote neighborhood of a thousand of them,) were bestridden by gallant looking fellows, also in stylish uniforms, and after the carriage followed another detachment of body-guards. Every body got out of the way; every body bowed to the Emperor and his friend the Sultan; and they went by on a swinging trot and disappeared.

I will not describe the *Bois de Boulogne*. I can not do it. It is simply a beautiful, cultivated, endless, wonderful wilderness. It is an enchanting place. It is in Paris, now, one may say, but a crumbling old cross in one portion of it reminds one that it was not always so. The cross marks the spot where a celebrated troubadour was waylaid and murdered in the fourteenth century. It was in this park that that fellow with an unpronounceable name made the attempt upon the Russian Czar's life last spring with a pistol. The bullet struck a tree. Ferguson showed us the place. Now in America that interesting tree would be chopped down or forgotten within the next five years, but it will be treasured here. The guides will point it out to visitors for the next eight hundred years, and when it decays and falls down they will put up another there and go on with the same old story just the same.

[Milan, from Chapter 19]

Here, in Milan, in an ancient tumble-down ruin of a church, is the mournful wreck of the most celebrated painting in the world—"The Last Supper," by Leonardo da Vinci. We are not infallible judges of pictures, but of course we went there to see this wonderful painting, once so beautiful, always so worshipped by masters in art, and forever to be famous in song and story. And the first thing that occurred was the infliction on us of a placard fairly reeking with wretched English. Take a morsel of it: "Bartholomew (that is the first figure on the left hand side at the spectator,) uncertain and doubtful about what he thinks to have heard, and upon which he wants to be assured by himself at Christ and by no others." Good, isn't it? And then Peter is described as "argumenting in a threatening and angrily condition at Judas Iscariot."

This paragraph recalls the picture. "The Last Supper" is painted on the dilapidated wall of what was a little chapel attached to the main church in ancient times, I suppose. It is battered and scarred in every direction, and stained and discolored by time, and Napoleon's horses kicked the legs off most the disciples when they (the horses, not the disciples,) were stabled there more than half a century ago.

I recognized the old picture in a moment—the Saviour with bowed head seated at the centre of a long, rough table with scattering fruits and dishes upon it, and six disciples on either side in their long robes, talking to each other—the picture from which all engravings and all copies have been made for three centuries. Perhaps no living man has ever known an attempt to paint the Lord's Supper differently. The world seems to have become settled in the belief, long ago, that it is not possible for human genius to outdo this creation of Da Vinci's. I suppose painters will go on copying it as long as any of the original is left visible to the eye. There were a dozen easels in the room, and as many artists transferring the great picture to their canvases. Fifty proofs of steel engravings and lithographs were scattered around, too. And as usual, I could not help noticing how superior the copies were to the original, that is, to my inexperienced eye. Wherever you find a Raphael, a Rubens, a Michel Angelo, a Caracci, or a Da Vinci (and we see them every day,) you find artists copying them, and the copies are always the handsomest. May be the originals were handsome when they were new, but they are not now.

This picture is about thirty feet long, and ten or twelve high, I should think, and the figures are at least life size. It is one of the largest paintings in Europe.

The colors are dimmed with age; the countenances are scaled and marred, and nearly all expression is gone from them; the hair is a dead blur upon the wall, and there is no life in the eyes. Only the attitudes are certain.

People come here from all parts of the world, and glorify this masterpiece. They stand entranced before it with bated breath and parted lips, and when they speak, it is only in the catchy ejaculations of rapture:

"O, wonderful!"

"Such expression!"

"Such grace of attitude!"

"Such dignity!"

"Such faultless drawing!"

"Such matchless coloring!"

"Such feeling!"

"What delicacy of touch!"

"What sublimity of conception!"

"A vision! a vision!"

I only envy these people; I envy them their honest admiration, if it be honest—their delight, if they feel delight. I harbor no animosity toward any of them. But at the same time the thought *will* intrude itself upon me, How can they see what is not visible? What would you think of a man who looked at some decayed, blind, toothless, pock-marked Cleopatra, and said: "What matchless beauty! What soul! What expression!" What would you think of a man who gazed upon a dingy, foggy sunset, and said: "What sublimity! what feeling! what richness of coloring!" What would you think of a man who stared in ecstasy upon a desert of stumps and said: "Oh, my soul, my beating heart, what a noble forest is here!"

You would think that those men had an astonishing talent for seeing things that had already passed away. It was what I thought when I stood before the Last Supper and heard men apostrophizing wonders, and beauties and perfections which had faded out of the picture and gone, a hundred years before they were born. We can imagine the beauty that was once in an aged face; we can imagine the forest if we see the stumps; but we can not absolutely *see* these things when they are not there. I am willing to believe that the eye of the practiced artist can rest upon the Last Supper and renew a lustre where only a hint of it is left, supply a tint that has faded away, restore an expression that is gone; patch, and color, and add, to the dull canvas until at last its figures shall stand before him aglow with the life, the feeling, the freshness, yea, with all the noble beauty that was theirs when first they came from the hand of the master. But *I* can not work this miracle. Can those other uninspired visitors do it, or do they only happily imagine they do?

After reading so much about it, I am satisfied that the Last Supper was a very miracle of art once. But it was three hundred years ago.

It vexes me to hear people talk so glibly of "feeling," "expression," "tone," and those other easily acquired and inexpensive technicalities of art that make such a fine show in conversations concerning pictures. There is not one man in seventy-five hundred that can tell *what* a pictured face is intended to express. There is not one man in five hundred that can go into a court-room and be sure that he will not mistake some harmless innocent of a juryman for the black-hearted assassin on trial. Yet such people talk of "character" and presume to interpret "expression" in pictures. There is an old story that Matthews, the actor, was once lauding the ability of the human face to express the passions and emotions hidden in the breast. He said the countenance could disclose what was passing in the heart plainer than the tongue could.

"Now," he said, "observe my face—what does it express?"

"Despair!"

"Bah, it expresses peaceful resignation! What does *this* express?"

"Rage!"

"Stuff! it means terror! *This!*"

"Imbecility!"

"Fool! It is smothered ferocity! Now *this!*"

"Joy!"

"Oh, perdition! *Any* ass can see it means insanity!"

Expression! People coolly pretend to read it who would think themselves presumptuous if they pretended to interpret the hieroglyphics on the obelisks of Luxor—yet they are fully as competent to do the one thing as the other. I have heard two very intelligent critics speak of Murillo's Immaculate Conception (now in the museum at Seville,) within the past few days. One said: "Oh, the Virgin's face is full of the ecstasy of a joy that is complete—that leaves nothing more to be desired on earth!"

The other said: "Ah, that wonderful face is so humble, so pleading—it says as plainly as words could say it: 'I fear; I tremble; I am unworthy. But Thy will be done; sustain Thou Thy servant!'"

The reader can see the picture in any drawing-room; it can be easily recognized: the Virgin (the only young and really beautiful Virgin that was ever painted by one of the old masters, some of us think,) stands in the crescent of the new moon, with a multitude of cherubs hovering about her, and more coming; her hands are crossed upon her breast, and upon her uplifted countenance falls a glory out of the heavens. The reader may amuse himself, if he chooses, in trying to determine which of these gentlemen read the Virgin's "expression" aright, or if either of them did it.

Any one who is acquainted with the old masters will comprehend how much the Last Supper is damaged when I say that the spectator can not really tell, now, whether the disciples are Hebrews or Italians. These ancient painters never succeeded in denationalizing themselves. The Italian artists painted Italian Virgins, the Dutch painted Dutch Virgins, the Virgins of the French painters were Frenchwomen—none of them ever put

into the face of the Madonna that indescribable something which pro-
claims the Jewess, whether you find her in New York, in Constantinople,
in Paris, Jerusalem, or in the Empire of Morocco. I saw in the Sandwich
Islands, once, a picture, copied by a talented German artist from an engraving in one of the American illustrated papers. It was an allegory, representing Mr. Davis in the act of signing a secession act or some such
document. Over him hovered the ghost of Washington in warning attitude, and in the background a troop of shadowy soldiers in Continental uniform were limping with shoeless, bandaged feet through a driving
snow-storm. Valley Forge was suggested, of course. The copy seemed accurate, and yet there was a discrepancy somewhere. After a long examination I discovered what it was—the shadowy soldiers were all Germans!
Jeff. Davis was a German! even the hovering ghost was a German ghost!
The artist had unconsciously worked his nationality into the picture. To
tell the truth, I am getting a little perplexed about John the Baptist and
his portraits. In France I finally grew reconciled to him as a Frenchman;
here he is unquestionably an Italian. What next? Can it be possible that
the painters make John the Baptist a Spaniard in Madrid and an Irishman
in Dublin?

[Venice, from Chapter 23]

We have been pretty much every where in our gondola. We have bought
beads and photographs in the stores, and wax matches in the Great Square
of St. Mark. The last remark suggests a digression. Every body goes to
this vast square in the evening. The military bands play in the centre of it
and countless couples of ladies and gentlemen promenade up and down
on either side, and platoons of them are constantly drifting away toward
the old Cathedral, and by the venerable column with the Winged Lion of
St. Mark on its top, and out to where the boats lie moored; and other platoons are as constantly arriving from the gondolas and joining the great
throng. Between the promenaders and the side-walks are seated hundreds
and hundreds of people at small tables, smoking and taking *granita*, (a first
cousin to ice-cream;) on the side-walks are more employing themselves in
the same way. The shops in the first floor of the tall rows of buildings that
wall in three sides of the square are brilliantly lighted, the air is filled with
music and merry voices, and altogether the scene is as bright and spirited
and full of cheerfulness as any man could desire. We enjoy it thoroughly.

Very many of the young women are exceedingly pretty and dress with rare good taste. We are gradually and laboriously learning the ill-manners of staring them unflinchingly in the face—not because such conduct is agreeable to us, but because it is the custom of the country and they say the girls like it. We wish to learn all the curious, outlandish ways of all the different countries, so that we can "show off" and astonish people when we get home. We wish to excite the envy of our untraveled friends with our strange foreign fashions which we can't shake off. All our passengers are paying strict attention to this thing, with the end in view which I have mentioned. The gentle reader will never, never know what a consummate ass he can become, until he goes abroad. I speak now, of course, in the supposition that the gentle reader has not been abroad, and therefore is not already a consummate ass. If the case be otherwise, I beg his pardon and extend to him the cordial hand of fellowship and call him brother. I shall always delight to meet an ass after my own heart when I shall have finished my travels.

On this subject let me remark that there are Americans abroad in Italy who have actually forgotten their mother tongue in three months—forgot it in France. They can not even write their address in English in a hotel register. I append these evidences, which I copied *verbatim* from the register of a hotel in a certain Italian city:

"John P. Whitcomb, *Etats Unis.*

"Wm. L. Ainsworth, *travailleur* (he meant traveler, I suppose,) *Etats Unis.*

"George P. Morton *et fils, d'Amerique.*

"Lloyd B. Williams, *et trois amis, ville de* Boston, *Amerique.*

"J. Ellsworth Baker, *tout de suite de France, place de naissance de Amerique, destination la Grand Bretagne.*"

I love this sort of people. A lady passenger of ours tells of a fellow-citizen of hers who spent eight weeks in Paris and then returned home and addressed his dearest old bosom friend Herbert as Mr. "Er-bare!" He apologized, though, and said, "'Pon my soul it is aggravating, but I cahn't help it—I have got so used to speaking nothing but French, my dear Erbare—damme there it goes again!—got so used to French pronunciation that I cahn't get rid of it—it is positively annoying, I assure you." This entertaining idiot, whose name was Gordon, allowed himself to be hailed three times in the street before he paid any attention, and then begged a thousand pardons and said he had grown so accustomed to hearing himself addressed as "M'sieu Gor-r-*dong,*" with a roll to the r, that he had forgotten the legitimate sound of his name! He wore a rose in his buttonhole; he gave the French salutation—two flips of the hand in front of the face; he called Paris *Pairree* in ordinary English conversation; he carried envelopes bearing foreign postmarks protruding from his breast-pocket; he cultivated a moustache and imperial, and did what else he could to suggest to the beholder his pet fancy that he resembled Louis Napoleon—and in a spirit of thankfulness which is entirely unaccountable, considering the slim foundation there was for it, he praised his Maker that he was *as* he was, and went on enjoying his little life just the same as if he really *had* been deliberately designed and erected by the great Architect of the Universe.

Think of our Whitcombs, and our Ainsworths and our Williamses writing themselves down in dilapidated French in foreign hotel registers! We laugh at Englishmen, when we are at home, for sticking so sturdily to their national ways and customs, but we look back upon it from abroad very forgivingly. It is not pleasant to see an American thrusting his nationality forward *obtrusively* in a foreign land, but Oh, it is pitiable to see him making of himself a thing that is neither male nor female, neither fish, flesh, nor fowl—a poor, miserable, hermaphrodite Frenchman!

Among a long list of churches, art galleries, and such things, visited by us in Venice, I shall mention only one—the church of Santa Maria dei Frari. It is about five hundred years old, I believe, and stands on twelve hundred thousand piles. In it lie the body of Canova and the heart of Titian, under magnificent monuments. Titian died at the age of almost one hundred years. A plague which swept away fifty thousand lives was raging at the time, and there is notable evidence of the reverence in which the great painter was held, in the fact that to him alone the state permitted a public funeral in all that season of terror and death.

In this church, also, is a monument to the doge Foscari, whose name a once resident of Venice, Lord Byron, has made permanently famous.

The monument to the doge Giovanni Pesaro, in this church, is a curiosity in the way of mortuary adornment. It is eighty feet high and is fronted like some fantastic pagan temple. Against it stand four colossal Nubians, as black as night, dressed in white marble garments. The black legs are bare, and through rents in sleeves and breeches, the skin, of shiny black marble, shows. The artist was as ingenious as his funeral designs were absurd. There are two bronze skeletons bearing scrolls, and two great dragons uphold the sarcophagus. On high, amid all this grotesqueness, sits the departed doge.

In the conventual buildings attached to this church are the state archives of Venice. We did not see them, but they are said to number millions of documents. "They are the records of centuries of the most watchful, observant and suspicious government that ever existed—in which every thing was written down and nothing spoken out." They fill nearly three hundred rooms. Among them are manuscripts from the archives of nearly two thousand families, monasteries and convents. The secret history of Venice for a thousand years is here—its plots, its hidden trials, its assassinations, its commissions of hireling spies and masked bravoes—food, ready to hand, for a world of dark and mysterious romances.

Yes, I think we have seen all of Venice. We have seen, in these old churches, a profusion of costly and elaborate sepulchre ornamentation such as we never dreampt of before. We have stood in the dim religious light of these hoary sanctuaries, in the midst of long ranks of dusty monuments and effigies of the great dead of Venice, until we seemed drifting back, back, back, into the solemn past, and looking upon the scenes and mingling with the peoples of a remote antiquity. We have been in a half-waking sort of dream all the time. I do not know how else to describe the feeling. A part of our being has remained still in the nineteenth century, while another part of it has seemed in some unaccountable way walking among the phantoms of the tenth.

We have seen famous pictures until our eyes are weary with looking at them and refuse to find interest in them any longer. And what wonder, when there are twelve hundred pictures by Palma the Younger in Venice and fifteen hundred by Tintoretto? And behold there are Titians and the works of other artists in proportion. We have seen Titian's celebrated Cain and Abel, his David and Goliah, his Abraham's Sacrifice. We have seen Tintoretto's monster picture, which is seventy-four feet long and I do not know how many feet high, and thought it a very commodious picture. We have seen pictures of martyrs enough, and saints enough, to regenerate the world. I ought not to confess it, but still, since one has no opportunity in America to acquire a critical judgment in art, and since I could not hope to become educated in it in Europe in a few short weeks,

I may therefore as well acknowledge with such apologies as may be due, that to me it seemed that when I had seen one of these martyrs I had seen them all. They all have a marked family resemblance to each other, they dress alike, in coarse monkish robes and sandals, they are all bald headed, they all stand in about the same attitude, and without exception they are gazing heavenward with countenances which the Ainsworths, the Mortons and the Williamses, *et fils*, inform me are full of "expression." To me there is nothing tangible about these imaginary portraits, nothing that I can grasp and take a living interest in. If great Titian had only been gifted with prophecy, and had skipped a martyr, and gone over to England and painted a portrait of Shakspeare, even as a youth, which we could all have confidence in now, the world down to the latest generations would have forgiven him the lost martyr in the rescued seer. I think posterity could have spared one more martyr for the sake of a great historical picture of Titian's time and painted by his brush—such as Columbus returning in chains from the discovery of a world, for instance. The old masters did paint some Venetian historical pictures, and these we did not tire of looking at, notwithstanding representations of the formal introduction of defunct doges to the Virgin Mary in regions beyond the clouds clashed rather harshly with the proprieties, it seemed to us.

But humble as we are, and unpretending, in the matter of art, our researches among the painted monks and martyrs have not been wholly in vain. We have striven hard to learn. We have had some success. We have mastered some things, possibly of trifling import in the eyes of the learned, but to us they give pleasure, and we take as much pride in our little acquirements as do others who have learned far more, and we love to display them full as well. When we see a monk going about with a lion and looking tranquilly up to heaven, we know that that is St. Mark. When we see a monk with a book and a pen, looking tranquilly up to heaven, trying to think of a word, we know that that is St. Matthew. When we see a monk sitting on a rock, looking tranquilly up to heaven, with a human skull beside him, and without other baggage, we know that that is St. Jerome. Because we know that he always went flying light in the matter of baggage. When we see a party looking tranquilly up to heaven, unconscious that his body is shot through and through with arrows, we know that that is St. Sebastian. When we see other monks looking tranquilly up to heaven, but having no trade-mark, we always ask who those parties are. We do this because we humbly wish to learn. We have seen thirteen thousand St. Jeromes, and twenty-two thousand St. Marks, and sixteen thousand St. Matthews, and sixty thousand St. Sebastians, and four millions of assorted monks, undesignated, and we feel encouraged to believe that when we have seen some more of these various pictures, and had a larger experience, we shall begin to take an absorbing interest in them like our cultivated countrymen from *Amerique*.

Now it does give me real pain to speak in this almost unappreciative way of the old masters and their martyrs, because good friends of mine in the ship—friends who do thoroughly and conscientiously appreciate them and are in every way competent to discriminate between good pictures and inferior ones—have urged me for my own sake not to make public the fact that I lack this appreciation and this critical discrimination myself. I believe that what I have written and may still write about pictures will give them pain, and I am honestly sorry for it. I even promised that I would hide my uncouth sentiments in my own breast. But alas! I never could keep a promise. I do not blame myself for this weakness, because the fault must lie in my physical organization. It is likely that such a very liberal amount of space was given to the organ which enables me to *make* promises, that the organ which should enable me to keep them was crowded out. But I grieve not. I like no half-way things. I had rather have one faculty nobly developed than two faculties of mere ordinary capacity. I certainly meant to keep that promise, but I find I can not do it. It is impossible to travel through Italy without speaking of pictures, and can I see them through others' eyes?

[Rome, from Chapter 26]

Of course we have been to the monster Church of St. Peter, frequently. I knew its dimensions. I knew it was a prodigious structure. I knew it was just about the length of the capitol at Washington—say seven hundred and thirty feet. I knew it was three hundred and sixty-four feet wide, and consequently wider than the capitol. I knew that the cross on the top of the dome of the church was four hundred and thirty-eight feet above the ground, and therefore about a hundred or may be a hundred and twenty-five feet higher than the dome of the capitol.—Thus I had one gauge. I wished to come as near forming a correct idea of how it was going to look, as possible; I had a curiosity to see how much I would err. I erred considerably. St. Peter's did not look nearly so large as the capitol, and certainly not a twentieth part as beautiful, from the outside.

When we reached the door, and stood fairly within the church, it was impossible to comprehend that it was a *very* large building. I had to *cipher* a comprehension of it. I had to ransack my memory for some more similes. St. Peter's is bulky. Its height and size would represent two of the Washington capitol set one on top of the other—if the capitol were wider; or two blocks or two blocks and a half of ordinary buildings set one on top of the other. St. Peter's *was* that large, but it could and would not look so. The trouble was that every thing in it and about it was on such a scale of uniform vastness that there were no contrasts to judge by— none but the people, and I had not noticed them. They were insects. The statues of children holding vases of holy water were immense, according to the tables of figures, but so was every thing else around them. The mosaic pictures in the dome were huge, and were made of thousands and thousands of cubes of glass as large as the end of my little finger, but those pictures looked smooth, and gaudy of color, and in good proportion to the dome. Evidently they would not answer to measure by. Away down toward the far end of the church (I thought it was really clear at the far end, but discovered afterward that it was in the centre, under the dome,) stood the thing they call the *baldacchino*—a great bronze pyramidal frame-work like that which upholds a mosquito bar. It only looked like a considerably magnified bedstead—nothing more. Yet I knew it was a good deal more than half as high as Niagara Falls. It was overshadowed by a dome so mighty that its own height was snubbed. The four great square piers or pillars that stand equidistant from each other in the church, and support the roof, I could not work up to their real dimensions by any method of comparison. I knew that the faces of each were about the width of a very large dwelling-house front, (fifty or sixty feet,) and that they were twice as high as an ordinary three-story dwelling, but still they looked small. I tried all the different ways I could think of to compel myself to understand how large St. Peter's was, but with small success. The mosaic portrait of an Apostle who was writing with a pen six feet long seemed only an ordinary Apostle.

But the people attracted my attention after a while. To stand in the door of St. Peter's and look at men down toward its further extremity, two blocks away, has a diminishing effect on them; surrounded by the prodigious pictures and statues, and lost in the vast spaces, they look very much smaller than they would if they stood two blocks away in the open air. I "averaged" a man as he passed me and watched him as he drifted far down by the *baldacchino* and beyond—watched him dwindle to an insignificant school-boy, and then, in the midst of the silent throng of human pigmies gliding about him, I lost him. The church had lately been decorated, on the occasion of a great ceremony in honor of St. Peter, and men were engaged, now, in removing the flowers and gilt paper from the walls and pillars. As no ladders could reach the great heights, the men swung themselves down from balustrades and the capitals of pilasters by ropes, to do this work. The upper gallery which encircles the inner sweep of the dome is two hundred and forty feet above the floor of the church—very few steeples in America could reach up to it. Visitors always go up there to look down into the church because one gets the best idea of some of the heights and distances from that point. While we stood on the floor one of the workmen swung loose from that gallery at the end of a long rope. I had not supposed, before, that a man *could* look so much like a spider. He was insignificant in size, and his rope seemed only a thread. Seeing that he took up so little space, I could believe the story, then, that ten thousand troops went to St. Peter's, once, to hear mass, and their commanding officer came afterward, and not finding them, supposed they had not yet arrived. But they were in the church, nevertheless—they were in one of the transepts. Nearly fifty thousand persons assembled in St. Peter's to hear the publishing of the dogma of the Immaculate Conception. It is estimated that the floor of the church affords standing room for—for a large number of people; I have forgotten the exact figures. But it is no matter—it is near enough.

They have twelve small pillars, in St. Peter's, which came from Solomon's Temple. They have, also—which was far more interesting to me—a piece of the true cross, and some nails, and a part of the crown of thorns.

Of course we ascended to the summit of the dome, and of course we also went up into the gilt copper ball which is above it.—There was room there for a dozen persons, with a little crowding, and it was as close and hot as an oven. Some of those people who are so fond of writing their names in prominent places had been there before us—a million or two, I should think. From the dome of St. Peter's one can see every notable object in Rome, from the Castle of St. Angelo to the Coliseum. He can discern the seven hills upon which Rome is built. He can see the Tiber, and the locality of the bridge which Horatius kept "in the brave days of old" when Lars Porsena attempted to cross it with his invading host. He can see the spot where the Horatii and the Curatii fought their famous battle. He can see the broad green Campagna, stretching away toward the mountains, with its scattered arches and broken aqueducts of the olden time, so picturesque in their gray ruin, and so daintily festooned with vines. He can see the Alban Mountains, the Appenines, the Sabine Hills, and the blue Mediterranean. He can see a panorama that is varied, extensive, beautiful to the eye, and more illustrious in history than any other in Europe.—About his feet is spread the remnant of a city that once had a population of four million souls; and among its massed edifices stand the ruins of temples, columns, and triumphal arches that knew the Cæsars, and the noonday of Roman splendor; and close by them, in unimpaired strength, is a drain of arched and heavy masonry that belonged to that older city which stood here before Romulus and Remus were born or Rome thought of. The Appian Way is here yet, and looking much as it did, perhaps, when the triumphal processions of the Emperors moved over it in other days bringing fettered princes from the confines of the earth. We can not see the long array of chariots and mail-clad men laden with the spoils of conquest, but we can imagine the pageant, after a fashion. We look out upon many objects of interest from the dome of St. Peter's; and last of all, almost at our feet, our eyes rest upon the building which was once the Inquisition. How times changed, between the older ages and the new! Some seventeen or eighteen centuries ago, the ignorant men of Rome were wont to put Christians in the arena of the Coliseum yonder, and turn the wild beasts in upon them for a show. It was for a lesson as well. It was to teach the people to abhor and fear the new doctrine the followers of Christ were teaching. The beasts tore the victims limb from limb and made poor mangled corpses of them in the twinkling of an eye. But when the Christians came into power, when the holy Mother Church became mistress of the barbarians, she taught them the error of their ways by no such means. No, she put them in this pleasant Inquisition and pointed to the Blessed Redeemer, who was so gentle and so merciful toward all men, and they urged the barbarians to love him; and they did all they could to persuade them to love and honor him—first by twisting their thumbs out of joint with a screw; then by nipping their flesh with pincers—red-hot ones, because they are the most comfortable in cold weather; then by skinning them alive a little, and finally by roasting them in public. They always convinced those barbarians. The true religion, properly administered, as the good Mother Church used to administer it, is very, very soothing. It is wonderfully persuasive, also. There is a great difference between feeding parties to wild beasts and stirring up their finer feelings in an Inquisition. One is the system of degraded barbarians, the other of enlightened, civilized people. It is a great pity the playful Inquisition is no more.

I prefer not to describe St. Peter's. It has been done before. The ashes of Peter, the disciple of the Saviour, repose in a crypt under the *baldacchino*. We stood reverently in that place; so did we also in the Mamertine Prison, where he was confined, where he converted the soldiers, and where tradition says he caused a spring of water to flow in order that he might baptize them. But when they showed us the print of Peter's face in the hard stone of the prison wall and said he made that by falling up against it, we doubted. And when, also, the monk at the church of San Sebastian showed us a paving-stone with two great footprints in it and said that Peter's feet made those, we lacked confidence again. Such things do not impress one. The monk said that angels came and liberated Peter from prison by night, and he started away from Rome by the Appian Way. The Saviour met him and told him to go back, which he did. Peter left those footprints in the stone upon which he stood at the time. It was not stated how it was ever discovered whose footprints they were, seeing the interview occurred secretly and at night. The print of the face in the prison was that of a man of common size; the footprints were those of a man ten or twelve feet high. The discrepancy confirmed our unbelief.

We necessarily visited the Forum, where Cæsar was assassinated, and also the Tarpeian Rock. We saw the Dying Gladiator at the Capitol, and I think that even we appreciated that wonder of art; as much, perhaps, as we did that fearful story wrought in marble, in the Vatican—the Laocoon. And then the Coliseum.

Every body knows the picture of the Coliseum; every body recognizes at once that "looped and windowed" band-box with a side bitten out. Being rather isolated, it shows to better advantage than any other of the monuments of ancient Rome. Even the beautiful Pantheon, whose pagan altars uphold the cross, now, and whose Venus, tricked out in consecrated gimcracks, does reluctant duty as a Virgin Mary to-day, is built about with shabby houses and its stateliness sadly marred. But the monarch of all European ruins, the Coliseum, maintains that reserve and that royal seclusion which is proper to majesty. Weeds and flowers spring from its massy arches and its circling seats, and vines hang their fringes from its lofty walls. An impressive silence broods over the monstrous structure where such multitudes of men and women were wont to assemble in other days. The butterflies have taken the places of the queens of fashion and beauty of eighteen centuries ago, and the lizards sun themselves in the sacred seat of the Emperor. More vividly than all the written histories, the Coliseum tells the story of Rome's grandeur and Rome's decay. It is the worthiest type of both that exists. Moving about the Rome of to-day, we might find it hard to believe in her old magnificence and her millions of population; but with this stubborn evidence before us that she was obliged to have a theatre with sitting room for eighty thousand persons and standing room for twenty thousand more, to accommodate such of her citizens as required amusement, we find belief less difficult. The Coliseum is over one thousand six hundred feet long, seven hundred and fifty wide, and one hundred and sixty-five high. Its shape is oval.

In America we make convicts useful at the same time that we punish them for their crimes. We farm them out and compel them to earn money for the State by making barrels and building roads. Thus we combine business with retribution, and all things are lovely. But in ancient Rome they combined religious duty with pleasure. Since it was necessary that the new sect called Christians should be exterminated, the people judged it wise to make this work profitable to the State at the same time, and entertaining to the public. In addition to the gladiatorial combats and other shows, they sometimes threw members of the hated sect into the arena of the Coliseum and turned wild beasts in upon them. It is estimated that seventy thousand Christians suffered martyrdom in this place. This has made the Coliseum holy ground, in the eyes of the followers of the Saviour. And well it might; for if the chain that bound a saint, and the footprints a saint has left upon a stone he chanced to stand upon, be holy, surely the spot where a man gave up his life for his faith is holy.

Seventeen or eighteen centuries ago this Coliseum was *the* theatre of Rome, and Rome was mistress of the world. Splendid pageants were exhibited here, in presence of the Emperor, the great ministers of State, the nobles, and vast audiences of citizens of smaller consequence. Gladiators fought with gladiators and at times with warrior prisoners from many a distant land. It was *the* theatre of Rome—of the world—and the man of fashion who could not let fall in a casual and unintentional manner something about "my private box at the Coliseum" could not move in the first circles. When the clothing-store merchant wished to consume the corner grocery man with envy, he bought secured seats in the front row and let the thing be known. When the irresistible dry goods clerk wished to blight and destroy, according to his native instinct, he got himself up regardless of expense and took some other fellow's young lady to the Coliseum, and then accented the affront by cramming her with ice cream between the acts, or by approaching the cage and stirring up the martyrs with his whalebone cane for her edification. The Roman swell was in his true element only when he stood up against a pillar and fingered his moustache unconscious of the ladies; when he viewed the bloody combats through an opera-glass two inches long; when he excited the envy of provincials by criticisms which showed that he had been to the Coliseum many and many a time and was long ago over the novelty of it; when he turned away with a yawn at last and said, "*He* a star! handles his sword like an apprentice brigand! he'll do for the country, may be, but he don't answer for the metropolis!"

Glad was the contraband that had a seat in the pit at the Saturday matinee, and happy the Roman street-boy who ate his peanuts and guyed the gladiators from the dizzy gallery.

[Rome and Genoa, from Chapter 27]

In this place I may as well jot down a chapter concerning those necessary nuisances, European guides. Many a man has wished in his heart he could do without his guide; but knowing he could not, has wished he could get some amusement out of him as a remuneration for the affliction of his society. We accomplished this latter matter, and if our experience can be made useful to others they are welcome to it.

Guides know about enough English to tangle every thing up so that a man can make neither head or tail of it. They know their story by heart—the history of every statue, painting, cathedral or other wonder they show you. They know it and tell it as a parrot would—and if you interrupt, and throw them off the track, they have to go back and begin over again. All their lives long, they are employed in showing strange things to foreigners and listening to their bursts of admiration. It is human nature to take delight in exciting admiration. It is what prompts children to say "smart" things, and do absurd ones, and in other ways "show off" when company is present. It is what makes gossips turn out in rain and storm to go and be the first to tell a startling bit of news. Think, then, what a passion it becomes with a guide, whose privilege it is, every day, to show to strangers wonders that throw them into perfect ecstasies of admiration! He gets so that he could not by any possibility live in a soberer atmosphere. After we discovered this, we *never* went into ecstasies any more—we never admired any thing—we never showed any but impassible faces and stupid indifference in the presence of the sublimest wonders a guide had to display. We had found their weak point. We have made good use of it ever since. We have made some of those people savage, at times, but we have never lost our own serenity.

The doctor asks the questions, generally, because he can keep his countenance, and look more like an inspired idiot, and throw more imbecility into the tone of his voice than any man that lives. It comes natural to him.

The guides in Genoa are delighted to secure an American party, because Americans so much wonder, and deal so much in sentiment and emotion before any relic of Columbus. Our guide there fidgeted about as if he had swallowed a spring mattrass. He was full of animation—full of impatience. He said: "Come wis me, genteelmen!—come! I show you ze letter writing by Christopher Colombo!—write it himself!—write it wis his own hand!—come!"

He took us to the municipal palace. After much impressive fumbling of keys and opening of locks, the stained and aged document was spread before us. The guide's eyes sparkled. He danced about us and tapped the parchment with his finger: "What I tell you, genteelmen! Is it not so? See! hand-writing Christopher Colombo!—write it himself!"

We looked indifferent—unconcerned. The doctor examined the document very deliberately, during a painful pause.—Then he said, without any show of interest: "Ah—Ferguson—what—what did you say was the name of the party who wrote this?"

"Christopher Colombo! ze great Christopher Colombo!"

Another deliberate examination.

"Ah—did he write it himself, or—or how?"

"He write it himself!—Christopher Colombo! he's own hand-writing, write by himself!"

Then the doctor laid the document down and said: "Why, I have seen boys in America only fourteen years old that could write better than that."

"But zis is ze great Christo—"

"I don't care who it is! It's the worst writing I ever saw. Now you musn't think you can impose on us because we are strangers. We are not fools, by a good deal. If you have got any specimens of penmanship of real merit, trot them out!—and if you haven't, drive on!"

We drove on. The guide was considerably shaken up, but he made one more venture. He had something which he thought would overcome us. He said: "Ah, genteelmen, you come wis me! I show you beautiful, O, magnificent bust Christopher Colombo!—splendid, grand, magnificent!"

He brought us before the beautiful bust—for it *was* beautiful—and sprang back and struck an attitude: "Ah, look, genteelmen!—beautiful, grand,—bust Christopher Colombo!—beautiful bust, beautiful pedestal!"

The doctor put up his eye-glass—procured for such occasions: "Ah—what did you say this gentleman's name was?"

"Christopher Colombo!—ze great Christopher Colombo!"

"Christopher Colombo—the great Christopher Colombo. Well, what did *he* do?"

"Discover America!—discover America, Oh, ze devil!"

"Discover America. No—that statement will hardly wash. We are just from America ourselves. We heard nothing about it. Christopher Colombo—pleasant name—is—is he dead?"

"Oh, corpo di Baccho!—three hundred year!"

"What did he die of?"

"I do not know!—I can not tell."

"Small-pox, think?"

"I do not know, genteelmen!—I do not know *what* he die of!"

"Measles, likely?"

"May be—may be—I do *not* know—I think he die of somethings."

"Parents living?"

"Im-posseeble!"

"Ah—which is the bust and which is the pedestal?"

"Santa Maria!—*zis* ze bust!—*zis* ze pedestal!"

"Ah, I see, I see—happy combination—very happy combination, indeed. Is—is this the first time this gentleman was ever on a bust?"

That joke was lost on the foreigner—guides can not master the subtleties of the American joke.

We have made it interesting for this Roman guide. Yesterday we spent three or four hours in the Vatican, again, that wonderful world of curiosities. We came very near expressing interest, sometimes—even admiration—it was very hard to keep from it. We succeeded though. Nobody else ever did, in the Vatican museums. The guide was bewildered—non-plussed. He walked his legs off, nearly, hunting up extraordinary things, and exhausted all his ingenuity on us, but it was a failure; we never showed any interest in any thing. He had reserved what he considered to be his greatest wonder till the last—a royal Egyptian mummy, the best preserved in the world, perhaps. He took us there. He felt so sure, this time, that some of his old enthusiasm came back to him: "See, genteelmen!—Mummy! Mummy!"

The eye-glass came up as calmly, as deliberately as ever.

"Ah,—Ferguson—what did I understand you to say the gentleman's name was?"

"Name?—he got no name!—Mummy!—'Gyptian mummy!"

"Yes, yes. Born here?"

"No! *'Gyptian* mummy!"

"Ah, just so. Frenchman, I presume?"

"No! *not* Frenchman, not Roman!—born in Egypta!"

"Born in Egypta. Never heard of Egypta before. Foreign locality, likely. Mummy—mummy. How calm he is—how self-possessed. Is, ah—is he dead?"

"Oh, *sacre bleu,* been dead three thousan' year!"

The doctor turned on him savagely: "Here, now, what do you mean by such conduct as this! Playing us for Chinamen because we are strangers and trying to learn! Trying to impose your vile second-hand carcasses on *us!*—thunder and lightning, I've a notion to—to—if you've got a nice *fresh* corpse, fetch him out!—or by George we'll brain you!"

We make it exceedingly interesting for this Frenchman. However, he has paid us back, partly, without knowing it. He came to the hotel this morning to ask if we were up, and he endeavored as well as he could to describe us, so that the landlord would know which persons he meant. He finished with the casual remark that we were lunatics. The observation was so innocent and so honest that it amounted to a very good thing for a guide to say.

There is one remark (already mentioned,) which never yet has failed to disgust these guides. We use it always, when we can think of nothing else to say. After they have exhausted their enthusiasm pointing out to us and praising the beauties of some ancient bronze image or broken-legged statue, we look at it stupidly and in silence for five, ten, fifteen minutes— as long as we can hold out, in fact—and then ask: "Is—is he dead?"

That conquers the serenest of them. It is not what they are looking for—especially a new guide. Our Roman Ferguson is the most patient, unsuspecting, long-suffering subject we have had yet. We shall be sorry to part with him. We have enjoyed his society very much. We trust he has enjoyed ours, but we are harassed with doubts.

[Athens, Chapter 32]

Home, again! For the first time, in many weeks, the ship's entire family met and shook hands on the quarter-deck. They had gathered from many points of the compass and from many lands, but not one was missing; there was no tale of sickness or death among the flock to dampen the pleasure of the reunion. Once more there was a full audience on deck to listen to the sailors' chorus as they got the anchor up, and to wave an adieu to the land as we sped away from Naples. The seats were full at dinner again, the domino parties were complete, and the life and bustle on the upper deck in the fine moonlight at night was like old times—old times that had been gone weeks only, but yet they were weeks so crowded with incident, adventure and excitement, that they seemed almost like years. There was no lack of cheerfulness on board the *Quaker City*. For once, her title was a misnomer.

At seven in the evening, with the western horizon all golden from the sunken sun, and specked with distant ships, the full moon sailing high over head, the dark blue of the sea under foot, and a strange sort of twilight affected by all these different lights and colors around us and about us, we sighted superb Stromboli. With what majesty the monarch held his lonely state above the level sea! Distance clothed him in a purple gloom, and added a veil of shimmering mist that so softened his rugged features that we seemed to see him through a web of silver gauze. His torch was out; his fires were smoldering; a tall column of smoke that rose up and lost itself in the growing moonlight was all the sign he gave that he was a living Autocrat of the Sea and not the spectre of a dead one.

At two in the morning we swept through the Straits of Messina, and so bright was the moonlight that Italy on the one hand and Sicily on the other seemed almost as distinctly visible as though we looked at them from the middle of a street we were traversing. The city of Messina, milk-white, and starred and spangled all over with gaslights, was a fairy spectacle. A great party of us were on deck smoking and making a noise, and waiting to see famous Scylla and Charybdis. And presently the Oracle stepped out with his eternal spy-glass and squared himself on the deck like another Colossus of Rhodes. It was a surprise to see him abroad at such an hour. Nobody supposed he cared anything about an old fable like that of Scylla and Charybdis. One of the boys said: "Hello, doctor, what are you doing up here at this time of night?—What do you want to see this place for?"

"What do *I* want to see this place for? Young man, little do you know me, or you wouldn't ask such a question. I wish to see *all* the places that's mentioned in the Bible."

"Stuff—this place isn't mentioned in the Bible."

"It ain't mentioned in the Bible! *This* place ain't—well now, what place *is* this, since you know so much about it?"

"Why it's Scylla and Charybdis."

"Scylla and Cha—confound it, I thought it was Sodom and Gomorrah!"

And he closed up his glass and went below. The above is the ship story. Its plausibility is marred a little by the fact that the Oracle was not a biblical student, and did not spend much of his time instructing himself about Scriptural localities.—They say the Oracle complains, in this hot weather, lately, that the only beverage in the ship that is passable, is the butter. He did not mean butter, of course, but inasmuch as that article remains in a melted state now since we are out of ice, it is fair to give him the credit of getting one long word in the right place, anyhow, for once in his life. He said, in Rome, that the Pope was a noble-looking old man, but he never *did* think much of his Iliad.

We spent one pleasant day skirting along the Isles of Greece. They are very mountainous. Their prevailing tints are gray and brown, approaching to red. Little white villages surrounded by trees, nestle in the valleys or roost upon the lofty perpendicular sea-walls.

We had one fine sunset—a rich carmine flush that suffused the western sky and cast a ruddy glow far over the sea.—Fine sunsets seem to be rare in this part of the world—or at least, striking ones. They are soft, sensuous, lovely—they are exquisite, refined, effeminate, but we have seen no sunsets here yet like the gorgeous conflagrations that flame in the track of the sinking sun in our high northern latitudes.

But what were sunsets to us, with the wild excitement upon us of approaching the most renowned of cities! What cared we for outward visions, when Agamemnon, Achilles, and a thousand other heroes of the great Past were marching in ghostly procession through our fancies? What were sunsets to us, who were about to live and breathe and walk in actual Athens; yea, and go far down into the dead centuries and bid in person for the slaves, Diogenes and Plato, in the public market-place, or gossip with the neighbors about the siege of Troy or the splendid deeds of Marathon? We scorned to consider sunsets.

We arrived, and entered the ancient harbor of the Piræus at last. We dropped anchor within half a mile of the village. Away off, across the undulating Plain of Attica, could be seen a little square-topped hill with a something on it, which our glasses soon discovered to be the ruined edifices of the citadel of the Athenians, and most prominent among them loomed the venerable Parthenon. So exquisitely clear and pure is this wonderful atmosphere that every column of the noble structure was discernible through the telescope, and even the smaller ruins about it assumed some semblance of shape. This at a distance of five or six miles. In the valley, near the Acropolis, (the square-topped hill before spoken of,) Athens itself could be vaguely made out with an ordinary lorgnette. Every body was anxious to get ashore and visit these classic localities as quickly as possible. No land we had yet seen had aroused such universal interest among the passengers.

But bad news came. The commandant of the Piræus came in his boat, and said we must either depart or else get outside the harbor and remain imprisoned in our ship, under rigid quarantine, for eleven days! So we took up the anchor and moved outside, to lie a dozen hours or so, taking in supplies, and then sail for Constantinople. It was the bitterest disappointment we had yet experienced. To lie a whole day in sight of the Acropolis, and yet be obliged to go away without visiting Athens! Disappointment was hardly a strong enough word to describe the circumstances.

All hands were on deck, all the afternoon, with books and maps and glasses, trying to determine which "narrow rocky ridge" was the Areopagus, which sloping hill the Pnyx, which elevation the Museum Hill, and so on. And we got things confused. Discussion became heated, and party spirit ran high. Church members were gazing with emotion upon a hill which they said was the one St. Paul preached from, and another faction claimed that that hill was Hymettus, and another that it was Pentelicon! After all the trouble, we could be certain of only one thing—the square-topped hill was the Acropolis, and the grand ruin that crowned it was the Parthenon, whose picture we knew in infancy in the school books.

We inquired of every body who came near the ship, whether there were guards in the Piræus, whether they were strict, what the chances were of capture should any of us slip ashore, and in case any of us made the venture and were caught, what would be probably done to us? The answers were discouraging: There was a strong guard or police force; the Piræus was a small town, and any stranger seen in it would surely attract attention—capture would be certain. The commandant said the punishment would be "heavy;" when asked "how heavy?" he said it would be "very severe"—that was all we could get out of him.

At eleven o'clock at night, when most of the ship's company were abed, four of us stole softly ashore in a small boat, a clouded moon favoring the enterprise, and started two and two, and far apart, over a low hill, intending to go clear around the Piræus, out of the range of its police. Picking our way so stealthily over that rocky, nettle-grown eminence, made me feel a good deal as if I were on my way somewhere to steal something. My immediate comrade and I talked in an undertone about quarantine laws and their penalties, but we found nothing cheering in the subject. I was posted. Only a few days before, I was talking with our captain, and he mentioned the case of a man who swam ashore from a quarantined ship somewhere, and got imprisoned six months for it; and when he was in Genoa a few years ago, a captain of a quarantined ship went in his boat to a departing ship, which was already outside of the harbor, and put a letter on board to be taken to his family, and the authorities imprisoned him three months for it, and then conducted him and his ship fairly to sea, and warned him never to show himself in that port again while he lived. This kind of conversation did no good, further than to give a sort of dismal interest to our quarantine-breaking expedition, and so we dropped it. We made the entire circuit of the town without seeing any body but one man, who stared at us curiously, but said nothing, and a dozen persons asleep on the ground before their doors, whom we walked among and never woke—but we woke up dogs enough, in all conscience—we always had one or two barking at our heels, and several times we had as many as ten and twelve at once. They made such a preposterous din that persons aboard our ship said they could tell how we were progressing for a long time, and where we were, by the barking of the dogs. The clouded moon still favored us. When we had made the whole circuit, and were passing among the houses on the further side of the town, the moon came out splendidly, but we no longer feared the light. As we approached a well, near a house, to get a drink, the owner merely glanced at us and went within. He left the quiet, slumbering town at our mercy. I record it here proudly, that we didn't do any thing to it.

Seeing no road, we took a tall hill to the left of the distant Acropolis for a mark, and steered straight for it over all obstructions, and over a little rougher piece of country than exists any where else outside of the State of Nevada, perhaps. Part of the way it was covered with small, loose stones—we trod on six at a time, and they all rolled. Another part of it was dry, loose, newly-ploughed ground. Still another part of it was a long stretch of low grape-vines, which were tanglesome and troublesome, and which we took to be brambles. The Attic Plain, barring the grape-vines, was a barren, desolate, unpoetical waste—I wonder what it was in Greece's Age of Glory, five hundred years before Christ?

In the neighborhood of one o'clock in the morning, when we were heated with fast walking and parched with thirst, Denny exclaimed, "Why, these weeds are grape-vines!" and in five minutes we had a score of bunches of large, white, delicious grapes, and were reaching down for more when a dark shape rose mysteriously up out of the shadows beside us and said "Ho!" And so we left.

In ten minutes more we struck into a beautiful road, and unlike some others we had stumbled upon at intervals, it led in the right direction. We followed it. It was broad, and smooth, and white—handsome and in perfect repair, and shaded on both sides for a mile or so with single ranks of trees, and also with luxuriant vineyards. Twice we entered and stole grapes, and the second time somebody shouted at us from some invisible place. Whereupon we left again. We speculated in grapes no more on that side of Athens.

Shortly we came upon an ancient stone aqueduct, built upon arches, and from that time forth we had ruins all about us—we were approaching our journey's end. We could not see the Acropolis now or the high hill, either, and I wanted to follow the road till we were abreast of them, but the others overruled me, and we toiled laboriously up the stony hill immediately in our front—and from its summit saw another—climbed it and saw another! It was an hour of exhausting work. Soon we came upon a row of open graves, cut in the solid rock—(for a while one of them served Socrates for a prison)—we passed around the shoulder of the hill, and the citadel, in all its ruined magnificence, burst upon us! We hurried across the ravine and up a winding road, and stood on the old Acropolis, with the prodigious walls of the citadel towering above our heads. We did not stop to inspect their massive blocks of marble, or measure their height, or guess at their extraordinary thickness, but passed at once through a great arched passage like a railway tunnel, and went straight to the gate that leads to the ancient temples. It was locked! So, after all, it seemed that we were not to see the great Parthenon face to face. We sat down and held a council of war. Result: the gate was only a flimsy structure of wood—we would break it down. It seemed like desecration, but then we had traveled far, and our necessities were urgent. We could not hunt up guides and keepers—we must be on the ship before daylight. So we argued. This was all very fine, but when we came to break the gate, we could not do it. We moved around an angle of the wall and found a low bastion—eight feet high without—ten or twelve within. Denny prepared to scale it, and we got ready to follow. By dint of hard scrambling he finally straddled the top, but some loose stones crumbled away and fell with a crash into the court within. There was instantly a banging of doors and a shout. Denny dropped from the wall in a twinkling, and we retreated in disorder to the gate. Xerxes took that mighty citadel four hundred and eighty years before Christ, when his five millions of soldiers and camp-followers followed him to Greece, and if we four Americans could have remained unmolested five minutes longer, we would have taken it too.

The garrison had turned out—four Greeks. We clamored at the gate, and they admitted us. [Bribery and corruption.]

We crossed a large court, entered a great door, and stood upon a pavement of purest white marble, deeply worn by footprints. Before us, in the flooding moonlight, rose the noblest ruins we had ever looked upon—the Propylæ; a small Temple of Minerva; the Temple of Hercules, and the grand Parthenon. [We got these names from the Greek guide, who didn't seem to know more than seven men ought to know.] These edifices were all built of the whitest Pentelic marble, but have a pinkish stain upon them now. Where any part is broken, however, the fracture looks like fine loaf sugar. Six caryatides, or marble women, clad in flowing robes, support the portico of the Temple of Hercules, but the porticos and colonnades of the other structures are formed of massive Doric and Ionic pillars, whose flutings and capitals are still measurably perfect, notwithstanding the centuries that have gone over them and the sieges they have suffered. The Parthenon, originally, was two hundred and twenty-six feet long, one hundred wide, and seventy high, and had two rows of great columns, eight in each, at either end, and single rows of seventeen each down the sides, and was one of the most graceful and beautiful edifices ever erected.

Most of the Parthenon's imposing columns are still standing, but the roof is gone. It was a perfect building two hundred and fifty years ago, when a shell dropped into the Venetian magazine stored here, and the explosion which followed wrecked and unroofed it. I remember but little about the Parthenon, and I have put in one or two facts and figures for the use of other people with short memories. Got them from the guide-book.

As we wandered thoughtfully down the marble-paved length of this stately temple, the scene about us was strangely impressive. Here and there, in lavish profusion, were gleaming white statues of men and women, propped against blocks of marble, some of them armless, some without legs, others headless—but all looking mournful in the moonlight, and startlingly human! They rose up and confronted the midnight intruder on every side—they stared at him with stony eyes from unlooked-for nooks and recesses; they peered at him over fragmentary heaps far down the desolate corridors; they barred his way in the midst of the broad forum, and solemnly pointed with handless arms the way from the sacred fane; and through the roofless temple the moon looked down, and banded the floor and darkened the scattered fragments and broken statues with the slanting shadows of the columns.

What a world of ruined sculpture was about us! Set up in rows—stacked up in piles—scattered broadcast over the wide area of the Acropolis— were hundreds of crippled statues of all sizes and of the most exquisite workmanship; and vast fragments of marble that once belonged to the entablatures, covered with bas-reliefs representing battles and sieges, ships of war with three and four tiers of oars, pageants and processions—every thing one could think of. History says that the temples of the Acropolis were filled with the noblest works of Praxiteles and Phidias, and of many a great master in sculpture besides—and surely these elegant fragments attest it.

We walked out into the grass-grown, fragment-strewn court beyond the Parthenon. It startled us, every now and then, to see a stony white face stare suddenly up at us out of the grass with its dead eyes. The place seemed alive with ghosts. I half expected to see the Athenian heroes of twenty centuries ago glide out of the shadows and steal into the old temple they knew so well and regarded with such boundless pride.

The full moon was riding high in the cloudless heavens, now. We sauntered carelessly and unthinkingly to the edge of the lofty battlements of the citadel, and looked down—a vision! And such a vision! Athens by moonlight! The prophet that thought the splendors of the New Jerusalem were revealed to him, surely saw this instead! It lay in the level plain right under our feet—all spread abroad like a picture—and we looked down upon it as we might have looked from a balloon. We saw no semblance of a street, but every house, every window, every clinging vine, every projection, was as distinct and sharply marked as if the time were noon-day; and yet there was no glare, no glitter, nothing harsh or repulsive—the noiseless city was flooded with the mellowest light that ever streamed from the moon, and seemed like some living creature wrapped in peaceful slumber. On its further side was a little temple, whose delicate pillars and ornate front glowed with a rich lustre that chained the eye like a spell; and nearer by, the palace of the king reared its creamy walls out of the midst of a great garden of shrubbery that was flecked all over with a random shower of amber lights—a spray of golden sparks that lost their brightness in the glory of the moon, and glinted softly upon the sea of dark foliage like the pallid stars of the milky-way. Overhead the stately columns, majestic still in their ruin—under foot the dreaming city—in the distance the silver sea—not on the broad earth is there another picture half so beautiful!

As we turned and moved again through the temple, I wished that the illustrious men who had sat in it in the remote ages could visit it again and reveal themselves to our curious eyes—Plato, Aristotle, Demosthenes, Socrates, Phocion, Pythagoras, Euclid, Pindar, Xenophon, Herodotus, Praxiteles and Phidias, Zeuxis the painter. What a constellation of celebrated names! But more than all, I wished that old Diogenes, groping so patiently with his lantern, searching so zealously for one solitary honest man in all the world, might meander along and stumble on our party. I ought not to say it, may be, but still I suppose he would have put out his light.

We left the Parthenon to keep its watch over old Athens, as it had kept it for twenty-three hundred years, and went and stood outside the walls of the citadel. In the distance was the ancient, but still almost perfect Temple of Theseus, and close by, looking to the west, was the Bema, from whence Demosthenes thundered his philippics and fired the wavering patriotism of his countrymen. To the right was Mars Hill, where the Areopagus sat in ancient times and where St. Paul defined his position, and below was the market-place where he "disputed daily" with the gossip-loving Athenians. We climbed the stone steps St. Paul ascended, and stood in the square-cut place he stood in, and tried to recollect the Bible account of the matter—but for certain reasons, I could not recall the words. I have found them since:

"Now while Paul waited for them at Athens, his spirit was stirred in him, when he saw the city wholly given up to idolatry.

"Therefore disputed he in the synagogue with the Jews, and with the devout persons, and in the market daily with them that met with him.

"And they took him and brought him unto Areopagus, saying, May we know what this new doctrine whereof thou speakest is?

"Then Paul stood in the midst of Mars hill, and said, Ye men of Athens, I perceive that in all things ye are too superstitious;

"For as I passed by and beheld your devotions, I found an altar with this inscription: TO THE UNKNOWN GOD. Whom, therefore, ye ignorantly worship, him declare I unto you."—*Acts*, ch. xvii."

It occurred to us, after a while, that if we wanted to get home before daylight betrayed us, we had better be moving. So we hurried away. When far on our road, we had a parting view of the Parthenon, with the moonlight streaming through its open colonnades and touching its capitals with silver. As it looked then, solemn, grand, and beautiful it will always remain in our memories.

As we marched along, we began to get over our fears, and ceased to care much about quarantine scouts or any body else. We grew bold and reckless; and once, in a sudden burst of courage, I even threw a stone at a dog. It was a pleasant reflection, though, that I did not hit him, because his master might just possibly have been a policeman. Inspired by this happy failure, my valor became utterly uncontrollable, and at intervals I absolutely whistled, though on a moderate key. But boldness breeds boldness, and shortly I plunged into a vineyard, in the full light of the moon, and captured a gallon of superb grapes, not even minding the presence of a peasant who rode by on a mule. Denny and Birch followed my example. Now I had grapes enough for a dozen, but then Jackson was all swollen up with courage, too, and he was obliged to enter a vineyard presently. The first bunch he seized brought trouble. A frowsy, bearded brigand sprang into the road with a shout, and flourished a musket in the light of the moon! We sidled toward the Piræus—not running, you understand, but only advancing with celerity. The brigand shouted again, but still we advanced. It was getting late, and we had no time to fool away on every ass that wanted to drivel Greek platitudes to us. We would just as soon have talked with him as not if we had not been in a hurry. Presently Denny said, "Those fellows are following us!"

We turned, and, sure enough, there they were—three fantastic pirates armed with guns. We slackened our pace to let them come up, and in the meantime I got out my cargo of grapes and dropped them firmly but reluctantly into the shadows by the wayside. But I was not afraid. I only felt that it was not right to steal grapes. And all the more so when the owner was around—and not only around, but with his friends around also. The villains came up and searched a bundle Dr. Birch had in his hand, and scowled upon him when they found it had nothing in it but some holy rocks from Mars Hill, and these were not contraband. They evidently suspected him of playing some wretched fraud upon them, and seemed half inclined to scalp the party. But finally they dismissed us with a warning, couched in excellent Greek, I suppose, and dropped tranquilly in our wake. When they had gone three hundred yards they stopped, and we went on rejoiced. But behold, another armed rascal came out of the shadows and took their place, and followed us two hundred yards. Then he delivered us over to another miscreant, who emerged from some mysterious place, and he in turn to another! For a mile and a half our rear was guarded all the while by armed men. I never traveled in so much state before in all my life.

It was a good while after that before we ventured to steal any more grapes, and when we did we stirred up another troublesome brigand, and then we ceased all further speculation in that line. I suppose that fellow that rode by on the mule posted all the sentinels, from Athens to the Piræus, about us.

Every field on that long route was watched by an armed sentinel, some of whom had fallen asleep, no doubt, but were on hand, nevertheless. This shows what sort of a country modern Attica is—a community of questionable characters. These men were not there to guard their possessions against strangers, but against each other; for strangers seldom visit Athens and the Piræus, and when they do, they go in daylight, and can buy all the grapes they want for a trifle. The modern inhabitants are confiscators and falsifiers of high repute, if gossip speaks truly concerning them, and I freely believe it does.

Just as the earliest tinges of the dawn flushed the eastern sky and turned the pillared Parthenon to a broken harp hung in the pearly horizon, we closed our thirteenth mile of weary, round-about marching, and emerged upon the sea-shore abreast the ships, with our usual escort of fifteen hundred Piræan dogs howling at our heels. We hailed a boat that was two or three hundred yards from shore, and discovered in a moment that it was a police-boat on the lookout for any quarantine-breakers that might chance to be abroad. So we dodged—we were used to that by this time—and when the scouts reached the spot we had so lately occupied, we were absent. They cruised along the shore, but in the wrong direction, and shortly our own boat issued from the gloom and took us aboard. They had heard our signal on the ship. We rowed noiselessly away, and before the police-boat came in sight again, we were safe at home once more.

Four more of our passengers were anxious to visit Athens, and started half an hour after we returned; but they had not been ashore five minutes till the police discovered and chased them so hotly that they barely escaped to their boat again, and that was all. They pursued the enterprise no further.

[Constantinople, from Chapter 34]

When I think how I have been swindled by books of Oriental travel, I want a tourist for breakfast. For years and years I have dreamed of the wonders of the Turkish bath; for years and years I have promised myself that I would yet enjoy one. Many and many a time, in fancy, I have lain in the marble bath, and breathed the slumbrous fragrance of Eastern spices that filled the air; then passed through a weird and complicated system of pulling and hauling, and drenching and scrubbing, by a gang of naked savages who loomed vast and vaguely through the steaming mists, like demons; then rested for a while on a divan fit for a king; then passed through another complex ordeal, and one more fearful than the first; and, finally, swathed in soft fabrics, been conveyed to a princely saloon and laid on a bed of eider down, where eunuchs, gorgeous of costume, fanned me while I drowsed and dreamed, or contentedly gazed at the rich hangings of the apartment, the soft carpets, the sumptuous furniture, the pictures, and drank delicious coffee, smoked the soothing narghili, and dropped, at the last, into tranquil repose, lulled by sensuous odors from unseen censers, by the gentle influence of the narghili's Persian tobacco, and by the music of fountains that counterfeited the pattering of summer rain.

That was the picture, just as I got it from incendiary books of travel. It was a poor, miserable imposture. The reality is no more like it than the Five Points are like the Garden of Eden. They received me in a great court, paved with marble slabs; around it were broad galleries, one above another, carpeted with seedy matting, railed with unpainted balustrades, and furnished with huge rickety chairs, cushioned with rusty old mattresses, indented with impressions left by the forms of nine successive generations of men who had reposed upon them. The place was vast, naked, dreary; its court a barn, its galleries stalls for human horses. The cadaverous, half nude varlets that served in the establishment had nothing of poetry in their appearance, nothing of romance, nothing of Oriental splendor. They shed no entrancing odors—just the contrary. Their hungry eyes and their lank forms continually suggested one glaring, unsentimental fact—they wanted what they term in California "a square meal."

I went into one of the racks and undressed. An unclean starveling wrapped a gaudy table-cloth about his loins, and hung a white rag over my shoulders. If I had had a tub then, it would have come natural to me to take in washing. I was then conducted down stairs into the wet, slippery court, and the first things that attracted my attention were my heels. My fall excited no comment. They expected it, no doubt. It belonged in the list of softening, sensuous influences peculiar to this home of Eastern luxury. It was softening enough, certainly, but its application was not happy. They now gave me a pair of wooden clogs—benches in miniature, with leather straps over them to confine my feet (which they would have done, only I do not wear No. 13s.) These things dangled uncomfortably by the straps when I lifted up my feet, and came down in awkward and unexpected places when I put them on the floor again, and sometimes turned sideways and wrenched my ankles out of joint. However, it was all Oriental luxury, and I did what I could to enjoy it.

They put me in another part of the barn and laid me on a stuffy sort of pallet, which was not made of cloth of gold, or Persian shawls, but was merely the unpretending sort of thing I have seen in the negro quarters of Arkansas. There was nothing whatever in this dim marble prison but five more of these biers. It was a very solemn place. I expected that the spiced odors of Araby were going to steal over my senses now, but they did not. A copper-colored skeleton, with a rag around him, brought me a glass decanter of water, with a lighted tobacco pipe in the top of it, and a pliant stem a yard long, with a brass mouth-piece to it.

It was the famous "narghili" of the East—the thing the Grand Turk smokes in the pictures. This began to look like luxury. I took one blast at it, and it was sufficient; the smoke went in a great volume down into my stomach, my lungs, even into the uttermost parts of my frame. I exploded one mighty cough, and it was as if Vesuvius had let go. For the next five minutes I smoked at every pore, like a frame house that is on fire on the inside. Not any more narghili for me. The smoke had a vile taste, and the taste of a thousand infidel tongues that remained on that brass mouthpiece was viler still. I was getting discouraged. Whenever, hereafter, I see the cross-legged Grand Turk smoking his narghili, in pretended bliss, on the outside of a paper of Connecticut tobacco, I shall know him for the shameless humbug he is.

This prison was filled with hot air. When I had got warmed up sufficiently to prepare me for a still warmer temperature, they took me where it was—into a marble room, wet, slippery and steamy, and laid me out on a raised platform in the centre. It was very warm. Presently my man sat me down by a tank of hot water, drenched me well, gloved his hand with a coarse mitten, and began to polish me all over with it. I began to smell disgreeably. The more he polished the worse I smelt. It was alarming. I said to him: "I perceive that I am pretty far gone. It is plain that I ought to be buried without any unnecessary delay. Perhaps you had better go after my friends at once, because the weather is warm, and I can not 'keep' long.'"

He went on scrubbing, and paid no attention. I soon saw that he was reducing my size. He bore hard on his mitten, and from under it rolled little cylinders, like maccaroni. It could not be dirt, for it was too white. He pared me down in this way for a long time. Finally I said: "It is a tedious process. It will take hours to trim me to the size you want me; I will wait; go and borrow a jack-plane."

He paid no attention at all.

After a while he brought a basin, some soap, and something that seemed to be the tail of a horse. He made up a prodigious quantity of soap-suds, deluged me with them from head to foot, without warning me to shut my eyes, and then swabbed me viciously with the horse-tail. Then he left me there, a snowy statue of lather, and went away. When I got tired of waiting I went and hunted him up. He was propped against the wall, in another room, asleep. I woke him. He was not disconcerted. He took me back and flooded me with hot water, then turbaned my head, swathed me with dry table-cloths, and conducted me to a latticed chicken-coop in one of the galleries, and pointed to one of those Arkansas beds. I mounted it, and vaguely expected the odors of Araby again. They did not come.

The blank, unornamented coop had nothing about it of that oriental voluptuousness one reads of so much. It was more suggestive of the county hospital than any thing else. The skinny servitor brought a narghili, and I got him to take it out again without wasting any time about it. Then he brought the world-renowned Turkish coffee that poets have sung so rapturously for many generations, and I seized upon it as the last hope that was left of my old dreams of Eastern luxury. It was another fraud. Of all the unchristian beverages that ever passed my lips, Turkish coffee is the worst. The cup is small, it is smeared with grounds; the coffee is black, thick, unsavory of smell, and execrable in taste. The bottom of the cup has a muddy sediment in it half an inch deep. This goes down your throat, and portions of it lodge by the way, and produce a tickling aggravation that keeps you barking and coughing for an hour.

Here endeth my experience of the celebrated Turkish bath, and here also endeth my dream of the bliss the mortal revels in who passes through it. It is a malignant swindle. The man who enjoys it is qualified to enjoy any thing that is repulsive to sight or sense, and he that can invest it with a charm of poetry is able to do the same with any thing else in the world that is tedious, and wretched, and dismal, and nasty.

[Syria, from Chapter 43]

Properly, with the sorry relics we bestrode, it was a three days' journey to Damascus. It was necessary that we should do it in less than two. It was necessary because our three pilgrims would not travel on the Sabbath day. We were all perfectly willing to keep the Sabbath day, but there are times when to keep the *letter* of a sacred law whose spirit is righteous, becomes a sin, and this was a case in point. We pleaded for the tired, ill-treated horses, and tried to show that their faithful service deserved kindness in return, and their hard lot compassion. But when did ever self-righteousness know the sentiment of pity? What were a few long hours added to the hardships of some over-taxed brutes when weighed against the peril of those human souls? It was not the most promising party to travel with and hope to gain a higher veneration for religion through the example of its devotees. We said the Saviour who pitied dumb beasts and taught that the ox must be rescued from the mire even on the Sabbath day, would not have counseled a forced march like this. We said the "long trip" was exhausting and therefore dangerous in the blistering heats of summer, even when the ordinary days' stages were traversed, and if we persisted in this hard march, some of us might be stricken down with the fevers of the country in consequence of it. Nothing could move the pilgrims. They *must* press on. Men might die, horses might die, but they must enter upon holy soil next week, with no Sabbath-breaking stain upon them.

Thus they were willing to commit a sin against the spirit of religious law, in order that they might preserve the letter of it. It was not worth while to tell them "the letter kills." I am talking now about personal friends; men whom I like; men who are good citizens; who are honorable, upright, conscientious; but whose idea of the Saviour's religion seems to me distorted. They lecture our shortcomings unsparingly, and every night they call us together and read to us chapters from the Testament that are full of gentleness, of charity, and of tender mercy; and then all the next day they stick to their saddles clear up to the summits of these rugged mountains, and clear down again. Apply the Testament's gentleness, and charity, and tender mercy to a toiling, worn and weary horse?—Nonsense—these are for God's human creatures, not His dumb ones. What the pilgrims choose to do, respect for their almost sacred character demands that I should allow to pass—but I would so like to catch any other member of the party riding his horse up one of these exhausting hills once!

We have given the pilgrims a good many examples that might benefit them, but it is virtue thrown away. They have never heard a cross word out of our lips toward each other—but *they* have quarreled once or twice. We love to hear them at it, after they have been lecturing us. The very first thing they did, coming ashore at Beirout, was to quarrel in the boat. I have said I like them, and I do like them—but every time they read me a scorcher of a lecture I mean to talk back in print.

Not content with doubling the legitimate stages, they switched off the main road and went away out of the way to visit an absurd fountain called Figia, because Baalam's ass had drank there once. So we journeyed on, through the terrible hills and deserts and the roasting sun, and then far into the night, seeking the honored pool of Baalam's ass, the patron saint of all pilgrims like us. I find no entry but this in my note-book:

"Rode to-day, altogether, thirteen hours, through deserts, partly, and partly over barren, unsightly hills, and latterly through wild, rocky scenery, and camped at about eleven o'clock at night on the banks of a limpid stream, near a Syrian village. Do not know its name—do not wish to know it—want to go to bed. Two horses lame (mine and Jack's) and the others worn out. Jack and I walked three or four miles, over the hills, and led the horses. Fun—but of a mild type."

Twelve or thirteen hours in the saddle, even in a Christian land and a Christian climate, and on a good horse, is a tiresome journey; but in an oven like Syria, in a ragged spoon of a saddle that slips fore-and-aft, and "thort-ships," and every way, and on a horse that is tired and lame, and yet must be whipped and spurred with hardly a moment's cessation all day long, till the blood comes from his side, and your conscience hurts you every time you strike, if you are half a man,—it is a journey to be remembered in bitterness of spirit and execrated with emphasis for a liberal division of a man's lifetime.

[Jerusalem, Chapter 53]

A fast walker could go outside the walls of Jerusalem and walk entirely around the city in an hour. I do not know how else to make one understand how small it is. The appearance of the city is peculiar. It is as knobby with countless little domes as a prison door is with bolt-heads. Every house has from one to half a dozen of these white plastered domes of stone, broad and low, sitting in the centre of, or in a cluster upon, the flat roof. Wherefore, when one looks down from an eminence, upon the compact mass of houses (so closely crowded together, in fact, that there is no appearance of streets at all, and so the city looks solid,) he sees the knobbiest town in the world, except Constantinople. It looks as if it might be roofed, from centre to circumference, with inverted saucers. The monotony of the view is interrupted only by the great Mosque of Omar, the Tower of Hippicus, and one or two other buildings that rise into commanding prominence.

The houses are generally two stories high, built strongly of masonry, whitewashed or plastered outside, and have a cage of wooden latticework projecting in front of every window. To reproduce a Jerusalem street, it would only be necessary to up-end a chicken-coop and hang it before each window in an alley of American houses.

The streets are roughly and badly paved with stone, and are tolerably crooked—enough so to make each street appear to close together constantly and come to an end about a hundred yards ahead of a pilgrim as long as he chooses to walk in it. Projecting from the top of the lower story of many of the houses is a very narrow porch-roof or shed, without supports from below; and I have several times seen cats jump across the street from one shed to the other when they were out calling. The cats could have jumped double the distance without extraordinary exertion. I mention these things to give an idea of how narrow the streets are. Since a cat can jump across them without the least inconvenience, it is hardly necessary to state that such streets are too narrow for carriages. These vehicles cannot navigate the Holy City.

The population of Jerusalem is composed of Moslems, Jews, Greeks, Latins, Armenians, Syrians, Copts, Abyssinians, Greek Catholics, and a handful of Protestants. One hundred of the latter sect are all that dwell now in this birthplace of Christianity. The nice shades of nationality comprised in the above list, and the languages spoken by them, are altogether too numerous to mention. It seems to me that all the races and colors and tongues of the earth must be represented among the fourteen thousand souls that dwell in Jerusalem. Rags, wretchedness, poverty and dirt, those signs and symbols that indicate the presence of Moslem rule more surely than the crescent-flag itself, abound. Lepers, cripples, the blind, and the idiotic, assail you on every hand, and they know but one word of but one language apparently—the eternal "bucksheesh." To see the numbers of maimed, malformed and diseased humanity that throng the holy places and obstruct the gates, one might suppose that the ancient days had come again, and that the angel of the Lord was expected to descend at any moment to stir the waters of Bethesda. Jerusalem is mournful, and dreary, and lifeless. I would not desire to live here.

One naturally goes first to the Holy Sepulchre. It is right in the city, near the western gate; it and the place of the Crucifixion, and, in fact, every other place intimately connected with that tremendous event, are ingeniously massed together and covered by one roof—the dome of the Church of the Holy Sepulchre.

Entering the building, through the midst of the usual assemblage of beggars, one sees on his left a few Turkish guards—for Christians of different sects will not only quarrel, but fight, also, in this sacred place, if allowed to do it. Before you is a marble slab, which covers the Stone of Unction, whereon the Saviour's body was laid to prepare it for burial. It was found necessary to conceal the real stone in this way in order to save it from destruction. Pilgrims were too much given to chipping off pieces of it to carry home. Near by is a circular railing which marks the spot where the Virgin stood when the Lord's body was anointed.

Entering the great Rotunda, we stand before the most sacred locality in Christendom—the grave of Jesus. It is in the centre of the church, and immediately under the great dome. It is inclosed in a sort of little temple of yellow and white stone, of fanciful design. Within the little temple is a portion of the very stone which was rolled away from the door of the Sepulchre, and on which the angel was sitting when Mary came thither "at early dawn." Stooping low, we enter the vault—the Sepulchre itself. It is only about six feet by seven, and the stone couch on which the dead Saviour lay extends from end to end of the apartment and occupies half its width. It is covered with a marble slab which has been much worn by the lips of pilgrims. This slab serves as an altar, now. Over it hang some fifty gold and silver lamps, which are kept always burning, and the place is otherwise scandalized by trumpery gewgaws and tawdry ornamentation.

All sects of Christians (except Protestants,) have chapels under the roof of the Church of the Holy Sepulchre, and each must keep to itself and not venture upon another's ground. It has been proven conclusively that they can not worship together around the grave of the Saviour of the World in peace. The chapel of the Syrians is not handsome; that of the Copts is the humblest of them all. It is nothing but a dismal cavern, roughly hewn in the living rock of the Hill of Calvary. In one side of it two ancient tombs are hewn, which are claimed to be those in which Nicodemus and Joseph of Aramathea were buried.

As we moved among the great piers and pillars of another part of the church, we came upon a party of black-robed, animal-looking Italian monks, with candles in their hands, who were chanting something in Latin, and going through some kind of religious performance around a disk of white marble let into the floor. It was there that the risen Saviour appeared to Mary Magdalen in the likeness of a gardener. Near by was a similar stone, shaped like a star—here the Magdalen herself stood, at the same time. Monks were performing in this place also. They perform every where—all over the vast building, and at all hours. Their candles are always flitting about in the gloom, and making the dim old church more dismal than there is any necessity that it should be, even though it is a tomb.

We were shown the place where our Lord appeared to His mother after the Resurrection. Here, also, a marble slab marks the place where St. Helena, the mother of the Emperor Constantine, found the crosses about three hundred years after the Crucifixion. According to the legend, this great discovery elicited extravagant demonstrations of joy. But they were of short duration. The question intruded itself: "Which bore the blessed Saviour, and which the thieves?" To be in doubt, in so mighty a matter as this—to be uncertain which one to adore—was a grievous misfortune. It turned the public joy to sorrow. But when lived there a holy priest who could not set so simple a trouble as this at rest? One of these soon hit upon a plan that would be a certain test. A noble lady lay very ill in Jerusalem. The wise priests ordered that the three crosses be taken to her bedside one at a time. It was done. When her eyes fell upon the first one, she uttered a scream that was heard beyond the Damascus Gate, and even upon the Mount of Olives, it was said, and then fell back in a deadly swoon. They recovered her and brought the second cross. Instantly she went into fearful convulsions, and it was with the greatest difficulty that six strong men could hold her. They were afraid, now, to bring in the third cross. They began to fear that possibly they had fallen upon the wrong crosses, and that the true cross was not with this number at all. However, as the woman seemed likely to die with the convulsions that were tearing her, they concluded that the third could do no more than put her out of her misery with a happy dispatch. So they brought it, and behold, a miracle! The woman sprang from her bed, smiling and joyful, and perfectly restored to health. When we listen to evidence like this, we can not but believe. We would be ashamed to doubt, and properly, too. Even the very part of Jerusalem where this all occurred is there yet. So there is really no room for doubt.

The priests tried to show us, through a small screen, a fragment of the genuine Pillar of Flagellation, to which Christ was bound when they scourged him. But we could not see it, because it was dark inside the screen. However, a baton is kept here, which the pilgrim thrusts through a hole in the screen, and then he no longer doubts that the true Pillar of Flagellation is in there. He can not have any excuse to doubt it, for he can feel it with the stick. He can feel it as distinctly as he could feel any thing.

Not far from here was a niche where they used to preserve a piece of the True Cross, but it is gone, now. This piece of the cross was discovered in the sixteenth century. The Latin priests say it was stolen away, long ago, by priests of another sect. That seems like a hard statement to make, but we know very well that it *was* stolen, because we have seen it ourselves in several of the cathedrals of Italy and France.

But the relic that touched us most was the plain old sword of that stout

Crusader, Godfrey of Bulloigne—King Godfrey of Jerusalem. No blade in Christendom wields such enchantment as this—no blade of all that rust in the ancestral halls of Europe is able to invoke such visions of romance in the brain of him who looks upon it—none that can prate of such chivalric deeds or tell such brave tales of the warrior days of old. It stirs within a man every memory of the Holy Wars that has been sleeping in his brain for years, and peoples his thoughts with mail-clad images, with marching armies, with battles and with sieges. It speaks to him of Baldwin, and Tancred, the princely Saladin, and great Richard of the Lion Heart. It was with just such blades as these that these splendid heroes of romance used to segregate a man, so to speak, and leave the half of him to fall one way and the other half the other. This very sword has cloven hundreds of Saracen Knights from crown to chin in those old times when Godfrey wielded it. It was enchanted, then, by a genius that was under the command of King Solomon. When danger approached its master's tent it always struck the shield and clanged out a fierce alarm upon the startled ear of night. In times of doubt, or in fog or darkness, if it were drawn from its sheath it would point instantly toward the foe, and thus reveal the way—and it would also attempt to start after them of its own accord. A Christian could not be so disguised that it would not know him and refuse to hurt him—nor a Moslem so disguised that it would not leap from its scabbard and take his life. These statements are all well authenticated in many legends that are among the most trustworthy legends the good old Catholic monks preserve. I can never forget old Godfrey's sword, now. I tried it on a Moslem, and clove him in twain like a doughnut. The spirit of Grimes was upon me, and if I had had a graveyard I would have destroyed all the infidels in Jerusalem. I wiped the blood off the old sword and handed it back to the priest—I did not want the fresh gore to obliterate those sacred spots that crimsoned its brightness one day six hundred years ago and thus gave Godfrey warning that before the sun went down his journey of life would end.

Still moving through the gloom of the Church of the Holy Sepulchre we came to a small chapel, hewn out of the rock—a place which has been known as "The Prison of Our Lord" for many centuries. Tradition says that here the Saviour was confined just previously to the crucifixion. Under an altar by the door was a pair of stone stocks for human legs.

These things are called the "Bonds of Christ," and the use they were once put to has given them the name they now bear.

The Greek Chapel is the most roomy, the richest and the showiest chapel in the Church of the Holy Sepulchre. Its altar, like that of all the Greek churches, is a lofty screen that extends clear across the chapel, and is gorgeous with gilding and pictures. The numerous lamps that hang before it are of gold and silver, and cost great sums.

But the feature of the place is a short column that rises from the middle of the marble pavement of the chapel, and marks the exact *centre of the earth*. The most reliable traditions tell us that this was known to be the earth's centre, ages ago, and that when Christ was upon earth he set all doubts upon the subject at rest forever, by stating with his own lips that the tradition was correct. Remember, He said that that particular column stood upon the centre of the world. If the centre of the world changes, the column changes its position accordingly. This column has moved three different times, of its own accord. This is because, in great convulsions of nature, at three different times, masses of the earth—whole ranges of mountains, probably—have flown off into space, thus lessening the diameter of the earth, and changing the exact locality of its centre by a point or two. This is a very curious and interesting circumstance, and is a withering rebuke to those philosophers who would make us believe that it is not possible for any portion of the earth to fly off into space.

To satisfy himself that this spot was really the centre of the earth, a sceptic once paid well for the privilege of ascending to the dome of the church to see if the sun gave him a shadow at noon. He came down perfectly convinced. The day was very cloudy and the sun threw no shadows at all; but the man was satisfied that if the sun had come out and made shadows it could not have made any for him. Proofs like these are not to be set aside by the idle tongues of cavilers. To such as are not bigoted, and are willing to be convinced, they carry a conviction that nothing can ever shake.

If even greater proofs than those I have mentioned are wanted, to satisfy the headstrong and the foolish that this is the genuine centre of the earth, they are here. The greatest of them lies in the fact that from under this very column was taken the *dust from which Adam was made*. This can surely be regarded in the light of a settler. It is not likely that the original first man would have been made from an inferior quality of earth when it was entirely convenient to get first quality from the world's centre. This will strike any reflecting mind forcibly. That Adam was formed of dirt procured in this very spot is amply proven by the fact that in six thousand years no man has ever been able to prove that the dirt was *not* procured here whereof he was made.

It is a singular circumstance that right under the roof of this same great church, and not far away from that illustrious column, Adam himself, the father of the human race, lies buried. There is no question that he is actually buried in the grave which is pointed out as his—there can be none—because it has never yet been proven that that grave is not the grave in which he is buried.

The tomb of Adam! How touching it was, here in a land of strangers, far away from home, and friends, and all who cared for me, thus to discover the grave of a blood relation. True, a distant one, but still a relation. The unerring instinct of nature thrilled its recognition. The fountain of my filial affection was stirred to its profoundest depths, and I gave way to tumultuous emotion. I leaned upon a pillar and burst into tears. I deem it no shame to have wept over the grave of my poor dead relative. Let him who would sneer at my emotion close this volume here, for he will find little to his taste in my journeyings through Holy Land. Noble old man—he did not live to see me—he did not live to see his child. And I—I—alas, I did not live to see *him*. Weighed down by sorrow and disappointment, he died before I was born—six thousand brief summers before I was born. But let us try to bear it with fortitude. Let us trust that he is better off, where he is. Let us take comfort in the thought that his loss is our eternal gain.

The next place the guide took us to in the holy church was an altar dedicated to the Roman soldier who was of the military guard that attended at the crucifixion to keep order, and who—when the vail of the Temple was rent in the awful darkness that followed; when the rock of Golgotha was split asunder by an earthquake; when the artillery of heaven thundered, and in the baleful glare of the lightnings the shrouded dead flitted about the streets of Jerusalem—shook with fear and said, "Surely this was the Son of God!" Where this altar stands now, that Roman soldier stood then, in full view of the crucified Saviour—in full sight and hearing of all the marvels that were transpiring far and wide about the circumference of the Hill of Calvary. And in this self-same spot the priests of the Temple beheaded him for those blasphemous words he had spoken.

In this altar they used to keep one of the most curious relics that human eyes ever looked upon—a thing that had power to fascinate the beholder in some mysterious way and keep him gazing for hours together. It was nothing less than the copper plate Pilate put upon the Saviour's cross, and upon which he wrote, "THIS IS THE KING OF THE JEWS." I think St. Helena, the mother of Constantine, found this wonderful memento when she was here in the third century. She traveled all over Palestine, and was always fortunate. Whenever the good old enthusiast found a thing mentioned in her Bible, Old or New, she would go and search for that thing, and never stop until she found it. If it was Adam, she would find Adam; if it was the Ark, she would find the Ark; if it was Goliah, or Joshua, she would find *them*. She found the inscription here that I was speaking of, I think. She found it in this very spot, close to where the martyred Roman soldier stood. That copper plate is in one of the churches in Rome, now. Any one can see it there. The inscription is very distinct.

We passed along a few steps and saw the altar built over the very spot where the good Catholic priests say the soldiers divided the raiment of the Saviour.

Then we went down into a cavern which cavilers say was once a cistern. It is a chapel, now, however—the Chapel of St. Helena. It is fifty-one feet long by forty-three wide. In it is a marble chair which Helena used to sit in while she superintended her workmen when they were digging and delving for the True Cross. In this place is an altar dedicated to St. Dimas, the penitent thief. A new bronze statue is here—a statue of St. Helena. It reminded us of poor Maximilian, so lately shot. He presented it to this chapel when he was about to leave for his throne in Mexico.

From the cistern we descended twelve steps into a large roughly-shaped grotto, carved wholly out of the living rock. Helena blasted it out when she was searching for the true cross. She had a laborious piece of work, here, but it was richly rewarded. Out of this place she got the crown of thorns, the nails of the cross, the true cross itself, and the cross of the penitent thief. When she thought she had found every thing and was about to stop, she was told in a dream to continue a day longer. It was very fortunate. She did so, and found the cross of the other thief.

The walls and roof of this grotto still weep bitter tears in memory of the event that transpired on Calvary, and devout pilgrims groan and sob when these sad tears fall upon them from the dripping rock. The monks call this apartment the "Chapel of the Invention of the Cross"—a name which is unfortunate, because it leads the ignorant to imagine that a tacit acknowledgment is thus made that the tradition that Helena found the true cross here is a fiction—an invention. It is a happiness to know, however, that intelligent people do not doubt the story in any of its particulars.

Priests of any of the chapels and denominations in the Church of the Holy Sepulchre can visit this sacred grotto to weep and pray and worship the gentle Redeemer. Two different congregations are not allowed to enter at the same time, however, because they always fight.

Still marching through the venerable Church of the Holy Sepulchre, among chanting priests in coarse long robes and sandals; pilgrims of all colors and many nationalities, in all sorts of strange costumes; under dusky arches and by dingy piers and columns; through a sombre cathedral gloom freighted with smoke and incense, and faintly starred with scores of candles that appeared suddenly and as suddenly disappeared, or drifted mysteriously hither and thither about the distant aisles like ghostly jack-o'-lanterns—we came at last to a small chapel which is called the "Chapel of the Mocking." Under the altar was a fragment of a marble column; this was the seat Christ sat on when he was reviled, and mockingly made King, crowned with a crown of thorns and sceptred with a reed. It was here that they blindfolded him and struck him, and said in derision, "Prophesy who it is that smote thee." The tradition that this is the identical spot of the mocking is a very ancient one. The guide said that Saewulf was the first to mention it. I do not know Saewulf, but still, I cannot well refuse to receive his evidence—none of us can.

They showed us where the great Godfrey and his brother Baldwin, the first Christian Kings of Jerusalem, once lay buried by that sacred sepulchre they had fought so long and so valiantly to wrest from the hands of the infidel. But the niches that had contained the ashes of these renowned crusaders were empty. Even the coverings of their tombs were gone—destroyed by devout members of the Greek Church, because Godfrey and Baldwin were Latin princes, and had been reared in a Christian faith whose creed differed in some unimportant respects from theirs.

We passed on, and halted before the tomb of Melchisedek! You will remember Melchisedek, no doubt; he was the King who came out and levied a tribute on Abraham the time that he pursued Lot's captors to Dan, and took all their property from them. That was about four thousand years ago, and Melchisedek died shortly afterward. However, his tomb is in a good state of preservation.

When one enters the Church of the Holy Sepulchre, the Sepulchre itself is the first thing he desires to see, and really is almost the first thing he does see. The next thing he has a strong yearning to see is the spot where the Saviour was crucified. But this they exhibit last. It is the crowning glory of the place. One is grave and thoughtful when he stands in the little Tomb of the Saviour—he could not well be otherwise in such a place—but he has not the slightest possible belief that ever the Lord lay there, and so the interest he feels in the spot is very, very greatly marred by that reflection. He looks at the place where Mary stood, in another part of the church, and where John stood, and Mary Magdalen; where the mob derided the Lord; where the angel sat; where the crown of thorns was found, and the true cross; where the risen Saviour appeared—he looks at all these places with interest, but with the same conviction he felt in the case of the Sepulchre, that there is nothing genuine about them, and that they are imaginary holy places created by the monks. But the place of the Crucifixion affects him differently. He fully believes that he is looking upon the very spot where the Saviour gave up his life. He remembers that Christ was very celebrated, long before he came to Jerusalem; he knows that his fame was so great that crowds followed him all the time; he is aware that his entry into the city produced a stirring sensation, and that his reception was a kind of ovation; he can not overlook the fact that when he was crucified there were very many in Jerusalem who believed that he was the true Son of God. To publicly execute such a personage was sufficient in itself to make the locality of the execution a memorable place for ages; added to this, the storm, the darkness, the earthquake, the rending of the vail of the Temple, and the untimely waking of the dead, were events calculated to fix the execution and the scene of it in the memory of even the most thoughtless witness. Fathers would tell their sons about the strange affair, and point out the spot; the sons would transmit the story to their children, and thus a period of three hundred years would easily be spanned {The thought is Mr. Prime's, not mine, and is full of good sense. I borrowed it from his "Tent Life."—M.T.}—at which time Helena came and built a church upon Calvary to commemorate the death and burial of the Lord and preserve the sacred place in the memories of men; since that time there has always been a church there. It is not possible that there can be any mistake about the locality of the Crucifixion. Not half a dozen persons knew where they buried the Saviour, perhaps, and a burial is not a startling event, any how; therefore, we can be pardoned for unbelief in the Sepulchre, but not in the place of the Crucifixion. Five hundred years hence there will be no vestige of Bunker Hill Monument left, but America will still know where the battle was fought and where Warren fell. The crucifixion of Christ was too notable an event in Jerusalem, and the Hill of Calvary made too celebrated by it, to be forgotten in the short space of three hundred years. I climbed the stairway in the church which brings one to the top of the small inclosed pinnacle of rock, and looked upon the place where the true cross once stood, with a far more absorbing interest than I had ever felt in any thing earthly before. I could not believe that the three holes in the top of the rock were the actual ones the crosses stood in, but I felt satisfied that those crosses had stood so near the place now occupied by them, that the few feet of possible difference were a matter of no consequence.

When one stands where the Saviour was crucified, he finds it all he can do to keep it strictly before his mind that Christ was not crucified in a Catholic Church. He must remind himself every now and then that the great event transpired in the open air, and not in a gloomy, candle-lighted cell in a little corner of a vast church, up-stairs—a small cell all bejeweled and bespangled with flashy ornamentation, in execrable taste.

Under a marble altar like a table, is a circular hole in the marble floor, corresponding with the one just under it in which the true cross stood. The first thing every one does is to kneel down and take a candle and examine this hole. He does this strange prospecting with an amount of gravity that can never be estimated or appreciated by a man who has not seen the operation. Then he holds his candle before a richly engraved picture of the Saviour, done on a massy slab of gold, and wonderfully rayed and starred with diamonds, which hangs above the hole within the altar, and his solemnity changes to lively admiration. He rises and faces the finely wrought figures of the Saviour and the malefactors uplifted upon their crosses behind the altar, and bright with a metallic lustre of many colors. He turns next to the figures close to them of the Virgin and Mary

Magdalen; next to the rift in the living rock made by the earthquake at the time of the Crucifixion, and an extension of which he had seen before in the wall of one of the grottoes below; he looks next at the show-case with a figure of the Virgin in it, and is amazed at the princely fortune in precious gems and jewelry that hangs so thickly about the form as to hide it like a garment almost. All about the apartment the gaudy trappings of the Greek Church offend the eye and keep the mind on the rack to remember that this is the Place of the Crucifixion—Golgotha—the Mount of Calvary. And the last thing he looks at is that which was also the first— the place where the true cross stood. That will chain him to the spot and compel him to look once more, and once again, after he has satisfied all curiosity and lost all interest concerning the other matters pertaining to the locality.

And so I close my chapter on the Church of the Holy Sepulchre—the most sacred locality on earth to millions and millions of men, and women, and children, the noble and the humble, bond and free. In its history from the first, and in its tremendous associations, it is the most illustrious edifice in Christendom. With all its clap-trap side-shows and unseemly impostures of every kind, it is still grand, reverend, venerable—for a god died there; for fifteen hundred years its shrines have been wet with the tears of pilgrims from the earth's remotest confines; for more than two hundred, the most gallant knights that ever wielded sword wasted their lives away in a struggle to seize it and hold it sacred from infidel pollution. Even in our own day a war, that cost millions of treasure and rivers of blood, was fought because two rival nations claimed the sole right to put a new dome upon it. History is full of this old Church of the Holy Sepulchre—full of blood that was shed because of the respect and the veneration in which men held the last resting-place of the meek and lowly, the mild and gentle, Prince of Peace!

[Egypt, from Chapter 58]

After years of waiting, it was before me at last. The great face was so sad, so earnest, so longing, so patient. There was a dignity not of earth in its mien, and in its countenance a benignity such as never any thing human wore. It was stone, but it seemed sentient. If ever image of stone thought, it was thinking. It was looking toward the verge of the landscape, yet looking *at* nothing—nothing but distance and vacancy. It was looking over and beyond every thing of the present, and far into the past. It was gazing out over the ocean of Time—over lines of century-waves which, further and further receding, closed nearer and nearer together, and blended at last into one unbroken tide, away toward the horizon of remote antiquity. It was thinking of the wars of departed ages; of the empires it had seen created and destroyed; of the nations whose birth it had witnessed, whose progress it had watched, whose annihilation it had noted; of the joy and sorrow, the life and death, the grandeur and decay, of five thousand slow revolving years. It was the type of an attribute of man—of a faculty of his heart and brain. It was MEMORY—RETROSPECTION—wrought into visible, tangible form. All who know what pathos there is in memories of days that are accomplished and faces that have vanished—albeit only a trifling score of years gone by—will have some appreciation of the pathos that dwells in these grave eyes that look so steadfastly back upon the things they knew before History was born—before Tradition had being—things that were, and forms that moved, in a vague era which even Poetry and Romance scarce know of—and passed one by one away and left the stony dreamer solitary in the midst of a strange new age, and uncomprehended scenes.

The Sphynx is grand in its loneliness; it is imposing in its magnitude; it is impressive in the mystery that hangs over its story. And there is that in the overshadowing majesty of this eternal figure of stone, with its accusing memory of the deeds of all ages, which reveals to one something of what he shall feel when he shall stand at last in the awful presence of God.

There are some things which, for the credit of America, should be left unsaid, perhaps; but these very things happen sometimes to be the very things which, for the real benefit of Americans, ought to have prominent notice. While we stood looking, a wart, or an excrescence of some kind, appeared on the jaw of the Sphynx. We heard the familiar clink of a hammer, and understood the case at once. One of our well-meaning reptiles—I mean relic-hunters—had crawled up there and was trying to break a "specimen" from the face of this the most majestic creation the hand of man has wrought. But the great image contemplated the dead ages as calmly as ever, unconscious of the small insect that was fretting at its jaw. Egyptian granite that has defied the storms and earthquakes of all time has nothing to fear from the tack-hammers of ignorant excursionists—

highwaymen like this specimen. He failed in his enterprise. We sent a sheik to arrest him if he had the authority, or to warn him, if he had not, that by the laws of Egypt the crime he was attempting to commit was punishable with imprisonment or the bastinado. Then he desisted and went away.

2. "The Miner's Dream," frontispiece from *Roughing It* (Hartford, CT: American Publishing Company, 1872).

2

Roughing It (1872)

"The Innocents at Home," a logical follow-up to Twain's highly popular *The Innocents Abroad*, was a preliminary title for the book that would eventually be published as *Roughing It*. However, this narrative related a series of "vagabondizing" adventures rather than a scheduled voyage like that of the *Quaker City*, and the events had occurred years before Mark Twain became a recognized author. Twain was here recalling events that began when he accompanied his older brother Orion in a move to Nevada Territory in 1861 after the Civil War had closed the Mississippi River to piloting. Twain would remain in the Far West for more than five years. His reminiscences in *Roughing It* were those of an established literary figure remembering his youthful meanderings, but its contents bear conscious parallels to a conventional travel book chronicling a tour of the mythic West.

Oddly enough, the subject matter of Twain's second book is rarely classified as "travel." Most readers consult it as an early segment of his autobiography, and a few scholars have even mounted arguments that its tale of a tenderfoot's initiation into rowdy conduct in a rugged terrain, though highly episodic, nonetheless qualifies as being novelistic. But the fact is that *Roughing It* was primarily Twain's first attempt at using techniques mastered as a travel correspondent to document his participation in the great adventure of reaching, exploring, settling, and mining the American Far West.

The opening chapters that recount Twain's grueling journey to the Nevada Territory are as vivid and compelling in their way as Charles Dickens's descriptions of stage coach travel through quaint English villages and countryside. By contrast, however, Twain's trip across the grasslands, mountains, and deserts gave him the opportunity to write one of the fullest depictions of the hardships of stage coach travel before the completion of the first transcontinental railroad in 1869 announced the demise of a storied mode of transportation. This section alone would rank *Roughing It* as an important—and humorous—final snapshot of an era's end.

Yet much, much more was accomplished in the ensuing chapters as the twenty-six-year-old Sam Clemens alighted in Carson City, held territorial political responsibilities, made repeated if fruitless attempts to uncover one of the silver fortunes being discovered all around him, ventured into California, gave up prospecting and took up newspaper journalism in Nevada under Joseph T. Goodman, met the famous humorist Artemus Ward who was touring the Southwest, moved to the California coast and wrote for San Francisco magazines and newspapers, and even voyaged across the Pacific to the Sandwich Islands. Only a few other intrepid writers like Jack London would have experiences to rival Twain's incredible days as a footloose, unmarried vagabond.

We know now that Twain was not always grateful or helpful to his older brother Orion, who had taken the trouble to bring him to the territory where Orion had been given a political appointment. Nonetheless, Orion's generosity to an out-of-work steamboat pilot resulted in one of the classic books about the American West written during the nineteenth century. Though *Roughing It* sold more copies in the first year than had *The Innocents Abroad,* its long-term popularity would never match that of the earlier book; all the same, by the first years of the dawning twentieth century it still ranked as Twain's third-best-selling work.

Twain polished, refined, and removed the coarser humor from letters he had written earlier about the region and which he used to summon up his memories. Nevertheless, there adheres a compelling freshness and sense of pleasure within the narrative—and a pride in having belonged to a truly historical American epoch—that sets *Roughing It* apart from his other books. Twain would refer again and again to his Western years in speeches and essays, but here is his fullest evocation of a period that shaped his thought and behavior for a lifetime.

From ROUGHING IT

[St. Louis to St. Joseph, Chapter 1]

My brother had just been appointed Secretary of Nevada Territory—an office of such majesty that it concentrated in itself the duties and dignities of Treasurer, Comptroller, Secretary of State, and Acting Governor in the Governor's absence. A salary of eighteen hundred dollars a year and the title of "Mr. Secretary," gave to the great position an air of wild and imposing grandeur. I was young and ignorant, and I envied my brother. I coveted his distinction and his financial splendor, but particularly and especially the long, strange journey he was going to make, and the curious new world he was going to explore. He was going to travel! I never had been away from home, and that word "travel" had a seductive charm for me. Pretty soon he would be hundreds and hundreds of miles away on the great plains and deserts, and among the mountains of the Far West, and would see buffaloes and Indians, and prairie dogs, and antelopes, and have all kinds of adventures, and may be get hanged or scalped, and have ever such a fine time, and write home and tell us all about it, and be a hero. And he would see the gold mines and the silver mines, and maybe go about of an afternoon when his work was done, and pick up two or three pailfuls of shining slugs, and nuggets of gold and silver on the hillside. And by and by he would become very rich, and return home by sea, and be able to talk as calmly about San Francisco and the ocean, and "the isthmus" as if it was nothing of any consequence to have seen those marvels face to face. What I suffered in contemplating his happiness, pen cannot describe. And so, when he offered me, in cold blood, the sublime position of private secretary under him, it appeared to me that the heavens and the earth passed away, and the firmament was rolled together as a scroll! I had nothing more to desire. My contentment was complete. At the end of an hour or two I was ready for the journey. Not much packing up was necessary, because we were going in the overland stage from the Missouri frontier to Nevada, and passengers were only allowed a small quantity of baggage apiece. There was no Pacific railroad in those fine times of ten or twelve years ago—not a single rail of it.

I only proposed to stay in Nevada three months—I had no thought of staying longer than that. I meant to see all I could that was new and strange, and then hurry home to business. I little thought that I would not see the end of that three-month pleasure excursion for six or seven uncommonly long years!

I dreamed all night about Indians, deserts, and silver bars, and in due time, next day, we took shipping at the St. Louis wharf on board a steamboat bound up the Missouri River.

We were six days going from St. Louis to "St. Jo."—a trip that was so dull, and sleepy, and eventless that it has left no more impression on my memory than if its duration had been six minutes instead of that many days. No record is left in my mind, now, concerning it, but a confused jumble of savage-looking snags, which we deliberately walked over with one wheel or the other; and of reefs which we butted and butted, and then retired from and climbed over in some softer place; and of sand-bars which we roosted on occasionally, and rested, and then got out our crutches and sparred over. In fact, the boat might almost as well have gone to St. Jo. by land, for she was walking most of the time, anyhow—climbing over reefs and clambering over snags patiently and laboriously all day long. The captain said she was a "bully" boat, and all she wanted was more "shear" and a bigger wheel. I thought she wanted a pair of stilts, but I had the deep sagacity not to say so.

[Overland to Nevada Territory, Chapter 2]

The first thing we did on that glad evening that landed us at St. Joseph was to hunt up the stage-office, and pay a hundred and fifty dollars apiece for tickets per overland coach to Carson City, Nevada.

The next morning, bright and early, we took a hasty breakfast, and hurried to the starting-place. Then an inconvenience presented itself which we had not properly appreciated before, namely, that one cannot make a heavy traveling trunk stand for twenty-five pounds of baggage—because it weighs a good deal more. But that was all we could take—twenty-five pounds each. So we had to snatch our trunks open, and make a selection in a good deal of a hurry. We put our lawful twenty-five pounds apiece all in one valise, and shipped the trunks back to St. Louis again. It was a sad parting, for now we had no swallow-tail coats and white kid gloves to wear at Pawnee receptions in the Rocky Mountains, and no stove-pipe hats nor patent-leather boots, nor anything else necessary to make life calm and peaceful. We were reduced to a war-footing. Each of us put on a rough, heavy suit of clothing, woolen army shirt and "stogy" boots included; and into the valise we crowded a few white shirts, some underclothing and such things. My brother, the Secretary, took along about four pounds of United States statutes and six pounds of Unabridged Dictionary; for we did not know—poor innocents—that such things could be bought in San Francisco on one day and received in Carson City the next. I was armed to the teeth with a pitiful little Smith & Wesson's seven-shooter, which carried a ball like a homœopathic pill, and it took the whole seven to make a dose for an adult. But I thought it was grand. It appeared to me to be a dangerous weapon. It only had one fault—you could not hit anything with it. One of our "conductors" practiced awhile on a cow with it, and as long as she stood still and behaved herself she was safe; but as soon as she went to moving about, and he got to shooting at other things, she came to grief. The Secretary had a small-sized Colt's revolver strapped around him for protection against the Indians, and to guard against accidents he carried it uncapped. Mr. George Bemis was dismally formidable. George Bemis was our fellow-traveler. We had never seen him before. He wore in his belt an old original "Allen" revolver, such as irreverent people called a "pepper-box." Simply drawing the trigger back, cocked and fired the pistol. As the trigger came back, the hammer would begin to rise and the barrel to turn over, and presently down would drop the hammer, and away would speed the ball. To aim along the turning barrel and hit the thing aimed at was a feat which was probably never done with an "Allen" in the world. But George's was a reliable weapon, nevertheless, because, as one of the stage-drivers afterward said, "If she didn't get what she went after, she would fetch something else." And so she did. She went after a deuce of spades nailed against a tree, once, and fetched a mule standing about thirty yards to the left of it. Bemis did not want the mule; but the owner came out with a double-barreled shot-gun and persuaded him to buy it, anyhow. It was a cheerful weapon—the "Allen." Sometimes all its six barrels would go off at once, and then there was no safe place in all the region round about, but behind it.

We took two or three blankets for protection against frosty weather in the mountains. In the matter of luxuries we were modest—we took none along but some pipes and five pounds of smoking tobacco. We had two large canteens to carry water in, between stations on the Plains, and we also took with us a little shot-bag of silver coin for daily expenses in the way of breakfasts and dinners.

By eight o'clock everything was ready, and we were on the other side of the river. We jumped into the stage, the driver cracked his whip, and we bowled away and left "the States" behind us. It was a superb summer morning, and all the landscape was brilliant with sunshine. There was a freshness and breeziness, too, and an exhilarating sense of emancipation from all sorts of cares and responsibilities, that almost made us feel that the years we had spent in the close, hot city, toiling and slaving, had been wasted and thrown away. We were spinning along through Kansas, and in the course of an hour and a half we were fairly abroad on the great Plains. Just here the land was rolling—a grand sweep of regular elevations and depressions as far as the eye could reach—like the stately heave and swell of the ocean's bosom after a storm. And everywhere were cornfields, accenting with squares of deeper green, this limitless expanse of grassy land. But presently this sea upon dry ground was to lose its "rolling" character and stretch away for seven hundred miles as level as a floor!

Our coach was a great swinging and swaying stage, of the most sumptuous description—an imposing cradle on wheels. It was drawn by six handsome horses, and by the side of the driver sat the "conductor," the legitimate captain of the craft; for it was his business to take charge and care of the mails, baggage, express matter, and passengers. We three were the only passengers, this trip. We sat on the back seat, inside. About all the rest of the coach was full of mail bags—for we had three days' delayed mails with us. Almost touching our knees, a perpendicular wall of mail matter rose up to the roof. There was a great pile of it strapped on top of the stage, and both the fore and hind boots were full. We had twenty-seven hundred pounds of it aboard, the driver said—"a little for Brigham, and Carson, and 'Frisco, but the heft of it for the Injuns, which is powerful troublesome 'thout they get plenty of truck to read." But as he just then got up a fearful convulsion of his countenance which was suggestive of a wink being swallowed by an earthquake, we guessed that his remark was intended to be facetious, and to mean that we would unload the most of our mail matter somewhere on the Plains and leave it to the Indians, or whosoever wanted it.

We changed horses every ten miles, all day long, and fairly flew over the hard, level road. We jumped out and stretched our legs every time the coach stopped, and so the night found us still vivacious and unfatigued.

After supper a woman got in, who lived about fifty miles further on, and we three had to take turns at sitting outside with the driver and conductor. Apparently she was not a talkative woman. She would sit there in the gathering twilight and fasten her steadfast eyes on a mosquito rooting into her arm, and slowly she would raise her other hand till she had got his range, and then she would launch a slap at him that would have jolted a cow; and after that she would sit and contemplate the corpse with tranquil satisfaction—for she never missed her mosquito; she was a dead shot at short range. She never removed a carcase, but left them there for bait. I sat by this grim Sphynx and watched her kill thirty or forty mosquitoes— watched her, and waited for her to say something, but she never did. So I finally opened the conversation myself. I said: "The mosquitoes are pretty bad, about here, madam."

"You bet!"

"What did I understand you to say, madam?"

"You BET!"

Then she cheered up, and faced around and said: "Danged if I didn't begin to think you fellers was deef and dumb. I did, b'gosh. Here I've sot, and sot, and sot, a-bust'n muskeeters and wonderin' what was ailin' ye. Fust I thot you was deef and dumb, then I thot you was sick or crazy, or suthin', and then by and by I begin to reckon you was a passel of sickly fools that couldn't think of nothing to say. Wher'd ye come from?"

The Sphynx was a Sphynx no more! The fountains of her great deep were broken up, and she rained the nine parts of speech forty days and forty nights, metaphorically speaking, and buried us under a desolating deluge of trivial gossip that left not a crag or pinnacle of rejoinder projecting above the tossing waste of dislocated grammar and decomposed pronunciation!

How we suffered, suffered, suffered! She went on, hour after hour, till I was sorry I ever opened the mosquito question and gave her a start. She never did stop again until she got to her journey's end toward daylight; and then she stirred us up as she was leaving the stage (for we were nodding, by that time), and said: "Now you git out at Cottonwood, you fellers, and lay over a couple o' days, and I'll be along some time to-night, and if I can do ye any good by edgin' in a word now and then, I'm right thar. Folks'll tell you 't I've always ben kind o' offish and partic'lar for a gal that's raised in the woods, and I *am*, with the rag-tag and bob-tail, and a gal *has* to be, if she wants to *be* anything, but when people comes along which is my equals, I reckon I'm a pretty sociable heifer after all."

We resolved not to "lay by at Cottonwood."

[Overland to Nevada Territory, Chapter 3]

About an hour and a half before daylight we were bowling along smoothly over the road—so smoothly that our cradle only rocked in a gentle, lulling way, that was gradually soothing us to sleep, and dulling our consciousness—when something gave away under us! We were dimly aware of it, but indifferent to it. The coach stopped. We heard the driver and conductor talking together outside, and rummaging for a lantern, and swearing because they could not find it—but we had no interest in whatever had happened, and it only added to our comfort to think of those people out there at work in the murky night, and we snug in our nest with the curtains drawn. But presently, by the sounds, there seemed to be an examination going on, and then the driver's voice said: "By George, the thoroughbrace is broke!"

This startled me broad awake—as an undefined sense of calamity is always apt to do. I said to myself: "Now, a thoroughbrace is probably part of a horse; and doubtless a vital part, too, from the dismay in the driver's voice. Leg, maybe—and yet how could he break his leg waltzing along such a road as this? No, it can't be his leg. That is impossible, unless he was reaching for the driver. Now, what can be the thoroughbrace of a horse, I wonder? Well, whatever comes, I shall not air my ignorance in this crowd, anyway."

Just then the conductor's face appeared at a lifted curtain, and his lantern glared in on us and our wall of mail matter. He said: "Gents, you'll have to turn out a spell. Thoroughbrace is broke."

We climbed out into a chill drizzle, and felt ever so homeless and dreary. When I found that the thing they called a "thoroughbrace" was the massive combination of belts and springs which the coach rocks itself in, I said to the driver: "I never saw a thoroughbrace used up like that, before, that I can remember. How did it happen?"

"Why, it happened by trying to make one coach carry three days' mail—that's how it happened," said he. "And right here is the very direction which is wrote on all the newspaper-bags which was to be put out for the Injuns for to keep 'em quiet. It's most uncommon lucky, becuz it's so nation dark I should 'a' gone by unbeknowns if that air thoroughbrace hadn't broke."

I knew that he was in labor with another of those winks of his, though I could not see his face, because he was bent down at work; and wishing him a safe delivery, I turned to and helped the rest get out the mail-sacks. It made a great pyramid by the roadside when it was all out. When they had mended the thoroughbrace we filled the two boots again, but put no mail on top, and only half as much inside as there was before. The conductor bent all the seat-backs down, and then filled the coach just half full of mail-bags from end to end. We objected loudly to this, for it left us no seats. But the conductor was wiser than we, and said a bed was better than seats, and moreover, this plan would protect his thoroughbraces. We never wanted any seats after that. The lazy bed was infinitely preferable. I had many an exciting day, subsequently, lying on it reading the statutes and the dictionary, and wondering how the characters would turn out.

The conductor said he would send back a guard from the next station to take charge of the abandoned mail-bags, and we drove on.

It was now just dawn; and as we stretched our cramped legs full length on the mail sacks, and gazed out through the windows across the wide wastes of greensward clad in cool, powdery mist, to where there was an expectant look in the eastern horizon, our perfect enjoyment took the form of a tranquil and contented ecstasy. The stage whirled along at a spanking gait, the breeze flapping curtains and suspended coats in a most exhilarating way; the cradle swayed and swung luxuriously, the pattering of the horses' hoofs, the cracking of the driver's whip, and his "Hi-yi! g'lang!" were music; the spinning ground and the waltzing trees appeared to give us a mute hurrah as we went by, and then slack up and look after us with interest, or envy, or something; and as we lay and smoked the pipe of peace and compared all this luxury with the years of tiresome city life that had gone before it, we felt that there was only one complete and satisfying happiness in the world, and we had found it.

After breakfast, at some station whose name I have forgotten, we three climbed up on the seat behind the driver, and let the conductor have our bed for a nap. And by and by, when the sun made me drowsy, I lay down on my face on top of the coach, grasping the slender iron railing, and slept for an hour or more. That will give one an appreciable idea of those matchless roads. Instinct will make a sleeping man grip a fast hold of the railing when the stage jolts, but when it only swings and sways, no grip is necessary. Overland drivers and conductors used to sit in their places and sleep thirty or forty minutes at a time, on good roads, while spinning along at the rate of eight or ten miles an hour. I saw them do it, often. There was no danger about it; a sleeping man *will* seize the irons in time when the coach jolts. These men were hard worked, and it was not possible for them to stay awake all the time.

By and by we passed through Marysville, and over the Big Blue and Little Sandy; thence about a mile, and entered Nebraska. About a mile further on, we came to the Big Sandy—one hundred and eighty miles from St. Joseph.

As the sun was going down, we saw the first specimen of an animal known familiarly over two thousand miles of mountain and desert—from Kansas clear to the Pacific Ocean—as the "jackass rabbit." He is well named. He is just like any other rabbit, except that he is from one third to twice as large, has longer legs in proportion to his size, and has the most preposterous ears that ever were mounted on any creature *but* a jackass. When he is sitting quiet, thinking about his sins, or is absent-minded or unapprehensive of danger, his majestic ears project above him conspicuously; but the breaking of a twig will scare him nearly to death, and then he tilts his ears back gently and starts for home. All you can see, then, for the next minute, is his long gray form stretched out straight and "streaking it" through the low sage-brush, head erect, eyes right, and ears just canted a little to the rear, but showing you where the animal is, all the time, the same as if he carried a jib. Now and then he makes a marvelous spring with his long legs, high over the stunted sage-brush, and scores a leap that would make a horse envious. Presently he comes down to a long, graceful "lope," and shortly he mysteriously disappears. He has crouched behind a sage-bush, and will sit there and listen and tremble until you get within six feet of him, when he will get under way again. But one must shoot at this creature once, if he wishes to see him throw his heart into his heels, and do the best he knows how. He is frightened clear through, now, and he lays his long ears down on his back, straightens himself out like a yard-stick every spring he makes, and scatters miles behind him with an easy indifference that is enchanting.

Our party made this specimen "hump himself," as the conductor said. The secretary started him with a shot from the Colt; I commenced spitting at him with my weapon; and all in the same instant the old "Allen's" whole broadside let go with a rattling crash, and it is not putting it too strong to say that the rabbit was frantic! He dropped his ears, set up his tail, and left for San Francisco at a speed which can only be described as a flash and a vanish! Long after he was out of sight we could hear him whiz.

I do not remember where we first came across "sage-brush," but as I have been speaking of it I may as well describe it. This is easily done, for if the reader can imagine a gnarled and venerable live oak-tree reduced to a little shrub two feet high, with its rough bark, its foliage, its twisted boughs, all complete, he can picture the "sage-brush" exactly. Often, on lazy afternoons in the mountains, I have lain on the ground with my face under a sage-bush, and entertained myself with fancying that the gnats among its foliage were liliputian birds, and that the ants marching and countermarching about its base were liliputian flocks and herds, and myself some vast loafer from Brobdignag waiting to catch a little citizen and eat him.

It is an imposing monarch of the forest in exquisite miniature, is the "sage-brush." Its foliage is a grayish green, and gives that tint to desert and mountain. It smells like our domestic sage, and "sage-tea" made from it tastes like the sage-tea which all boys are so well acquainted with. The sage-brush is a singularly hardy plant, and grows right in the midst of deep sand, and among barren rocks, where nothing else in the vegetable world would try to grow, except "bunch-grass." {"Bunch-grass" grows on the bleak mountain-sides of Nevada and neighboring territories, and offers excellent feed for stock, even in the dead of winter, wherever the snow is blown aside and exposes it; notwithstanding its unpromising home, bunch-grass is a better and more nutritious diet for cattle and horses than almost any other hay or grass that is known—so stock-men say.} The sage-bushes grow from three to six or seven feet apart, all over the mountains and deserts of the Far West, clear to the borders of California. There is not a tree of any kind in the deserts, for hundreds of miles—there is no vegetation at all in a regular desert, except the sage-brush and its cousin the "greasewood," which is so much like the sage-brush that the difference amounts to little. Camp-fires and hot suppers in the deserts would be impossible but for the friendly sage-brush. Its trunk is as large as a boy's wrist (and from that up to a man's arm), and its crooked branches are half as large as its trunk—all good, sound, hard wood, very like oak.

When a party camps, the first thing to be done is to cut sage-brush; and in a few minutes there is an opulent pile of it ready for use. A hole a foot wide, two feet deep, and two feet long, is dug, and sage-brush chopped up and burned in it till it is full to the brim with glowing coals. Then the cooking begins, and there is no smoke, and consequently no swearing. Such a fire will keep all night, with very little replenishing; and it makes a very sociable camp-fire, and one around which the most impossible reminiscences sound plausible, instructive, and profoundly entertaining.

Sage-brush is very fair fuel, but as a vegetable it is a distinguished failure. Nothing can abide the taste of it but the jackass and his illegitimate child the mule. But their testimony to its nutritiousness is worth nothing, for they will eat pine knots, or anthracite coal, or brass filings, or lead pipe, or old bottles, or anything that comes handy, and then go off looking as grateful as if they had had oysters for dinner. Mules and donkeys and camels have appetites that anything will relieve temporarily, but nothing satisfy. In Syria, once, at the head-waters of the Jordan, a camel took charge of my overcoat while the tents were being pitched, and examined it with a critical eye, all over, with as much interest as if he had an idea of getting one made like it; and then, after he was done figuring on it as an article of apparel, he began to contemplate it as an article of diet. He put his foot on it, and lifted one of the sleeves out with his teeth, and chewed and chewed at it, gradually taking it in, and all the while opening and closing his eyes in a kind of religious ecstasy, as if he had never tasted anything as good as an overcoat before, in his life. Then he smacked his lips once or twice, and reached after the other sleeve. Next he tried the velvet collar, and smiled a smile of such contentment that it was plain to see that he regarded that as the daintiest thing about an overcoat. The tails went next, along with some percussion caps and cough candy, and some fig-paste from Constantinople. And then my newspaper correspondence dropped out, and he took a chance in that—manuscript letters written for the home papers. But he was treading on dangerous ground, now. He began to come across solid wisdom in those documents that was rather weighty on his stomach; and occasionally he would take a joke that would shake him up till it loosened his teeth; it was getting to be perilous times with him, but he held his grip with good courage and hopefully, till at last he began to stumble on statements that not even a camel could swallow with impunity. He began to gag and gasp, and his eyes to stand out, and his forelegs to spread, and in about a quarter of a minute he fell over as stiff as a carpenter's work-bench, and died a death of indescribable agony. I went and pulled the manuscript out of his mouth, and found that the sensitive creature had choked to death on one of the mildest and gentlest statements of fact that I ever laid before a trusting public.

I was about to say, when diverted from my subject, that occasionally one finds sage-bushes five or six feet high, and with a spread of branch and foliage in proportion, but two or two and a half feet is the usual height.

[Overland to Nevada Territory, Chapter 4]

As the sun went down and the evening chill came on, we made preparation for bed. We stirred up the hard leather letter-sacks, and the knotty canvas bags of printed matter (knotty and uneven because of projecting ends and corners of magazines, boxes and books). We stirred them up and redisposed them in such a way as to make our bed as level as possible. And we *did* improve it, too, though after all our work it had an upheaved and billowy look about it, like a little piece of a stormy sea. Next we hunted up our boots from odd nooks among the mail-bags where they had settled, and put them on. Then we got down our coats, vests, pantaloons and heavy woolen shirts, from the arm-loops where they had been swinging all day, and clothed ourselves in them—for, there being no ladies either at the stations or in the coach, and the weather being hot, we had looked to our comfort by stripping to our underclothing, at nine o'clock in the morning. All things being now ready, we stowed the uneasy Dictionary where it would lie as quiet as possible, and placed the water-canteens and pistols where we could find them in the dark. Then we smoked a final pipe, and swapped a final yarn; after which, we put the pipes, tobacco and bag of coin in snug holes and caves among the mail-bags, and then fastened down the coach curtains all around, and made the place as "dark as the inside of a cow," as the conductor phrased it in his picturesque way. It was certainly as dark as any place could be—nothing was even dimly visible in it. And finally, we rolled ourselves up like silk-worms, each person in his own blanket, and sank peacefully to sleep.

Whenever the stage stopped to change horses, we would wake up, and try to recollect where we were—and succeed—and in a minute or two the stage would be off again, and we likewise. We began to get into country, now, threaded here and there with little streams. These had high, steep banks on each side, and every time we flew down one bank and scrambled up the other, our party inside got mixed somewhat. First we would all be down in a pile at the forward end of the stage, nearly in a sitting posture, and in a second we would shoot to the other end, and stand on our heads. And we would sprawl and kick, too, and ward off ends and corners of mail-bags that came lumbering over us and about us; and as the dust rose from the tumult, we would all sneeze in chorus, and the majority of us would grumble, and probably say some hasty thing, like: "Take your elbow out of my ribs!—can't you quit crowding?"

Every time we avalanched from one end of the stage to the other, the Unabridged Dictionary would come too; and every time it came it damaged somebody. One trip it "barked" the Secretary's elbow; the next trip it hurt me in the stomach, and the third it tilted Bemis's nose up till he could look down his nostrils—he said. The pistols and coin soon settled to the bottom, but the pipes, pipe-stems, tobacco and canteens clattered and floundered after the Dictionary every time it made an assault on us, and aided and abetted the book by spilling tobacco in our eyes, and water down our backs.

Still, all things considered, it was a very comfortable night. It wore gradually away, and when at last a cold gray light was visible through the puckers and chinks in the curtains, we yawned and stretched with satisfaction, shed our cocoons, and felt that we had slept as much as was necessary. By and by, as the sun rose up and warmed the world, we pulled off our clothes and got ready for breakfast. We were just pleasantly in time, for five minutes afterward the driver sent the weird music of his bugle winding over the grassy solitudes, and presently we detected a low hut or two in the distance. Then the rattling of the coach, the clatter of our six horses' hoofs, and the driver's crisp commands, awoke to a louder and stronger emphasis, and we went sweeping down on the station at our smartest speed. It was fascinating—that old overland stage-coaching.

We jumped out in undress uniform. The driver tossed his gathered reins out on the ground, gaped and stretched complacently, drew off his heavy buckskin gloves with great deliberation and insufferable dignity—taking not the slightest notice of a dozen solicitous inquiries after his health, and humbly facetious and flattering accostings, and obsequious tenders of service, from five or six hairy and half-civilized station-keepers and hostlers who were nimbly unhitching our steeds and bringing the fresh team out of the stables—for in the eyes of the stage-driver of that

day, station-keepers and hostlers were a sort of good enough low creatures, useful in their place, and helping to make up a world, but not the
kind of beings which a person of distinction could afford to concern himself with; while, on the contrary, in the eyes of the station-keeper and the
hostler, the stage-driver was a hero—a great and shining dignitary, the
world's favorite son, the envy of the people, the observed of the nations.
When they spoke to him they received his insolent silence meekly, and as
being the natural and proper conduct of so great a man; when he opened
his lips they all hung on his words with admiration (he never honored a
particular individual with a remark, but addressed it with a broad gener-
ality to the horses, the stables, the surrounding country *and* the human
underlings); when he discharged a facetious insulting personality at a hostler, that hostler was happy for the day; when he uttered his one jest—
old as the hills, coarse, profane, witless, and inflicted on the same audience, in the same language, every time his coach drove up there—the
varlets roared, and slapped their thighs, and swore it was the best thing
they'd ever heard in all their lives. And how they would fly around when
he wanted a basin of water, a gourd of the same, or a light for his pipe!—
but they would instantly insult a passenger if he so far forgot himself as to
crave a favor at their hands. They could do that sort of insolence as well as
the driver they copied it from—for, let it be borne in mind, the overland
driver had but little less contempt for his passengers than he had for his
hostlers.

The hostlers and station-keepers treated the really powerful *conductor*
of the coach merely with the best of what was their idea of civility, but the
driver was the only being they bowed down to and worshipped. How ad-
miringly they would gaze up at him in his high seat as he gloved himself
with lingering deliberation, while some happy hostler held the bunch of
reins aloft, and waited patiently for him to take it! And how they would
bombard him with glorifying ejaculations as he cracked his long whip and
went careering away.

The station buildings were long, low huts, made of sun-dried, mud-
colored bricks, laid up without mortar (*adobes*, the Spaniards call these
bricks, and Americans shorten it to '*dobies*). The roofs, which had no slant
to them worth speaking of, were thatched and then sodded or covered
with a thick layer of earth, and from this sprung a pretty rank growth
of weeds and grass. It was the first time we had ever seen a man's front

yard on top of his house. The buildings consisted of barns, stable-room for twelve or fifteen horses, and a hut for an eating-room for passengers. This latter had bunks in it for the station-keeper and a hostler or two. You could rest your elbow on its eaves, and you had to bend in order to get in at the door. In place of a window there was a square hole about large enough for a man to crawl through, but this had no glass in it. There was no flooring, but the ground was packed hard. There was no stove, but the fireplace served all needful purposes. There were no shelves, no cupboards, no closets. In a corner stood an open sack of flour, and nestling against its base were a couple of black and venerable tin coffee-pots, a tin teapot, a little bag of salt, and a side of bacon.

By the door of the station-keeper's den, outside, was a tin wash-basin, on the ground. Near it was a pail of water and a piece of yellow bar soap, and from the eaves hung a hoary blue woolen shirt, significantly—but this latter was the station-keeper's private towel, and only two persons in all the party might venture to use it—the stage-driver and the conductor. The latter would not, from a sense of decency; the former would not, because he did not choose to encourage the advances of a station-keeper. We had towels—in the valise; they might as well have been in Sodom and Gomorrah. We (and the conductor) used our handkerchiefs, and the driver his pantaloons and sleeves. By the door, inside, was fastened a small old-fashioned looking-glass frame, with two little fragments of the original mirror lodged down in one corner of it. This arrangement afforded a pleasant double-barreled portrait of you when you looked into it, with one half of your head set up a couple of inches above the other half. From the glass frame hung the half of a comb by a string—but if I had to describe that patriarch or die, I believe I would order some sample coffins. It had come down from Esau and Samson, and had been accumulating hair ever since—along with certain impurities. In one corner of the room stood three or four rifles and muskets, together with horns and pouches of ammunition. The station-men wore pantaloons of coarse, country-woven stuff, and into the seat and the inside of the legs were sewed ample additions of buckskin, to do duty in place of leggings, when the man rode horseback—so the pants were half dull blue and half yellow, and unspeakably picturesque. The pants were stuffed into the tops of high boots, the heels whereof were armed with great Spanish spurs, whose little iron clogs and chains jingled with every step. The man wore a huge beard and mustachios, an old slouch hat, a blue woolen shirt, no suspenders, no vest, no coat—in a leathern sheath in his belt, a great long "navy" revolver (slung on right side, hammer to the front), and projecting from his boot a horn-handled bowie-knife. The furniture of the hut was neither gorgeous nor much in the way. The rocking-chairs and sofas were not present, and never had been, but they were represented by two three-legged stools, a pine-board bench four feet long, and two empty candle-boxes. The table was a greasy board on stilts, and the table-cloth and napkins had not come—and they were not looking for them, either. A battered tin platter, a knife and fork, and a tin pint cup, were at each man's place, and the driver had a queensware saucer that had seen better days. Of course this duke sat at the head of the table. There was one isolated piece of table furniture that bore about it a touching air of grandeur in misfortune. This was the caster. It was German silver, and crippled and rusty, but it was so preposterously out of place there that it was suggestive of a tattered exiled king among barbarians, and the majesty of its native position compelled respect even in its degradation. There was only one cruet left, and that was a stopperless, fly-specked, broken-necked thing, with two inches of vinegar in it, and a dozen preserved flies with their heels up and looking sorry they had invested there.

The station-keeper upended a disk of last week's bread, of the shape and size of an old-time cheese, and carved some slabs from it which were as good as Nicholson pavement, and tenderer.

He sliced off a piece of bacon for each man, but only the experienced old hands made out to eat it, for it was condemned army bacon which the United States would not feed to its soldiers in the forts, and the stage company had bought it cheap for the sustenance of their passengers and employees. We may have found this condemned army bacon further out on the plains than the section I am locating it in, but we *found* it—there is no gainsaying that.

Then he poured for us a beverage which he called "*Slumgullion*," and it is hard to think he was not inspired when he named it. It really pretended to be tea, but there was too much dish-rag, and sand, and old bacon-rind in it to deceive the intelligent traveler. He had no sugar and no milk—not even a spoon to stir the ingredients with.

We could not eat the bread or the meat, nor drink the "slumgullion." And when I looked at that melancholy vinegar-cruet, I thought of the anecdote (a very, very old one, even at that day) of the traveler who sat down to a table which had nothing on it but a mackerel and a pot of mustard. He asked the landlord if this was all. The landlord said: "*All!* Why, thunder and lightning, I should think there was mackerel enough there for six."

"But I don't like mackerel."

"Oh—then help yourself to the mustard."

In other days I had considered it a good, a very good, anecdote, but there was a dismal plausibility about it, here, that took all the humor out of it.

Our breakfast was before us, but our teeth were idle.

I tasted and smelt, and said I would take coffee, I believed. The station-boss stopped dead still, and glared at me speechless. At last, when he came to, he turned away and said, as one who communes with himself upon a matter too vast to grasp: "*Coffee!* Well, if that don't go clean ahead of me, I'm d—d!"

We could not eat, and there was no conversation among the hostlers and herdsmen—we all sat at the same board. At least there was no conversation further than a single hurried request, now and then, from one employee to another. It was always in the same form, and always gruffly friendly. Its western freshness and novelty startled me, at first, and interested me; but it presently grew monotonous, and lost its charm. It was: "Pass the bread, you son of a skunk!" No, I forget—skunk was not the word; it seems to me it was still stronger than that; I know it was, in fact, but it is gone from my memory, apparently. However, it is no matter— probably it was too strong for print, anyway. It is the landmark in my memory which tells me where I first encountered the vigorous new vernacular of the occidental plains and mountains.

We gave up the breakfast, and paid our dollar apiece and went back to our mail-bag bed in the coach, and found comfort in our pipes. Right here we suffered the first diminution of our princely state. We left our six fine horses and took six mules in their place. But they were wild Mexican fellows, and a man had to stand at the head of each of them and hold him fast while the driver gloved and got himself ready. And when at last he grasped the reins and gave the word, the men sprung suddenly away from the mules' heads and the coach shot from the station as if it had issued from a cannon. How the frantic animals did scamper! It was a fierce and furious gallop—and the gait never altered for a moment till we reeled off ten or twelve miles and swept up to the next collection of little station-huts and stables.

So we flew along all day. At 2 P.M. the belt of timber that fringes the North Platte and marks its windings through the vast level floor of the Plains came in sight. At 4 P.M. we crossed a branch of the river, and at 5 P.M. we crossed the Platte itself, and landed at Fort Kearney, *fifty-six hours out from St. Joe*—THREE HUNDRED MILES!

[Overland to Nevada Territory, Chapter 18]

At eight in the morning we reached the remnant and ruin of what had been the important military station of "Camp Floyd," some forty-five or fifty miles from Salt Lake City. At four P.M. we had doubled our distance and were ninety or a hundred miles from Salt Lake. And now we entered upon one of that species of deserts whose concentrated hideousness shames the diffused and diluted horrors of Sahara—an "*alkali*" desert. For sixty-eight miles there was but one break in it. I do not remember that this was really a break; indeed it seems to me that it was nothing but a watering depot *in the midst* of the stretch of sixty-eight miles. If my memory serves me, there was no well or spring at this place, but the water was hauled there by mule and ox teams from the further side of the desert. There was a stage station there. It was forty-five miles from the beginning of the desert, and twenty-three from the end of it.

We plowed and dragged and groped along, the whole live-long night, and at the end of this uncomfortable twelve hours we finished the forty-five-mile part of the desert and got to the stage station where the imported water was. The sun was just rising. It was easy enough to cross a desert in the night while we were asleep; and it was pleasant to reflect, in the morning, that we in actual person *had* encountered an absolute desert and could always speak knowingly of deserts in presence of the ignorant thenceforward. And it was pleasant also to reflect that this was not an obscure, back country desert, but a very celebrated one, the metropolis itself, as you may say. All this was very well and very comfortable and satisfactory—but now we were to cross a desert in *daylight*. This was fine—novel—romantic—dramatically adventurous—*this*, indeed, was worth living for, worth traveling for! We would write home all about it.

This enthusiasm, this stern thirst for adventure, wilted under the sultry August sun and did not last above one hour. One poor little hour—

and then we were ashamed that we had "gushed" so. The poetry was all in the anticipation—there is none in the reality. Imagine a vast, waveless ocean stricken dead and turned to ashes; imagine this solemn waste tufted with ash-dusted sage-bushes; imagine the lifeless silence and solitude that belong to such a place; imagine a coach, creeping like a bug through the midst of this shoreless level, and sending up tumbled volumes of dust as if it were a bug that went by steam; imagine this aching monotony of toiling and plowing kept up hour after hour, and the shore still as far away as ever, apparently; imagine team, driver, coach and passengers so deeply coated with ashes that they are all one colorless color; imagine ash-drifts roosting above moustaches and eyebrows like snow accumulations on boughs and bushes. This is the reality of it.

The sun beats down with dead, blistering, relentless malignity; the perspiration is welling from every pore in man and beast, but scarcely a sign of it finds its way to the surface—it is absorbed before it gets there; there is not the faintest breath of air stirring; there is not a merciful shred of cloud in all the brilliant firmament; there is not a living creature visible in any direction whither one searches the blank level that stretches its monotonous miles on every hand; there is not a sound—not a sigh—not a whisper—not a buzz, or a whir of wings, or distant pipe of bird—not even a sob from the lost souls that doubtless people that dead air. And so the occasional sneezing of the resting mules, and the champing of the bits, grate harshly on the grim stillness, not dissipating the spell but accenting it and making one feel more lonesome and forsaken than before.

The mules, under violent swearing, coaxing and whip-cracking, would make at stated intervals a "spurt," and drag the coach a hundred or may be two hundred yards, stirring up a billowy cloud of dust that rolled back, enveloping the vehicle to the wheel-tops or higher, and making it seem afloat in a fog. Then a rest followed, with the usual sneezing and bit-champing. Then another "spurt" of a hundred yards and another rest at the end of it. All day long we kept this up, without water for the mules and without ever changing the team. At least we kept it up ten hours, which, I take it, is a day, and a pretty honest one, in an alkali desert. It was from four in the morning till two in the afternoon. And it was so hot! and so close! and our water canteens went dry in the middle of the day and we got so thirsty! It was so stupid and tiresome and dull! and the tedious hours did lag and drag and limp along with such a cruel deliberation! It was so trying to give one's watch a good long undisturbed spell and then take it out and find that it had been fooling away the time and not trying to get ahead any! The alkali dust cut through our lips, it persecuted our eyes, it ate through the delicate membranes and made our noses bleed and *kept* them bleeding—and truly and seriously the romance all faded far away and disappeared, and left the desert trip nothing but a harsh reality—a thirsty, sweltering, longing, hateful reality!

Two miles and a quarter an hour for ten hours—that was what we accomplished. It was hard to bring the comprehension away down to such a snail-pace as that, when we had been used to making eight and ten miles an hour. When we reached the station on the farther verge of the desert, we were glad, for the first time, that the dictionary was along, because we never could have found language to tell how glad we were, in any sort of dictionary but an unabridged one with pictures in it. But there could not have been found in a whole library of dictionaries language sufficient to tell how tired those mules were after their twenty-three mile pull. To try to give the reader an idea of how *thirsty* they were, would be to "gild refined gold or paint the lily."

Somehow, now that it is there, the quotation does not seem to fit—but no matter, let it stay, anyhow. I think it is a graceful and attractive thing, and therefore have tried time and time again to work it in where it *would* fit, but could not succeed. These efforts have kept my mind distracted and ill at ease, and made my narrative seem broken and disjointed, in places. Under these circumstances it seems to me best to leave it in, as above, since this will afford at least a temporary respite from the wear and tear of trying to "lead up" to this really apt and beautiful quotation.

[Lake Tahoe, Chapter 22]

It was the end of August, and the skies were cloudless and the weather superb. In two or three weeks I had grown wonderfully fascinated with the curious new country, and concluded to put off my return to "the States" awhile. I had grown well accustomed to wearing a damaged slouch hat, blue woolen shirt, and pants crammed into boot-tops, and gloried in the absence of coat, vest and braces. I felt rowdyish and "bully," (as the historian Josephus phrases it, in his fine chapter upon the destruction of the

Temple). It seemed to me that nothing could be so fine and so romantic. I had become an officer of the government, but that was for mere sublimity. The office was an unique sinecure. I had nothing to do and no salary. I was private Secretary to his majesty the Secretary and there was not yet writing enough for two of us. So Johnny K— and I devoted our time to amusement. He was the young son of an Ohio nabob and was out there for recreation. He got it. We had heard a world of talk about the marvellous beauty of Lake Tahoe, and finally curiosity drove us thither to see it. Three or four members of the Brigade had been there and located some timber lands on its shores and stored up a quantity of provisions in their camp. We strapped a couple of blankets on our shoulders and took an axe apiece and started—for we intended to take up a wood ranch or so ourselves and become wealthy. We were on foot. The reader will find it advantageous to go horseback. We were told that the distance was eleven miles. We tramped a long time on level ground, and then toiled laboriously up a mountain about a thousand miles high and looked over. No lake there. We descended on the other side, crossed the valley and toiled up another mountain three or four thousand miles high, apparently, and looked over again. No lake yet. We sat down tired and perspiring, and hired a couple of Chinamen to curse those people who had beguiled us. Thus refreshed, we presently resumed the march with renewed vigor and determination. We plodded on, two or three hours longer, and at last the Lake burst upon us—a noble sheet of blue water lifted six thousand three hundred feet above the level of the sea, and walled in by a rim of snow-clad mountain peaks that towered aloft full three thousand feet higher still! It was a vast oval, and one would have to use up eighty or a hundred good miles in traveling around it. As it lay there with the shadows of the mountains brilliantly photographed upon its still surface I thought it must surely be the fairest picture the whole earth affords.

We found the small skiff belonging to the Brigade boys, and without loss of time set out across a deep bend of the lake toward the landmarks that signified the locality of the camp. I got Johnny to row—not because I mind exertion myself, but because it makes me sick to ride backwards when I am at work. But I steered. A three-mile pull brought us to the camp just as the night fell, and we stepped ashore very tired and wolfishly hungry. In a "cache" among the rocks we found the provisions and the cooking utensils, and then, all fatigued as I was, I sat down on a boulder and superintended while Johnny gathered wood and cooked supper. Many a man who had gone through what I had, would have wanted to rest.

It was a delicious supper—hot bread, fried bacon, and black coffee. It was a delicious solitude we were in, too. Three miles away was a saw-mill and some workmen, but there were not fifteen other human beings throughout the wide circumference of the lake. As the darkness closed down and the stars came out and spangled the great mirror with jewels, we smoked meditatively in the solemn hush and forgot our troubles and our pains. In due time we spread our blankets in the warm sand between two large boulders and soon feel asleep, careless of the procession of ants that passed in through rents in our clothing and explored our persons. Nothing could disturb the sleep that fettered us, for it had been fairly earned, and if our consciences had any sins on them they had to adjourn court for that night, any way. The wind rose just as we were losing consciousness, and we were lulled to sleep by the beating of the surf upon the shore.

It is always very cold on that lake shore in the night, but we had plenty of blankets and were warm enough. We never moved a muscle all night, but waked at early dawn in the original positions, and got up at once, thoroughly refreshed, free from soreness, and brim full of friskiness. There is no end of wholesome medicine in such an experience. That morning we could have whipped ten such people as we were the day before—sick ones at any rate. But the world is slow, and people will go to "water cures" and "movement cures" and to foreign lands for health. Three months of camp life on Lake Tahoe would restore an Egyptian mummy to his pristine vigor, and give him an appetite like an alligator. I do not mean the oldest and driest mummies, of course, but the fresher ones. The air up there in the clouds is very pure and fine, bracing and delicious. And why shouldn't it be?—it is the same the angels breathe. I think that hardly any amount of fatigue can be gathered together that a man cannot sleep off in one night on the sand by its side. Not under a roof, but under the sky; it seldom or never rains there in the summer time. I know a man who went there to die. But he made a failure of it. He was a skeleton when he came, and could barely stand. He had no appetite, and did nothing but read tracts and reflect on the future. Three months later he was sleeping out of doors regularly, eating all he could hold, three times a day, and chasing game over mountains three thousand feet high for recreation. And he was a skeleton no longer, but weighed part of a ton. This is no fancy sketch, but the truth. His disease was consumption. I confidently commend his experience to other skeletons.

I superintended again, and as soon as we had eaten breakfast we got in the boat and skirted along the lake shore about three miles and disembarked. We liked the appearance of the place, and so we claimed some three hundred acres of it and stuck our "notices" on a tree. It was yellow pine timber land—a dense forest of trees a hundred feet high and from one to five feet through at the butt. It was necessary to fence our property or we could not hold it. That is to say, it was necessary to cut down trees here and there and make them fall in such a way as to form a sort of enclosure (with pretty wide gaps in it). We cut down three trees apiece, and found it such heart-breaking work that we decided to "rest our case" on those; if they held the property, well and good; if they didn't, let the property spill out through the gaps and go; it was no use to work ourselves to death merely to save a few acres of land. Next day we came back to build a house—for a house was also necessary, in order to hold the property. We decided to build a substantial log-house and excite the envy of the Brigade boys; but by the time we had cut and trimmed the first log it seemed unnecessary to be so elaborate, and so we concluded to build it of saplings. However, two saplings, duly cut and trimmed, compelled recognition of the fact that a still modester architecture would satisfy the law, and so we concluded to build a "brush" house. We devoted the next day to this work, but we did so much "sitting around" and discussing, that by the middle of the afternoon we had achieved only a half-way sort of affair which one of us had to watch while the other cut brush, lest if both turned our backs we might not be able to find it again, it had such a strong family resemblance to the surrounding vegetation. But we were satisfied with it.

We were land owners now, duly seized and possessed, and within the protection of the law. Therefore we decided to take up our residence on our own domain and enjoy that large sense of independence which only such an experience can bring. Late the next afternoon, after a good long rest, we sailed away from the Brigade camp with all the provisions and cooking utensils we could carry off—borrow is the more accurate word— and just as the night was falling we beached the boat at our own landing.

If there is any life that is happier than the life we led on our timber ranch for the next two or three weeks, it must be a sort of life which I have not read of in books or experienced in person. We did not see a human being but ourselves during the time, or hear any sounds but those that were made by the wind and the waves, the sighing of the pines, and now and then the far-off thunder of an avalanche. The forest about us was dense and cool, the sky above us was cloudless and brilliant with sunshine, the broad lake before us was glassy and clear, or rippled and breezy, or black and storm-tossed, according to Nature's mood; and its circling border of mountain domes, clothed with forests, scarred with land-slides, cloven by cañons and valleys, and helmeted with glittering snow, fitly framed and finished the noble picture. The view was always fascinating, bewitching, entrancing. The eye was never tired of gazing, night or day, in calm or storm; it suffered but one grief, and that was that it could not look always, but must close sometimes in sleep.

We slept in the sand close to the water's edge, between two protecting boulders, which took care of the stormy night-winds for us. We never took any paregoric to make us sleep. At the first break of dawn we were always up and running foot-races to tone down excess of physical vigor and exuberance of spirits. That is, Johnny was—but I held his hat. While smoking the pipe of peace after breakfast we watched the sentinel peaks put on the glory of the sun, and followed the conquering light as it swept down among the shadows, and set the captive crags and forests free. We watched the tinted pictures grow and brighten upon the water till every little detail of forest, precipice and pinnacle was wrought in and finished, and the miracle of the enchanter complete. Then to "business."

That is, drifting around in the boat. We were on the north shore. There, the rocks on the bottom are sometimes gray, sometimes white. This gives the marvelous transparency of the water a fuller advantage than it has elsewhere on the lake. We usually pushed out a hundred yards or so from shore, and then lay down on the thwarts, in the sun, and let the boat drift by the hour whither it would. We seldom talked. It interrupted the Sabbath stillness, and marred the dreams the luxurious rest and indolence brought. The shore all along was indented with deep, curved bays and coves, bordered by narrow sand-beaches; and where the sand ended, the steep mountain-sides rose right up aloft into space—rose up like a vast wall a little out of the perpendicular, and thickly wooded with tall pines.

So singularly clear was the water, that where it was only twenty or thirty feet deep the bottom was so perfectly distinct that the boat seemed floating in the air! Yes, where it was even *eighty* feet deep. Every little pebble was distinct, every speckled trout, every hand's-breadth of sand. Often, as we lay on our faces, a granite boulder, as large as a village church, would start out of the bottom apparently, and seem climbing up rapidly to the surface, till presently it threatened to touch our faces, and we could not resist the impulse to seize an oar and avert the danger. But the boat would float on, and the boulder descend again, and then we could see that when we had been exactly above it, it must still have been twenty or thirty feet below the surface. Down through the transparency of these great depths, the water was not *merely* transparent, but dazzlingly, brilliantly so. All objects seen through it had a bright, strong vividness, not only of outline, but of every minute detail, which they would not have had when seen simply through the same depth of atmosphere. So empty and airy did all spaces seem below us, and so strong was the sense of floating high aloft in mid-nothingness, that we called these boat-excursions "balloon-voyages."

We fished a good deal, but we did not average one fish a week. We could see trout by the thousand winging about in the emptiness under us, or sleeping in shoals on the bottom, but they would not bite—they could see the line too plainly, perhaps. We frequently selected the trout we wanted, and rested the bait patiently and persistently on the end of his nose at a depth of eighty feet, but he would only shake it off with an annoyed manner, and shift his position.

We bathed occasionally, but the water was rather chilly, for all it looked so sunny. Sometimes we rowed out to the "blue water," a mile or two from shore. It was as dead blue as indigo there, because of the immense depth. By official measurement the lake in its centre is one thousand five hundred and twenty-five feet deep!

Sometimes, on lazy afternoons, we lolled on the sand in camp, and smoked pipes and read some old well-worn novels. At night, by the camp-fire, we played euchre and seven-up to strengthen the mind—and played them with cards so greasy and defaced that only a whole summer's acquaintance with them could enable the student to tell the ace of clubs from the jack of diamonds.

We never slept in our "house." It never recurred to us, for one thing; and besides, it was built to hold the ground, and that was enough. We did not wish to strain it.

By and by our provisions began to run short, and we went back to the old camp and laid in a new supply. We were gone all day, and reached home again about night-fall, pretty tired and hungry. While Johnny was carrying the main bulk of the provisions up to our "house" for future use, I took the loaf of bread, some slices of bacon, and the coffee-pot, ashore, set them down by a tree, lit a fire, and went back to the boat to get the frying-pan. While I was at this, I heard a shout from Johnny, and looking up I saw that my fire was galloping all over the premises!

Johnny was on the other side of it. He had to run through the flames to get to the lake shore, and then we stood helpless and watched the devastation.

The ground was deeply carpeted with dry pine-needles, and the fire touched them off as if they were gunpowder. It was wonderful to see with what fierce speed the tall sheet of flame traveled! My coffee-pot was gone, and everything with it. In a minute and a half the fire seized upon a dense growth of dry manzanita chapparal six or eight feet high, and then the roaring and popping and crackling was something terrific. We were driven to the boat by the intense heat, and there we remained, spell-bound.

Within half an hour all before us was a tossing, blinding tempest of flame! It went surging up adjacent ridges—surmounted them and disappeared in the cañons beyond—burst into view upon higher and farther ridges, presently—shed a grander illumination abroad, and dove again—flamed out again, directly, higher and still higher up the mountain-side—threw out skirmishing parties of fire here and there, and sent them trailing their crimson spirals away among remote ramparts and ribs and gorges, till as far as the eye could reach the lofty mountain-fronts were webbed as it were with a tangled network of red lava streams. Away across the water the crags and domes were lit with a ruddy glare, and the firmament above was a reflected hell!

Every feature of the spectacle was repeated in the glowing mirror of the lake! Both pictures were sublime, both were beautiful; but that in the lake had a bewildering richness about it that enchanted the eye and held it with the stronger fascination.

We sat absorbed and motionless through four long hours. We never thought of supper, and never felt fatigue. But at eleven o'clock the conflagration had traveled beyond our range of vision, and then darkness stole down upon the landscape again.

Hunger asserted itself now, but there was nothing to eat. The provisions were all cooked, no doubt, but we did not go to see. We were homeless wanderers again, without any property. Our fence was gone, our house burned down; no insurance. Our pine forest was well scorched, the dead trees all burned up, and our broad acres of manzanita swept away. Our blankets were on our usual sand-bed, however, and so we lay down and went to sleep. The next morning we started back to the old camp, but while out a long way from shore, so great a storm came up that we dared not try to land. So I baled out the seas we shipped, and Johnny pulled heavily through the billows till we had reached a point three or four miles beyond the camp. The storm was increasing, and it became evident that it was better to take the hazard of beaching the boat than go down in a hundred fathoms of water; so we ran in, with tall white-caps following, and I sat down in the stern-sheets and pointed her head-on to the shore. The instant the bow struck, a wave came over the stern that washed crew and cargo ashore, and saved a deal of trouble. We shivered in the lee of a boulder all the rest of the day, and froze all the night through. In the morning the tempest had gone down, and we paddled down to the camp without any unnecessary delay. We were so starved that we ate up the rest of the Brigade's provisions, and then set out to Carson to tell them about it and ask their forgiveness. It was accorded, upon payment of damages.

We made many trips to the lake after that, and had many a hair-breadth escape and blood-curdling adventure which will never be recorded in any history.

[San Francisco, Chapter 56]

We rumbled over the plains and valleys, climbed the Sierras to the clouds, and looked down upon summer-clad California. And I will remark here, in passing, that all scenery in California requires *distance* to give it its highest charm. The mountains are imposing in their sublimity and their majesty of form and altitude, from any point of view—but one must have distance to soften their ruggedness and enrich their tintings; a Californian forest is best at a little distance, for there is a sad poverty of variety in species, the trees being chiefly of one monotonous family—redwood, pine, spruce, fir—and so, at a near view there is a wearisome sameness of attitude in their rigid arms, stretched downward and outward in one continued and reiterated appeal to all men to "Sh!—don't say a word!—you might disturb somebody!" Close at hand, too, there is a reliefless and relentless smell of pitch and turpentine; there is a ceaseless melancholy in their sighing and complaining foliage; one walks over a soundless carpet of beaten yellow bark and dead spines of the foliage till he feels like a wandering spirit bereft of a footfall; he tires of the endless tufts of needles and yearns for substantial, shapely leaves; he looks for moss and grass to loll upon, and finds none, for where there is no bark there is naked clay and dirt, enemies to pensive musing and clean apparel. Often a grassy plain in California, is what it should be, but often, too, it is best contemplated at a distance, because although its grass blades are tall, they stand up vindictively straight and self-sufficient, and are unsociably wide apart, with uncomely spots of barren sand between.

One of the queerest things I know of, is to hear tourists from "the States" go into ecstasies over the loveliness of "ever-blooming California." And they always do go into that sort of ecstasies. But perhaps they would modify them if they knew how old Californians, with the memory full upon them of the dust-covered and questionable summer greens of Californian "verdure," stand astonished, and filled with worshipping admiration, in the presence of the lavish richness, the brilliant green, the infinite freshness, the spend-thrift variety of form and species and foliage that make an Eastern landscape a vision of Paradise itself. The idea of a man falling into raptures over grave and sombre California, when that man has seen New England's meadow-expanses and her maples, oaks and cathedral-windowed elms decked in summer attire, or the opaline splendors of autumn descending upon her forests, comes very near being funny—would be, in fact, but that it is so pathetic. No land with an unvarying climate can be very beautiful. The tropics are not, for all the sentiment that is wasted on them. They seem beautiful at first, but sameness impairs the charm by and by. *Change* is the handmaiden Nature requires to do her miracles with. The land that has four well-defined seasons, cannot lack beauty, or pall with monotony. Each season brings a world of enjoyment and interest in the watching of its unfolding, its gradual, harmonious development, its culminating graces—and just as one begins to tire of it, it passes away and a radical change comes, with new witcheries and new glories in its train. And I think that to one in sympathy with nature, each season, in its turn, seems the loveliest.

San Francisco, a truly fascinating city to live in, is stately and handsome at a fair distance, but close at hand one notes that the architecture is mostly old-fashioned, many streets are made up of decaying, smoke-grimed, wooden houses, and the barren sand-hills toward the outskirts obtrude themselves too prominently. Even the kindly climate is sometimes pleasanter when read about than personally experienced, for a lovely, cloudless sky wears out its welcome by and by, and then when the longed for rain does come it *stays*. Even the playful earthquake is better contemplated at a dis—

However there are varying opinions about that.

The climate of San Francisco is mild and singularly equable. The thermometer stands at about seventy degrees the year round. It hardly changes at all. You sleep under one or two light blankets Summer and Winter, and never use a mosquito bar. Nobody ever wears Summer clothing. You wear black broadcloth—if you have it—in August and January, just the same. It is no colder, and no warmer, in the one month than the other. You do not use overcoats and you do not use fans. It is as pleasant a climate as could well be contrived, take it all around, and is doubtless the most unvarying in the whole world. The wind blows there a good deal in the Summer months, but then you can go over to Oakland, if you choose—three or four miles away—it does not blow there. It has only snowed twice in San Francisco in nineteen years, and then it only remained on the ground long enough to astonish the children, and set them to wondering what the feathery stuff was.

During eight months of the year, straight along, the skies are bright and cloudless, and never a drop of rain falls. But when the other four months come along, you will need to go and steal an umbrella. Because you will require it. Not just one day, but one hundred and twenty days in hardly varying succession. When you want to go visiting, or attend church, or the theatre, you never look up at the clouds to see whether it is likely to rain or not—you look at the almanac. If it is Winter, it will *rain*—and if it is Summer, it *won't* rain, and you cannot help it. You never need a lightning-rod, because it never thunders and it never lightens. And after you have listened for six or eight weeks, every night, to the dismal monotony of those quiet rains, you will wish in your heart the thunder *would* leap and crash and roar along those drowsy skies once, and make everything alive—you will wish the prisoned lightnings *would* cleave the dull firmament asunder and light it with a blinding glare for *one* little instant. You would give *anything* to hear the old familiar thunder again and see the lightning strike somebody. And along in the Summer, when you have suffered about four months of lustrous, pitiless sunshine, you are ready to go down on your knees and plead for rain—hail—snow—thunder and lightning—anything to break the monotony—you will take an earthquake, if you cannot do any better. And the chances are that you'll get it, too.

San Francisco is built on sand hills, but they are prolific sand hills. They yield a generous vegetation. All the rare flowers which people in "the States" rear with such patient care in parlor flower-pots and green-houses, flourish luxuriantly in the open air there all the year round. Calla lilies, all sorts of geraniums, passion flowers, moss roses—I do not know the names of a tenth part of them. I only know that while New Yorkers are burdened with banks and drifts of snow, Californians are burdened with banks and drifts of flowers, if they only keep their hands off and let them grow. And I have heard that they have also that rarest and most curious of all the flowers, the beautiful *Espiritu Santo*, as the Spaniards call it—or flower of the Holy Spirit—though I thought it grew only in Central America—down on the Isthmus. In its cup is the daintiest little facsimile of a dove, as pure as snow. The Spaniards have a superstitious reverence for it. The blossom has been conveyed to the States, submerged in ether; and the bulb has been taken thither also, but every attempt to make it bloom after it arrived, has failed.

I have elsewhere spoken of the endless Winter of Mono, California, and but this moment of the eternal Spring of San Francisco. Now if we travel a hundred miles in a straight line, we come to the eternal Summer of Sacramento. One never sees Summer-clothing or mosquitoes in San Francisco—but they can be found in Sacramento. Not always and unvaryingly, but about one hundred and forty-three months out of twelve years, perhaps. Flowers bloom there, always, the reader can easily believe—people suffer and sweat, and swear, morning, noon and night, and wear out their stanchest energies fanning themselves. It gets hot there, but if you go down to Fort Yuma you will find it hotter. Fort Yuma is probably the hottest place on earth. The thermometer stays at one hundred and twenty in the shade there all the time—except when it varies and goes higher. It is a U.S. military post, and its occupants get so used to the terrific heat that they suffer without it. There is a tradition (attributed to John Phoenix) {It has been purloined by fifty different scribblers who were too poor to invent a fancy but not ashamed to steal one.—M. T.} that a very, very wicked soldier died there, once, and of course, went straight to the hottest corner of perdition,—and the next day he *telegraphed back for his blankets*. There is no doubt about the truth of this statement—there can be no doubt about it. I have seen the place where that soldier used to board. In Sacramento it is fiery Summer always, and you can gather roses, and eat strawberries and ice-cream, and wear white linen clothes, and pant and perspire, at eight or nine o'clock in the morning, and then take the cars, and at noon put on your furs and your skates, and go skimming over frozen Donner Lake, seven thousand feet above the valley, among snow banks fifteen feet deep, and in the shadow of grand mountain peaks that lift their frosty crags ten thousand feet above the level of the sea. There is a transition for you! Where will you find another like it in the Western hemisphere? And some of us have swept around snow-walled curves of the Pacific Railroad in that vicinity, six thousand feet above the sea, and looked down as the birds do, upon the deathless Summer of the Sacramento Valley, with its fruitful fields, its feathery foliage, its silver streams, all slumbering in the mellow haze of its enchanted atmosphere, and all infinitely softened and spiritualized by distance—a dreamy, exquisite glimpse of fairyland, made all the more charming and striking that it was caught through a forbidden gateway of ice and snow, and savage crags and precipices.

[Hawaiian Islands, Chapter 63]

On a certain bright morning the Islands hove in sight, lying low on the lonely sea, and everybody climbed to the upper deck to look. After two thousand miles of watery solitude the vision was a welcome one. As we approached, the imposing promontory of Diamond Head rose up out of the ocean its rugged front softened by the hazy distance, and presently the details of the land began to make themselves manifest: first the line of beach; then the plumed cocoanut trees of the tropics; then cabins of the natives; then the white town of Honolulu, said to contain between twelve and fifteen thousand inhabitants spread over a dead level; with streets from twenty to thirty feet wide, solid and level as a floor, most of them straight as a line and few as crooked as a corkscrew.

The further I traveled through the town the better I liked it. Every step revealed a new contrast—disclosed something I was unaccustomed to. In place of the grand mud-colored brown fronts of San Francisco, I saw dwellings built of straw, adobies, and cream-colored pebble-and-shell-conglomerated coral, cut into oblong blocks and laid in cement; also a great number of neat white cottages, with green window-shutters; in place of front yards like billiard-tables with iron fences around them, I saw these homes surrounded by ample yards, thickly clad with green grass, and shaded by tall trees, through whose dense foliage the sun could scarcely penetrate; in place of the customary geranium, calla lily, etc., languishing in dust and general debility, I saw luxurious banks and thickets of flowers, fresh as a meadow after a rain, and glowing with the richest dyes; in place of the dingy horrors of San Francisco's pleasure grove, the "Willows," I saw huge-bodied, wide-spreading forest trees, with strange names and stranger appearance—trees that cast a shadow like a thunder-cloud, and were able to stand alone without being tied to green poles; in place of gold fish, wiggling around in glass globes, assuming countless shades and degrees of distortion through the magnifying and diminishing qualities of their transparent prison houses, I saw cats—Tom-cats, Mary Ann cats, long-tailed cats, bob-tailed cats, blind cats, one-eyed cats, wall-eyed cats, cross-eyed cats, gray cats, black cats, white cats, yellow cats, striped cats, spotted cats, tame cats, wild cats, singed cats, individual cats, groups of cats, platoons of cats, companies of cats, regiments of cats, armies of cats, multitudes of cats, millions of cats, and all of them sleek, fat, lazy and sound asleep.

I looked on a multitude of people, some white, in white coats, vests, pantaloons, even white cloth shoes, made snowy with chalk duly laid on every morning; but the majority of the people were almost as dark as negroes—women with comely features, fine black eyes, rounded forms, inclining to the voluptuous, clad in a single bright red or white garment

that fell free and unconfined from shoulder to heel, long black hair falling loose, gypsy hats, encircled with wreaths of natural flowers of a brilliant carmine tint; plenty of dark men in various costumes, and some with
nothing on but a battered stove-pipe hat tilted on the nose, and a very
scant breech-clout;—certain smoke-dried children were clothed in nothing but sunshine—a very neat fitting and picturesque apparel indeed.

In place of roughs and rowdies staring and blackguarding on the corners, I saw long-haired, saddle-colored Sandwich Island maidens sitting
on the ground in the shade of corner houses, gazing indolently at whatever or whoever happened along; instead of wretched cobble-stone pavements, I walked on a firm foundation of coral, built up from the bottom
of the sea by the absurd but persevering insect of that name, with a light
layer of lava and cinders overlying the coral, belched up out of fathomless
perdition long ago through the seared and blackened crater that stands
dead and harmless in the distance now; instead of cramped and crowded
street-cars, I met dusky native women sweeping by, free as the wind, on
fleet horses and astride, with gaudy riding-sashes, streaming like banners
behind them; instead of the combined stenches of Chinadom and Bran-
nan street slaughter-houses, I breathed the balmy fragrance of jessamine,
oleander, and the Pride of India; in place of the hurry and bustle and noisy
confusion of San Francisco, I moved in the midst of a Summer calm as
tranquil as dawn in the Garden of Eden; in place of the Golden City's
skirting sand hills and the placid bay, I saw on the one side a frame-work
of tall, precipitous mountains close at hand, clad in refreshing green, and
cleft by deep, cool, chasm-like valleys—and in front the grand sweep of
the ocean: a brilliant, transparent green near the shore, bound and bordered by a long white line of foamy spray dashing against the reef, and
further out the dead blue water of the deep sea, flecked with "white caps,"
and in the far horizon a single, lonely sail—a mere accent-mark to em-
phasize a slumberous calm and a solitude that were without sound or
limit. When the sun sunk down—the one intruder from other realms and
persistent in suggestions of them—it was tranced luxury to sit in the per-
fumed air and forget that there was any world but these enchanted islands.

It was such ecstacy to dream, and dream—till you got a bite. A scorpion bite. Then the first duty was to get up out of the grass and kill the

scorpion; and the next to bathe the bitten place with alcohol or brandy; and the next to resolve to keep out of the grass in future. Then came an adjournment to the bed-chamber and the pastime of writing up the day's journal with one hand and the destruction of mosquitoes with the other—a whole community of them at a slap. Then, observing an enemy approaching,—a hairy tarantula on stilts—why not set the spittoon on him? It is done, and the projecting ends of his paws give a luminous idea of the magnitude of his reach. Then to bed and become a promenade for a centipede with forty-two legs on a side and every foot hot enough to burn a hole through a raw-hide. More soaking with alcohol, and a resolution to examine the bed before entering it, in future. Then wait, and suffer, till all the mosquitoes in the neighborhood have crawled in under the bar, then slip out quickly, shut them in and sleep peacefully on the floor till morning. Meantime it is comforting to curse the tropics in occasional wakeful intervals.

We had an abundance of fruit in Honolulu, of course. Oranges, pine-apples, bananas, strawberries, lemons, limes, mangoes, guavas, melons, and a rare and curious luxury called the chirimoya, which is delicious-ness itself. Then there is the tamarind. I thought tamarinds were made to eat, but that was probably not the idea. I ate several, and it seemed to me that they were rather sour that year. They pursed up my lips, till they resembled the stem-end of a tomato, and I had to take my suste-nance through a quill for twenty-four hours. They sharpened my teeth till I could have shaved with them, and gave them a "wire edge" that I was afraid would stay; but a citizen said "no, it will come off when the enamel does"—which was comforting, at any rate. I found, afterward, that only strangers eat tamarinds—but they only eat them once.

[Hawaiian Islands, from Chapter 73]

At noon, we hired a Kanaka to take us down to the ancient ruins at Hon-aunau in his canoe—price two dollars—reasonable enough, for a sea voy-age of eight miles, counting both ways.

The native canoe is an irresponsible looking contrivance. I cannot think of anything to liken it to but a boy's sled runner hollowed out, and that does not quite convey the correct idea. It is about fifteen feet long, high and pointed at both ends, is a foot and a half or two feet deep, and so narrow that if you wedged a fat man into it you might not get him out again. It sits on top of the water like a duck, but it has an outrigger and does not upset easily, if you keep still. This outrigger is formed of two long bent sticks like plow handles, which project from one side, and to their outer ends is bound a curved beam composed of an extremely light wood, which skims along the surface of the water and thus saves you from an upset on that side, while the outrigger's weight is not so easily lifted as to make an upset on the other side a thing to be greatly feared. Still, until one gets used to sitting perched upon this knife-blade, he is apt to reason within himself that it would be more comfortable if there were just an outrigger or so on the other side also.

I had the bow seat, and Billings sat amidships and faced the Kanaka, who occupied the stern of the craft and did the paddling. With the first stroke the trim shell of a thing shot out from the shore like an arrow. There was not much to see. While we were on the shallow water of the reef, it was pastime to look down into the limpid depths at the large bunches of branching coral—the unique shrubbery of the sea. We lost that, though, when we got out into the dead blue water of the deep. But we had the picture of the surf, then, dashing angrily against the crag-bound shore and sending a foaming spray high into the air. There was interest in this beetling border, too, for it was honey-combed with quaint caves and arches and tunnels, and had a rude semblance of the dilapidated architecture of ruined keeps and castles rising out of the restless sea. When this novelty ceased to be a novelty, we turned our eyes shoreward and gazed at the long mountain with its rich green forests stretching up into the curtaining clouds, and at the specks of houses in the rearward distance and the diminished schooner riding sleepily at anchor. And when these grew tiresome we dashed boldly into the midst of a school of huge, beastly porpoises engaged at their eternal game of arching over a wave and disappearing, and then doing it over again and keeping it up—always circling over, in that way, like so many well-submerged wheels. But the porpoises wheeled themselves away, and then we were thrown upon our own resources. It did not take many minutes to discover that the sun was blazing like a bonfire, and that the weather was of a melting temperature. It had a drowsing effect, too.

In one place we came upon a large company of naked natives, of both sexes and all ages, amusing themselves with the national pastime of surf-bathing. Each heathen would paddle three or four hundred yards out to sea, (taking a short board with him), then face the shore and wait for a particularly prodigious billow to come along; at the right moment he would fling his board upon its foamy crest and himself upon the board, and here he would come whizzing by like a bombshell! It did not seem that a lightning express train could shoot along at a more hair-lifting speed. I tried surf-bathing once, subsequently, but made a failure of it. I got the board placed right, and at the right moment, too; but missed the connection myself.—The board struck the shore in three quarters of a second, without any cargo, and I struck the bottom about the same time, with a couple of barrels of water in me. None but natives ever master the art of surf-bathing thoroughly.

At the end of an hour, we had made the four miles, and landed on a level point of land, upon which was a wide extent of old ruins, with many a tall cocoanut tree growing among them. Here was the ancient City of Refuge—a vast inclosure, whose stone walls were twenty feet thick at the base, and fifteen feet high; an oblong square, a thousand and forty feet one way and a fraction under seven hundred the other. Within this inclosure, in early times, has been three rude temples; each two hundred and ten feet long by one hundred wide, and thirteen high.

In those days, if a man killed another anywhere on the island the relatives were privileged to take the murderer's life; and then a chase for life and liberty began—the outlawed criminal flying through pathless forests and over mountain and plain, with his hopes fixed upon the protecting walls of the City of Refuge, and the avenger of blood following hotly after him! Sometimes the race was kept up to the very gates of the temple, and the panting pair sped through long files of excited natives, who watched the contest with flashing eye and dilated nostril, encouraging the hunted refugee with sharp, inspiriting ejaculations, and sending up a ringing shout of exultation when the saving gates closed upon him and the cheated pursuer sank exhausted at the threshold. But sometimes the flying criminal fell under the hand of the avenger at the very door, when one more brave stride, one more brief second of time would have brought his feet upon the sacred ground and barred him against all harm. Where did these isolated pagans get this idea of a City of Refuge—this ancient Oriental custom?

This old sanctuary was sacred to all—even to rebels in arms and invading armies. Once within its walls, and confession made to the priest and absolution obtained, the wretch with a price upon his head could go forth without fear and without danger—he was *tabu,* and to harm him was death. The routed rebels in the lost battle for idolatry fled to this place to claim sanctuary, and many were thus saved.

Close to the corner of the great inclosure is a round structure of stone, some six or eight feet high, with a level top about ten or twelve in diameter. This was the place of execution. A high palisade of cocoanut piles shut out the cruel scenes from the vulgar multitude. Here criminals were killed, the flesh stripped from the bones and burned, and the bones secreted in holes in the body of the structure. If the man had been guilty of a high crime, the entire corpse was burned.

The walls of the temple are a study. The same food for speculation that is offered the visitor to the Pyramids of Egypt he will find here— the mystery of how they were constructed by a people unacquainted with science and mechanics. The natives have no invention of their own for hoisting heavy weights, they had no beasts of burden, and they have never even shown any knowledge of the properties of the lever. Yet some of the lava blocks quarried out, brought over rough, broken ground, and built into this wall, six or seven feet from the ground, are of prodigious size and would weigh tons. How did they transport and how raise them?

Both the inner and outer surfaces of the walls present a smooth front and are very creditable specimens of masonry. The blocks are of all manner of shapes and sizes, but yet are fitted together with the neatest exactness. The gradual narrowing of the wall from the base upward is accurately preserved.

No cement was used, but the edifice is firm and compact and is capable of resisting storm and decay for centuries. Who built this temple, and how was it built, and when, are mysteries that may never be unraveled.

Outside of these ancient walls lies a sort of coffin-shaped stone eleven feet four inches long and three feet square at the small end (it would weigh a few thousand pounds), which the high chief who held sway over this district many centuries ago brought thither on his shoulder one day to use as a lounge! This circumstance is established by the most reliable traditions. He used to lie down on it, in his indolent way, and keep an eye on his subjects at work for him and see that there was no "soldiering" done.

And no doubt there was not any done to speak of, because he was a man of that sort of build that incites to attention to business on the part of an employee. He was fourteen or fifteen feet high. When he stretched himself at full length on his lounge, his legs hung down over the end, and when he snored he woke the dead. These facts are all attested by irrefragable tradition.

[Hawaiian Islands, from Chapter 74]

We got back to the schooner in good time, and then sailed down to Kau, where we disembarked and took final leave of the vessel. Next day we bought horses and bent our way over the summer-clad mountain-terraces, toward the great volcano of Kilauea (Ke-low-way-ah). We made nearly a two days' journey of it, but that was on account of laziness. Toward sunset on the second day, we reached an elevation of some four thousand feet above sea level, and as we picked our careful way through billowy wastes of lava long generations ago stricken dead and cold in the climax of its tossing fury, we began to come upon signs of the near presence of the volcano—signs in the nature of ragged fissures that discharged jets of sulphurous vapor into the air, hot from the molten ocean down in the bowels of the mountain.

Shortly the crater came into view. I have seen Vesuvius since, but it was a mere toy, a child's volcano, a soup-kettle, compared to this. Mount Vesuvius is a shapely cone thirty-six hundred feet high; its crater an inverted cone only three hundred feet deep, and not more than a thousand feet in diameter, if as much as that; its fires meagre, modest, and docile.— But here was a vast, perpendicular, walled cellar, nine hundred feet deep in some places, thirteen hundred in others, level-floored, and *ten miles in circumference!* Here was a yawning pit upon whose floor the armies of Russia could camp, and have room to spare.

Perched upon the edge of the crater, at the opposite end from where we stood, was a small look-out house—say three miles away. It assisted us, by comparison, to comprehend and appreciate the great depth of the basin— it looked like a tiny martin-box clinging at the eaves of a cathedral. After some little time spent in resting and looking and ciphering, we hurried on to the hotel.

By the path it is half a mile from the Volcano House to the lookout-house. After a hearty supper we waited until it was thoroughly dark and then started to the crater. The first glance in that direction revealed a scene of wild beauty. There was a heavy fog over the crater and it was splendidly illuminated by the glare from the fires below. The illumination was two miles wide and a mile high, perhaps; and if you ever, on a dark night and at a distance beheld the light from thirty or forty blocks of distant buildings all on fire at once, reflected strongly against over-hanging clouds, you can form a fair idea of what this looked like.

A colossal column of cloud towered to a great height in the air immediately above the crater, and the outer swell of every one of its vast folds was dyed with a rich crimson luster, which was subdued to a pale rose tint in the depressions between. It glowed like a muffled torch and stretched upward to a dizzy height toward the zenith. I thought it just possible that its like had not been seen since the children of Israel wandered on their long march through the desert so many centuries ago over a path illuminated by the mysterious "pillar of fire." And I was sure that I now had a vivid conception of what the majestic "pillar of fire" was like, which almost amounted to a revelation.

Arrived at the little thatched lookout house, we rested our elbows on the railing in front and looked abroad over the wide crater and down over the sheer precipice at the seething fires beneath us. The view was a startling improvement on my daylight experience. I turned to see the effect on the balance of the company and found the reddest-faced set of men I almost ever saw. In the strong light every countenance glowed like red-hot iron, every shoulder was suffused with crimson and shaded rearward into dingy, shapeless obscurity! The place below looked like the infernal regions and these men like half-cooled devils just come up on a furlough.

I turned my eyes upon the volcano again. The "cellar" was tolerably well lighted up. For a mile and a half in front of us and half a mile on either side, the floor of the abyss was magnificently illuminated; beyond these limits the mists hung down their gauzy curtains and cast a deceptive gloom over all that made the twinkling fires in the remote corners of the crater seem countless leagues removed—made them seem like the campfires of a great army far away. Here was room for the imagination to work! You could imagine those lights the width of a continent away—and that hidden under the intervening darkness were hills, and winding rivers, and weary wastes of plain and desert—and even then the tremendous vista stretched on, and on, and on!—to the fires and far beyond! You could not compass it—it was the idea of eternity made tangible—and the longest end of it made visible to the naked eye!

The greater part of the vast floor of the desert under us was as black as ink, and apparently smooth and level; but over a mile square of it was ringed and streaked and striped with a thousand branching streams of liquid and gorgeously brilliant fire! It looked like a colossal railroad map of the State of Massachusetts done in chain lightning on a midnight sky. Imagine it—imagine a coal-black sky shivered into a tangled net-work of angry fire!

Here and there were gleaming holes a hundred feet in diameter, broken in the dark crust, and in them the melted lava—the color a dazzling white just tinged with yellow—was boiling and surging furiously; and from these holes branched numberless bright torrents in many directions, like the spokes of a wheel, and kept a tolerably straight course for a while and then swept round in huge rainbow curves, or made a long succession of sharp worm-fence angles, which looked precisely like the fiercest jagged lightning. These streams met other streams, and they mingled with and crossed and recrossed each other in every conceivable direction, like skate tracks on a popular skating ground. Sometimes streams twenty or thirty feet wide flowed from the holes to some distance without dividing—and through the opera-glasses we could see that they ran down small, steep hills and were genuine cataracts of fire, white at their source, but soon cooling and turning to the richest red, grained with alternate lines of black and gold. Every now and then masses of the dark crust broke away and floated slowly down these streams like rafts down a river. Occasionally the molten lava flowing under the superincumbent crust broke through—split a daz-zling streak, from five hundred to a thousand feet long, like a sudden flash of lightning, and then acre after acre of the cold lava parted into frag-ments, turned up edgewise like cakes of ice when a great river breaks up, plunged downward and were swallowed in the crimson cauldron. Then the wide expanse of the "thaw" maintained a ruddy glow for a while, but shortly cooled and became black and level again. During a "thaw," every dismembered cake was marked by a glittering white border which was superbly shaded inward by aurora borealis rays, which were a flaming yellow where they joined the white border, and from thence toward their points tapered into glowing crimson, then into a rich, pale carmine, and finally into a faint blush that held its own a moment and then dimmed and turned black. Some of the streams preferred to mingle together in a tangle of fantastic circles, and then they looked something like the confusion of ropes one sees on a ship's deck when she has just taken in sail and dropped anchor—provided one can imagine those ropes on fire.

Through the glasses, the little fountains scattered about looked very beautiful. They boiled, and coughed, and spluttered, and discharged sprays of stringy red fire—of about the consistency of mush, for instance—from ten to fifteen feet into the air, along with a shower of brilliant white sparks—a quaint and unnatural mingling of gouts of blood and snowflakes!

We had circles and serpents and streaks of lightning all twined and wreathed and tied together, without a break throughout an area more than a mile square (that amount of ground was covered, though it was not strictly "square"), and it was with a feeling of placid exultation that we reflected that many years had elapsed since any visitor had seen such a splendid display—since any visitor had seen anything more than the now snubbed and insignificant "North" and "South" lakes in action. We had been reading old files of Hawaiian newspapers and the "Record Book" at the Volcano House, and were posted.

I could see the North Lake lying out on the black floor away off in the outer edge of our panorama, and knitted to it by a web-work of lava streams. In its individual capacity it looked very little more respectable than a schoolhouse on fire. True, it was about nine hundred feet long and two or three hundred wide, but then, under the present circumstances, it necessarily appeared rather insignificant, and besides it was so distant from us.

I forgot to say that the noise made by the bubbling lava is not great, heard as we heard it from our lofty perch. It makes three distinct sounds—a rushing, a hissing, and a coughing or puffing sound; and if you stand on the brink and close your eyes it is no trick at all to imagine that you are sweeping down a river on a large low-pressure steamer, and that you hear the hissing of the steam about her boilers, the puffing from her escape-pipes and the churning rush of the water abaft her wheels. The smell of sulphur is strong, but not unpleasant to a sinner.

We left the lookout house at ten o'clock in a half cooked condition, because of the heat from Pele's furnaces, and wrapping up in blankets, for the night was cold, we returned to our Hotel.

3. "The Caravan," from *A Tramp Abroad* (Hartford, CT: American Publishing Company, 1880).

3

A Tramp Abroad (1880)

Although Twain had become an emerging lion of American literature in the eleven years following publication of *The Innocents Abroad*, his literary reputation and his financial success were in some peril. After a propitious beginning provided by his first two travel books, by the mid-1870s his career had leveled off with the sales figures of his fictional works *The Gilded Age* (1873), co-authored with Charles Dudley Warner, and *The Adventures of Tom Sawyer* (1876). He needed rejuvenation in the public eye out of professional necessity. To regain that momentum, he returned to Europe and to travel writing, intent upon saving money by living abroad and making money by turning the experience into a narrative. In other words, Twain instinctively started to move again.

A Tramp Abroad, unlike Twain's first foray into Europe, has no distinct itinerary, no grand program. The writer who worked his way across the Atlantic as a correspondent in *The Innocents Abroad* has returned as a middle-aged epicure eager to maintain the trajectory that his younger self had launched. Though for many readers the narrative suffers as a result of its lack of a compulsory route and timetable, the rambling structure does indeed accurately capture the changing emphasis for American tourists at large, a shift from *seeing* the world to *being* at the center of it. Twain's condition matches that of his nation on the whole—now more settled, more affluent, more experienced. Indeed, Twain returned to Europe this time with his own entourage, traveling the continent at will and in comfort, a luxury paid for from his own pockets rather than those of the *Alta California*. The theme of astonished disappointment, so prominent in *The Innocents Abroad*, occurs only sporadically in this sequel. The focus more often is on Twain himself as a leisured tourist, aspiring artist, annoyed hotel guest, struggling German language student, and clueless mountain-climbing adventurer. The disappointments derive from his comic and ever-failing efforts at self improvement. Satire and parody within the narrative, then, depend not on what he sees but on what he does (or fails to do). The "spectacle" in *A Tramp Abroad* is not Europe; it is Twain himself, no longer an innocent voyager but an affluent tramp with an unbridled desire for distraction.

In April of 1878, Twain traveled to Europe on the *Holsatia* for what would be sixteen months. He brought along his wife, Olivia; their two daughters, Susy and Clara; a longtime friend of Livy's, Clara Spaulding; the nursemaid and German language teacher for his children, Rosina Hay; and the family butler, George Griffin. Joseph Twichell joined them later in the summer, at Twain's request and on Twain's dime, and provided the foil for much of the narrative action as the purported "agent" referred to as "Harris" in the subsequent narrative. The Clemenses spent considerable time in Heidelberg and Munich but would visit numerous cities in the ensuing months, including Hamburg, Frankfurt, Venice, Rome, and Paris.

Despite the frustrations Twain faced in establishing and completing a workable structure, *A Tramp Abroad* offers readers a wealth of wit and satire that matches his other travel books. Although virtually forgotten by modern readers, it sold well upon its publication and earned mostly positive reviews. The following selections represent a sampling of Twain's experiences as a man who had become famous but no less irascible. To him the Old World is no longer intimidating or even inspiring, yet he nonetheless discerns beauty, grace, and, occasionally, comic absurdity. If he is not always guided by a clear purpose, at least his quips are fully charged and this time sharpest when directed at himself, a much larger target than ever before.

From A TRAMP ABROAD

[Heidelberg and Heilbronn, Chapter 11]

The summer days passed pleasantly in Heidelberg. We had a skilled trainer, and under his instructions we were getting our legs in the right condition for the contemplated pedestrian tours; we were well satisfied with the progress which we had made in the German language, and more than satisfied with what we had accomplished in Art. We had had the best instructors in drawing and painting in Germany,—Häemmerling, Vogel, Müller, Dietz and Schumann. Häemmerling taught us landscape painting. Vogel taught us figure drawing, Müller taught us to do still-life, and Dietz and Schumann gave us a finishing course in two specialties,—battle-pieces and shipwrecks. Whatever I am in Art I owe to these men. I have something of the manner of each and all of them; but they all said that I had also a manner of my own, and that it was conspicuous. They said there was a marked individuality about my style,—insomuch that if I ever painted the commonest type of a dog, I should be sure to throw a something into the aspect of that dog which would keep him from being mistaken for the creation of any other artist. Secretly I wanted to believe all these kind sayings, but I could not; I was afraid that my masters' partiality for me, and pride in me, biased their judgment. So I resolved to make a test. Privately, and unknown to any one, I painted my great picture, "Heidelberg Castle Illuminated,"—my first really important work in oils,—and had it hung up in the midst of a wilderness of oil pictures in the Art Exhibition, with no name attached to it. To my great gratification it was instantly recognized as mine. All the town flocked to see it, and people even came from neighboring localities to visit it. It made more stir than any other work in the Exhibition. But the most gratifying thing of all, was, that chance strangers, passing through, who had not heard of my picture, were not only drawn to it, as by a lodestone, the moment they entered the gallery, but always took it for a "Turner."

Mr. Harris was graduated in Art about the same time with myself, and we took a studio together. We waited awhile for some orders; then as time began to drag a little, we concluded to make a pedestrian tour. After much consideration, we determined on a trip up the shores of the beautiful Neckar to Heilbronn. Apparently nobody had ever done that. There were ruined castles on the overhanging cliffs and crags all the way; these were said to have their legends, like those on the Rhine, and what was better still, they had never been in print. There was nothing in the books about that lovely region; it had been neglected by the tourist, it was virgin soil for the literary pioneer.

Meantime the knapsacks, the rough walking suits and the stout walking shoes which we had ordered, were finished and brought to us. A Mr. X. and a young Mr. Z. had agreed to go with us. We went around one evening and bade good-bye to our friends, and afterwards had a little farewell banquet at the hotel. We got to bed early, for we wanted to make an early start, so as to take advantage of the cool of the morning.

We were out of bed at break of day, feeling fresh and vigorous, and took a hearty breakfast, then plunged down through the leafy arcades of the Castle grounds, toward the town. What a glorious summer morning it was, and how the flowers did pour out their fragrance, and how the birds did sing! It was just the time for a tramp through the woods and mountains.

We were all dressed alike: broad slouch hats, to keep the sun off; gray knapsacks; blue army shirts; blue overalls; leathern gaiters buttoned tight from knee down to ankle; high-quarter coarse shoes snugly laced. Each man had an opera glass, a canteen, and a guide-book case slung over his shoulder, and carried an alpenstock in one hand and a sun umbrella in the other. Around our hats were wound many folds of soft white muslin, with the ends hanging and flapping down our backs,—an idea brought from the Orient and used by tourists all over Europe. Harris carried the little watch-like machine called a "pedometer," whose office is to keep count of a man's steps and tell how far he has walked. Everybody stopped to admire our costumes and give us a hearty: "Pleasant march to you!"

When we got down town I found that we could go by rail to within five miles of Heilbronn. The train was just starting, so we jumped aboard and went tearing away in splendid spirits. It was agreed all around that we had done wisely, because it would be just as enjoyable to walk *down* the Neckar as up it, and it could not be needful to walk both ways. There were some nice German people in our compartment. I got to talking some pretty private matters presently, and Harris became nervous; so he nudged me and said,—"Speak in German—these Germans may understand English."

I did so, and it was well I did; for it turned out that there was not a German in that party who did not understand English perfectly. It is curious how wide-spread our language is in Germany. After a while some of those folks got out and a German gentleman and his two young daughters got in. I spoke in German to one of the latter several times, but without result. Finally she said,—"Ich verstehe nur Deutch und Englische,"—or words to that effect. That is, "I don't understand any language but German and English."

And sure enough, not only she but her father and sister spoke English. So after that we had all the talk we wanted; and we wanted a good deal, for they were very agreeable people. They were greatly interested in our costumes; especially the alpenstocks, for they had not seen any before. They said that the Neckar road was perfectly level, so we must be going to Switzerland or some other rugged country; and asked us if we did not find the walking pretty fatiguing in such warm weather. But we said no.

We reached Wimpfen,—I think it was Wimpfen,—in about three hours, and got out, not the least tired; found a good hotel and ordered beer and dinner,—then took a stroll through the venerable old village. It was very picturesque and tumble-down, and dirty and interesting. It had queer houses five hundred years old in it and a military tower, 115 feet high, which had stood there more than ten centuries. I made a little sketch of it. I kept a copy, but gave the original to the Burgomaster. I think the original was better than the copy, because it had more windows in it and the grass stood up better and had a brisker look. There was none around the tower though; I composed the grass myself, from studies I made in a field by Heidelberg in Häemmerling's time. The man on top, looking at the view, is apparently too large, but I found he could not be made smaller, conveniently. I wanted him there, and I wanted him visible, so I thought out a way to manage it; I composed the picture from two points of view; the spectator is to observe the man from about where that flag is, and he must observe the tower itself from the ground. This harmonizes the seeming discrepancy.

Near an old Cathedral, under a shed, were three crosses of stone,—mouldy and damaged things, bearing life-size stone figures. The two thieves were dressed in the fanciful court costumes of the middle of the sixteenth century, while the Savior was nude, with the exception of a cloth around the loins.

We had dinner under the green trees in a garden belonging to the hotel and overlooking the Neckar; then, after a smoke, we went to bed. We had a refreshing nap, then got up about three in the afternoon and put on our panoply. As we tramped gaily out at the gate of the town, we overtook a peasant's cart, partly laden with odds and ends of cabbages and similar vegetable rubbish, and drawn by a small cow and a smaller donkey yoked together. It was a pretty slow concern, but it got us into Heilbronn before dark,—five miles, or possibly it was seven.

We stopped at the very same inn which the famous old robber knight and rough fighter Götz von Berlichingen, abode in after he got out of

4. "The Tower," from *A Tramp Abroad* (Hartford, CT: American Publishing Company, 1880).

captivity in the Square Tower of Heilbronn between three hundred and fifty and four hundred years ago. Harris and I occupied the same room which he had occupied and the same paper had not all peeled off the walls yet. The furniture was quaint old carved stuff, full four hundred years old, and some of the smells were over a thousand. There was a hook in the wall, which the landlord said the terrific old Götz used to hang his iron hand on when he took it off to go to bed. This room was very large,—it might be called immense,—and it was on the first floor; which means it was in the second story, for in Europe the houses are so high that they do not count the first story, else they would get tired climbing before they got to the top. The wall paper was a fiery red, with huge gold figures in it, well smirched by time, and it covered all the doors. These doors fitted so snugly and continued the figures of the paper so unbrokenly, that when they were closed one had to go feeling and searching along the wall to find them. There was a stove in the corner,—one of those tall, square, stately white porcelain things that looks like a monument and keeps you thinking of death when you ought to be enjoying your travels. The windows looked out on a little alley, and over that into a stable and some poultry and pig yards in the rear of some tenement houses. There were the customary two beds in the room, one in one end of it, the other in the other, about an old-fashioned brass-mounted, single-barreled pistol-shot apart. They were fully as narrow as the usual German bed, too, and had the German bed's ineradicable habit of spilling the blankets on the floor every time you forgot yourself and went to sleep.

A round-table as large as King Arthur's stood in the centre of the room; while the waiters were getting ready to serve our dinner on it we all went out to see the renowned clock on the front of the municipal buildings.

[The Neckar River, Chapter 14]

When the landlord learned that I and my agent were artists, our party rose perceptibly in his esteem; we rose still higher when he learned that we were making a pedestrian tour of Europe.

He told us all about the Heidelberg road, and which were the best places to avoid and which the best ones to tarry at; he charged me less than cost for the things I broke in the night; he put up a fine luncheon for us and added to it a quantity of great light-green plums, the pleasantest fruit in Germany; he was so anxious to do us honor that he would not allow us to walk out of Heilbronn, but called up Götz von Berlichingen's horse and cab and made us ride.

I made a sketch of the turn-out. It is not a Work, it is only what artists call a "study"—a thing to make a finished picture from. This sketch has several blemishes in it; for instance, the wagon is not traveling as fast as the horse is. This is wrong. Again, the person trying to get out of the way is too small; he is out of perspective, as we say. The two upper lines are not the horse's back, they are the reins;—there seems to be a wheel missing—this would be corrected in a finished Work, of course. That thing flying out behind is not a flag, it is a curtain. That other thing up there is the sun, but I didn't get enough distance on it. I do not remember, now, what that thing is that is in front of the man who is running, but I think it is a haystack or a woman. This study was exhibited in the Paris Salon of 1879, but did not take any medal; they do not give medals for studies.

We discharged the carriage at the bridge. The river was full of logs,— long, slender, barkless pine logs,—and we leaned on the rails of the bridge and watched the men put them together into rafts. These rafts were of a shape and construction to suit the crookedness and extreme narrowness of the Neckar. They were from 50 to 100 yards long, and they gradually tapered from a 9-log breadth at their sterns, to a 3-log breadth at their bow-ends. The main part of the steering is done at the bow, with a pole; the 3-

5. "Leaving Heilbronn," from *A Tramp Abroad* (Hartford, CT: American Publishing Company, 1880).

log breadth there furnishes room for only the steersman, for these little logs are not larger around than an average young lady's waist. The connections of the several sections of the raft are slack and pliant, so that the raft may be readily bent into any sort of curve required by the shape of the river.

The Neckar is in many places so narrow that a person can throw a dog across it, if he has one; when it is also sharply curved in such places, the raftsman has to do some pretty nice snug piloting to make the turns. The river is not always allowed to spread over its whole bed,—which is as much as 30, and sometimes 40, yards wide,—but is split into three equal bodies of water, by stone dikes which throw the main volume, depth, and current into the central one. In low water these neat narrow-edged dikes project four or five inches above the surface, like the comb of a submerged roof, but in high water they are overflowed. A hatful of rain makes high water in the Neckar, and a basketful produces an overflow.

There are dikes abreast the Schloss Hotel, and the current is violently swift at that point. I used to sit for hours in my glass cage, watching the long, narrow rafts slip along through the central channel, grazing the right-bank dike and aiming carefully for the middle arch of the stone bridge below; I watched them in this way, and lost all this time hoping to see one of them hit the bridge-pier and wreck itself sometime or other, but was always disappointed. One was smashed there one morning, but I had just stepped into my room a moment to light a pipe, so I lost it.

While I was looking down upon the rafts that morning in Heilbronn, the dare-devil spirit of adventure came suddenly upon me, and I said to my comrades,—"*I* am going to Heidelberg on a raft. Will you venture with me?"

Their faces paled a little, but they assented with as good a grace as they could. Harris wanted to cable his mother,—thought it his duty to do that, as he was all she had in this world,—so, while he attended to this, I went down to the longest and finest raft and hailed the captain with a hearty "Ahoy, shipmate!" which put us upon pleasant terms at once, and we entered upon business. I said we were on a pedestrian tour to Heidelberg, and would like to take passage with him. I said this partly through young Z, who spoke German very well, and partly through Mr. X, who spoke it peculiarly. I can *understand* German as well as the maniac that invented it, but I *talk* it best through an interpreter.

The captain hitched up his trowsers, then shifted his quid thoughtfully. Presently he said just what I was expecting he would say,—that he had no license to carry passengers, and therefore was afraid the law would be after him in case the matter got noised about or any accident happened. So I *chartered* the raft and the crew and took all the responsibilities on myself.

With a rattling song the starboard watch bent to their work and hove the cable short, then got the anchor home, and our bark moved off with a stately stride, and soon was bowling along at about two knots an hour.

Our party were grouped amidships. At first the talk was a little gloomy, and ran mainly upon the shortness of life, the uncertainty of it, the perils which beset it, and the need and wisdom of being always prepared for the worst; this shaded off into low-voiced references to the dangers of the deep, and kindred matters; but as the gray east began to redden and the mysterious solemnity and silence of the dawn to give place to the joy-songs of the birds, the talk took a cheerier tone, and our spirits began to rise steadily.

Germany, in the summer, is the perfection of the beautiful, but nobody has understood, and realized, and enjoyed the utmost possibilities of this soft and peaceful beauty unless he has voyaged down the Neckar on a raft. The motion of a raft is the needful motion; it is gentle, and gliding, and smooth, and noiseless; it calms down all feverish activities, it soothes to sleep all nervous hurry and impatience; under its restful influence all the troubles and vexations and sorrows that harass the mind vanish away, and existence becomes a dream, a charm, a deep and tranquil ecstasy. How it contrasts with hot and perspiring pedestrianism, and dusty and deafening railroad rush, and tedious jolting behind tired horses over blinding white roads!

We went slipping silently along, between the green and fragrant banks, with a sense of pleasure and contentment that grew, and grew, all the time. Sometimes the banks were over-hung with thick masses of willows that wholly hid the ground behind; sometimes we had noble hills on one hand, clothed densely with foliage to their tops, and on the other hand open levels blazing with poppies, or clothed in the rich blue of the corn-flower; sometimes we drifted in the shadow of forests, and sometimes along the margin of long stretches of velvety grass, fresh and green and bright, a tireless charm to the eye. And the birds!—they were everywhere; they swept back and forth across the river constantly, and their jubilant music was never stilled.

It was a deep and satisfying pleasure to see the sun create the new morning, and gradually, patiently, lovingly, clothe it on with splendor after splendor, and glory after glory, till the miracle was complete. How different is this marvel observed from a raft, from what it is when one observes it through the dingy windows of a railway station in some wretched village while he munches a petrified sandwich and waits for the train.

[The Neckar River, from Chapter 15]

Men and women and cattle were at work in the dewy fields by this time. The people often stepped aboard the raft, as we glided along the grassy shores, and gossiped with us and with the crew for a hundred yards or so, then stepped ashore again, refreshed by the ride.

Only the men did this; the women were too busy. The women do all kinds of work on the continent. They dig, they hoe, they reap, they sow, they bear monstrous burdens on their backs, they shove similar ones long distances on wheelbarrows, they drag the cart when there is no dog or lean cow to drag it,—and when there is, they assist the dog or cow. Age is no matter,—the older the woman, the stronger she is, apparently. On the farm a woman's duties are not defined,—she does a little of everything; but in the towns it is different, there she only does certain things, the men do the rest. For instance, a hotel chambermaid has nothing to do but make beds and fires in fifty or sixty rooms, bring towels and candles, and fetch several tons of water up several flights of stairs, a hundred pounds at a time, in prodigious metal pitchers. She does not have to work more than eighteen or twenty hours a day, and she can always get down on her knees and scrub the floors of halls and closets when she is tired and needs a rest.

As the morning advanced and the weather grew hot, we took off our outside clothing and sat in a row along the edge of the raft and enjoyed the scenery, with our sun umbrellas over our heads and our legs dangling in the water. Every now and then we plunged in and had a swim. Every projecting grassy cape had its joyous group of naked children, the boys to themselves and the girls to themselves, the latter usually in care of some motherly dame who sat in the shade of a tree with her knitting. The little boys swam out to us, sometimes, but the little maids stood knee deep in the water and stopped their splashing and frolicking to inspect the raft with their innocent eyes as it drifted by. Once we turned a corner suddenly and surprised a slender girl of twelve years or upward, just stepping into the water. She had not time to run, but she did what answered just as well; she promptly drew a lithe young willow bough athwart her white body with one hand, and then contemplated us with a simple and untroubled interest. Thus she stood while we glided by. She was a pretty creature, and she and her willow bough made a very pretty picture, and one which could not offend the modesty of the most fastidious spectator. Her white skin had a low bank of fresh green willows for background and effective contrast,—for she stood against them,—and above and out of them projected the eager faces and white shoulders of two smaller girls.

Towards noon we heard the inspiriting cry,—"Sail ho!"

"Where away?" shouted the captain.

"Three points off the weather bow!"

We ran forward to see the vessel. It proved to be a steamboat,—for they had begun to run a steamer up the Neckar, for the first time in May. She was a tug, and one of very peculiar build and aspect. I had often watched her from the hotel, and wondered how she propelled herself, for apparently she had no propeller or paddles. She came churning along, now, making a deal of noise of one kind or another, and aggravating it every now and then by blowing a hoarse whistle. She had nine keel-boats hitched on behind and following after her in a long, slender rank. We met her in a narrow place, between dikes, and there was hardly room for us both in the cramped passage. As she went grinding and groaning by, we perceived the secret of her moving impulse. She did not drive her-self up the river with paddles or propeller, she pulled herself by hauling on a great chain. This chain is laid in the bed of the river and is only fas-tened at the two ends. It is seventy miles long. It comes in over the boat's bow, passes around a drum, and is payed out astern. She pulls on that chain, and so drags herself up the river or down it. She has neither bow nor stern, strictly speaking, for she has a long-bladed rudder on each end and she never turns around. She uses both rudders all the time, and they are powerful enough to enable her to turn to the right or the left and steer around curves, in spite of the strong resistance of the chain. I would not have believed that that impossible thing could be done; but I saw it done, and therefore I know that there is one impossible thing which *can* be done. What miracle will man attempt next?

We met many big keel boats on their way up, using sails, mule power, and profanity—a tedious and laborious business. A wire rope led from the foretop mast to the file of mules on the tow-path a hundred yards ahead, and by dint of much banging and swearing and urging, the detachment of drivers managed to get a speed of two or three miles an hour out of the mules against the stiff current. The Neckar has always been used as a canal, and thus has given employment to a great many men and animals; but now that this steamboat is able, with a small crew and a bushel or so of coal, to take nine keel boats farther up the river in one hour than thirty men and thirty mules can do it in two, it is believed that the old-fashioned towing industry is on its death-bed. A second steamboat began work in the Neckar three months after the first one was put in service.

At noon we stepped ashore and bought some bottled beer and got some chickens cooked, while the raft waited; then we immediately put to sea again, and had our dinner while the beer was cold and the chick-ens hot. There is no pleasanter place for such a meal than a raft that is gliding down the winding Neckar past green meadows and wooded hills, and slumbering villages, and craggy heights graced with crumbling tow-ers and battlements.

In one place we saw a nicely dressed German gentleman without any spectacles. Before I could come to anchor he had got away. It was a great pity. I so wanted to make a sketch of him. The captain comforted me for my loss, however, by saying that the man was without any doubt a fraud who had spectacles, but kept them in his pocket in order to make himself conspicuous.

Below Hassmersheim we passed Hornberg, Götz von Berlichingen's old castle. It stands on a bold elevation 200 feet above the surface of the river; it has high vine-clad walls enclosing trees, and a peaked tower about 75 feet high. The steep hillside, from the castle clear down to the water's edge, is terraced, and clothed thick with grape vines. This is like farming a mansard roof. All the steeps along that part of the river which furnish the proper exposure, are given up to the grape. That region is a great producer of Rhine wines. The Germans are exceedingly fond of Rhine wines; they are put up in tall, slender bottles, and are considered a pleasant beverage. One tells them from vinegar by the label.

[Lake Lucerne, Chapter 27]

Close by the Lion of Lucerne is what they call the "Glacier Garden,"— and it is the only one in the world. It is on high ground. Four or five years ago, some workmen who were digging foundations for a house came upon this interesting relic of a long departed age. Scientific men perceived in it a confirmation of their theories concerning the glacial period; so through their persuasions the little tract of ground was bought and permanently protected against being built upon. The soil was removed, and there lay the rasped and guttered track which the ancient glacier had made as it moved along upon its slow and tedious journey. This track was perforated by huge pot-shaped holes in the bed-rock, formed by the furious washing-around in them of boulders by the turbulent torrent which flows beneath all glaciers. These huge round boulders still remain in the holes; they and the walls of the holes are worn smooth by the long continued chafing which they gave each other in those old days. It took a mighty force to churn these big lumps of stone around in that vigorous way. The neighboring country had a very different shape, at that time,—the valleys have risen up and become hills, since, and the hills have become valleys. The boulders discovered in the pots had traveled a great distance, for there is no rock like them nearer than the distant Rhone Glacier.

For some days we were content to enjoy looking at the blue lake Lucerne and at the piled-up masses of snow mountains that border it all around,—an enticing spectacle, this last, for there is a strange and fascinating beauty and charm about a majestic snow-peak with the sun blazing upon it or the moonlight softly enriching it,—but finally we concluded to try a bit of excursioning around on a steamboat, and a dash on foot at the Rigi. Very well, we had a delightful trip to Fluelen, on a breezy, sunny day. Everybody sat on the upper deck, on benches, under an awning; everybody talked, laughed, and exclaimed at the wonderful scenery; in truth, a trip on that lake is almost the perfection of pleasuring. The mountains were a never ceasing marvel. Sometimes they rose straight up out of the lake, and towered aloft and overshadowed our pygmy steamer with their prodigious bulk in the most impressive way. Not snow-clad mountains, these, yet they climbed high enough toward the sky to meet the clouds and veil their foreheads in them. They were not barren and repulsive, but clothed in green, and restful and pleasant to the eye. And they were so almost straight-up-and-down, sometimes, that one could not imagine a man being able to keep his footing upon such a surface, yet there are paths, and the Swiss people go up and down them every day.

Sometimes one of these monster precipices had the slight inclination of the huge ship-houses in dockyards,—then high aloft, toward the sky, it took a little stronger inclination, like that of a mansard roof,—and perched on this dizzy mansard one's eye detected little things like martin boxes, and presently perceived that these were the dwellings of peasants,—an airy place for a home, truly. And suppose a peasant should walk in his sleep, or his child should fall out of the front yard?—the friends would have a tedious long journey down out of those cloud-heights before they found the remains. And yet those far-away homes looked ever so seductive, they were so remote from the troubled world, they dozed in such an atmosphere of peace and dreams,—surely no one who had learned to live up there would ever want to live on a meaner level.

We swept through the prettiest little curving arms of the lake, among these colossal green walls, enjoying new delights, always, as the stately panorama unfolded itself before us and re-rolled and hid itself behind us; and now and then we had the thrilling surprise of bursting suddenly upon a tremendous white mass like the distant and dominating Jungfrau, or some kindred giant, looming head and shoulders above a tumbled waste of lesser Alps.

Once, while I was hungrily taking in one of these surprises, and doing my best to get all I possibly could of it while it should last, I was interrupted by a young and care-free voice, "You're an American, I think,—so'm I."

He was about eighteen, or possibly nineteen; slender and of medium height; open, frank, happy face; a restless but independent eye; a snub nose, which had the air of drawing back with a decent reserve from the silky new-born mustache below it until it should be introduced; a loosely hung jaw, calculated to work easily in the sockets. He wore a low-crowned, narrow-brimmed straw hat, with a broad blue ribbon around it which had a white anchor embroidered on it in front; nobby short-tailed coat, pantaloons, vest, all trim and neat and up with the fashion; red-striped stockings, very low-quarter patent leather shoes, tied with black ribbon; blue ribbon around his neck, wide-open collar; tiny diamond studs; wrinkleless kids; projecting cuffs, fastened with large oxidized silver sleeve-buttons, bearing the device of a dog's face,—English pug. He carried a slim cane, surmounted with an English pug's head with red glass eyes. Under his arm he carried a German grammar,—Otto's. His hair was short, straight and smooth, and presently when he turned his head a moment, I saw that it was nicely parted behind. He took a cigarette out of a dainty box, stuck it into a meerschaum holder which he carried in a morocco case, and reached for my cigar. While he was lighting, I said,—"Yes,—I am an American."

"I knew it,—I can always tell them. What ship did you come over in?"

"Holsatia."

"We came in the Batavia,—Cunard, you know. What kind of passage did you have?"

"Tolerably rough."

"So did we. Captain said he'd hardly ever seen it rougher. Where are you from?"

"New England."

"So'm I. I'm from New Bloomfield. Anybody with you?"

"Yes,—a friend."

"Our whole family's along. It's awful slow, going around alone,—don't you think so?"

"Rather slow."

"Ever been over here before?"

"Yes."

"I haven't. My first trip. But we've been all around,—Paris and everywhere. I'm to enter Harvard next year. Studying German all the time, now. Can't enter till I know German. I know considerable French,—I get along pretty well in Paris, or anywhere where they speak French. What hotel are you stopping at?"

"Schweitzerhof."

"No! is that so? I never see you in the reception room. I go to the reception room a good deal of the time, because there's so many Americans there. I make lots of acquaintances. I know an American as soon as I see him,—and so I speak to him and make his acquaintance. I like to be always making acquaintances, don't you?"

"Lord, yes!"

"You see it breaks up a trip like this, first rate. I never get bored on a trip like this, if I can make acquaintances and have somebody to talk to. But I think a trip like this would be an awful bore, if a body couldn't find anybody to get acquainted with and talk to on a trip like this. I'm fond of talking, ain't you?"

"Passionately."

"Have you felt bored, on this trip?"

"Not all the time, part of it."

"That's it!—you see you ought to go around and get acquainted, and talk. That's my way. That's the way I always do,—I just go 'round, 'round, 'round, and talk, talk, talk,—I never get bored. You been up the Rigi yet?"

"No."

"Going?"

"I think so."

"What hotel you going to stop at?"

"I don't know. Is there more than one?"

"Three. You stop at the Schreiber—you'll find it full of Americans. What ship did you say you came over in?"

"City of Antwerp."

"German, I guess. You going to Geneva?"

"Yes."

"What hotel you going to stop at?"

"Hotel de l' Ecu de Genève."

"Don't you do it! No Americans there! You stop at one of those big hotels over the bridge,—they're packed full of Americans."

"But I want to practice my Arabic."

"Good gracious, do you speak Arabic?"

"Yes,—well enough to get along."

"Why, hang it, you won't get along in Geneva,—*they* don't speak Arabic, they speak French. What hotel are you stopping at here?"

"Hotel Pension-Beaurivage."

"Sho, you ought to stop at the Schweitzerhof. Didn't you know the Schweitzerhof was the best hotel in Switzerland?—look at your Baedeker."

"Yes, I know,—but I had an idea there warn't any Americans there."

"No Americans! Why bless your soul it's just alive with them! I'm in the great reception room most all the time. I make lots of acquaintances there. Not as many as I did at first, because now only the new ones stop in there,—the others go right along through. Where are you from?"

"Arkansaw."

"Is that so? I'm from New England,—New Bloomfield's my town when I'm at home. I'm having a mighty good time to-day, ain't you?"

"Divine."

"That's what I call it. I like this knocking around, loose and easy, and making acquaintances and talking. I know an American, soon as I see him; so I go and speak to him and make his acquaintance. I ain't ever bored, on a trip like this, if I can make new acquaintances and talk. I'm awful fond of talking when I can get hold of the right kind of a person, ain't you?"

"I prefer it to any other dissipation."

"That's my notion, too. Now some people like to take a book and sit down and read, and read, and read, or moon around yawping at the lake or these mountains and things, but that ain't my way; no, sir, if they like it, let 'em do it, I don't object; but as for me, talking's what *I* like. You been up the Rigi?"

"Yes."

"What hotel did you stop at?"

"Schreiber."

"That's the place!—I stopped there too. *Full* of Americans, *wasn't* it? It always is,—always is. That's what they say. Everybody says that. What ship did you come over in?"

"Ville de Paris."

"French, I reckon. What kind of a passage did . . . excuse me a minute, there's some Americans I haven't seen before."

And away he went. He went uninjured, too,—I had the murderous impulse to harpoon him in the back with my alpenstock, but as I raised the weapon the disposition left me; I found I hadn't the heart to kill him, he was such a joyous, innocent, good-natured numscull.

Half an hour later I was sitting on a bench inspecting, with strong interest, a noble monolith which we were skimming by,—a monolith not shaped by man, but by Nature's free great hand,—a massy pyramidal rock eighty feet high, devised by Nature ten million years ago against the day when a man worthy of it should need it for his monument. The time came at last, and now this grand remembrancer bears Schiller's name in huge letters upon its face. Curiously enough, this rock was not degraded or defiled in any way. It is said that two years ago a stranger let himself down from the top of it with ropes and pulleys, and painted all over it, in blue letters bigger than those in Schiller's name, these words:

"Try Sozodont;"

"Buy Sun Stove Polish;"

"Helmbold's Buchu;"

"Try Benzaline for the Blood."

He was captured, and it turned out that he was an American. Upon his trial the judge said to him,—"You are from a land where any insolent that wants to is privileged to profane and insult Nature, and through her, Nature's God, if by so doing he can put a sordid penny in his pocket. But here the case is different. Because you are a foreigner and ignorant, I will make your sentence light; if you were a native I would deal strenuously with you.—Hear and obey: You will immediately remove every trace of your offensive work from the Schiller monument; you will pay a fine of ten thousand francs; you will suffer two years' imprisonment at hard labor; you will then be horsewhipped, tarred and feathered, deprived of your ears, ridden on a rail to the confines of the canton, and banished forever. The severer penalties are omitted in your case,—not as a grace to you, but to that great republic which had the misfortune to give you birth."

The steamer's benches were ranged back to back across the deck. My back hair was mingling innocently with the back hair of a couple of ladies.

Presently they were addressed by someone and I overheard this conversation:

"You are Americans, I think? So'm I."

"Yes—we are Americans."

"I knew it,—I can always tell them. What ship did you come over in?"

"City of Chester."

"Oh, yes,—Inman line. We came in the Batavia,—Cunard you know. What kind of a passage did you have?"

"Pretty fair."

"That was luck. We had it awful rough. Captain said he'd hardly ever seen it rougher. Where are you from?"

"New Jersey."

"So'm I. No—I didn't mean that; I'm from New England. New Bloomfield's my place. These your children?—belong to both of you?"

"Only to one of us; they are mine; my friend is not married."

"Single, I reckon? So'm I. Are you two ladies traveling alone?"

"No,—my husband is with us."

"Our whole family's along. It's awful slow, going around alone,—don't you think so?"

"I suppose it must be."

"Hi, there's Mount Pilatus coming in sight again. Named after Pontius Pilate, you know, that shot the apple off of William Tell's head. Guidebook tells all about it, they say. I didn't read it—an American told me. I don't read when I'm knocking around like this, having a good time. Did you ever see the chapel where William Tell used to preach?"

"I did not know he ever preached there."

"O, yes he did. That American told me so. He don't ever shut up his guide-book. He knows more about this lake than the fishes in it. Besides, they *call* it 'Tell's Chapel'—you know that yourself. You ever been over here before?"

"Yes."

"I haven't. It's my first trip. But we've been all around,—Paris and everywhere. I'm to enter Harvard next year.—Studying German all the time now. Can't enter till I know German. This book's Otto's grammar. It's a mighty good book to get the *ich habe gehabt haben*'s out of. But I don't really study when I'm knocking around this way. If the notion takes me, I just run over my little old *ich habe gehabt, du hast gehabt, er hat gehabt, wir haben gehabt, ihr habet gehabt, sie haben gehabt,*—kind of 'Now-I-lay-me-down-to-sleep' fashion, you know, and after that, maybe I don't buckle to it again for three days. It's awful undermining to the intellect, German is; you want to take it in small doses, or first you know your brains all run together, and you feel them sloshing around in your head same as so much drawn butter. But French is different; *French* ain't anything. I ain't any more afraid of French than a tramp's afraid of pie; I can rattle off my little *j'ai, tu as, il a,* and the rest of it, just as easy as a-b-c. I get along pretty well in Paris, or anywhere where they speak French. What hotel are you stopping at?"

"The Schweitzerhof."

"No! is that so? I never see you in the big reception room. I go in there a good deal of the time, because there's so many Americans there. I make lots of acquaintances. You been up the Rigi yet?"

"No."

"Going?"

"We think of it."

"What hotel you going to stop at?"

"I don't know."

"Well, then, you stop at the Schreiber,—it's full of Americans. What ship did you come over in?"

"City of Chester."

"O, yes, I remember I asked you that before. But I always ask everybody what ship they came over in, and so sometimes I forget and ask again. You going to Geneva?"

"Yes."

"What hotel you going to stop at?"

"We expect to stop in a pension."

"I don't hardly believe you'll like that: there's very few Americans in the pensions. What hotel are you stopping at here?"

"The Schweitzerhof."

"O, yes, I asked you that before, too. But I always ask everybody what hotel they're stopping at, and so I've got my head all mixed up with hotels. But it makes talk, and I love to talk. It refreshes me up so,—don't it you—on a trip like this?"

"Yes,—sometimes."

"Well, it does me, too. As long as I'm talking I never feel bored,—ain't that the way with you?"

"Yes—generally. But there are exception to the rule."

"O, of course. *I* don't care to talk to everybody, *myself.* If a person starts in to jabber-jabber-jabber about scenery, and history, and pictures, and all sorts of tiresome things, I get the fan-tods mighty soon. I say 'Well, I must be going now,—hope I'll see you again'—and then I take a walk. Where you from?"

"New Jersey."

"Why, bother it all, I asked you *that* before, too. Have you seen the Lion of Lucerne?"

"Not yet."

"Nor I, either. But the man who told me about Mount Pilatus says it's one of the things to see. It's twenty-eight feet long. It don't seem reasonable, but he said so, anyway. He saw it yesterday; said it was dying, then, so I reckon it's dead by this time. But that ain't any matter, of course they'll stuff it. Did you say the children are yours,—or *hers?*"

"Mine."

"O, so you did. Are you going up the . . . no, I asked you that. What ship . . . no, I asked you that, too. What hotel are you . . . no, you told me that. Let me see . . . um . . . O, what kind of voy . . . no, we've been over that ground, too. Um . . . um . . . well, I believe that is all. *Bonjour*—I am very glad to have made your acquaintance, ladies. *Guten tag.*"

[Rigi-Kulm, Chapter 28]

The Rigi-Kulm is an imposing Alpine mass, 6,000 feet high, which stands by itself, and commands a mighty prospect of blue lakes, green valleys, and snowy mountains—a compact and magnificent picture three hundred miles in circumference. The ascent is made by rail, or horseback, or on foot, as one may prefer. I and my agent panoplied ourselves in walking costume, one bright morning, and started down the lake on the steamboat; we got ashore at the village of Wäggis; three quarters of an hour distant from Lucerne. This village is at the foot of the mountain.

We were soon tramping leisurely up the leafy mule-path, and then the talk began to flow, as usual. It was twelve o'clock noon, and a breezy, cloudless day; the ascent was gradual, and the glimpses, from under the curtaining boughs, of blue water, and tiny sailboats, and beetling cliffs, were as charming as glimpses of dreamland. All the circumstances were perfect—and the anticipations, too, for we should soon be enjoying, for the first time, that wonderful spectacle, an Alpine sunrise—the object of our journey. There was (apparently) no real need for hurry, for the guide-book made the walking distance from Wäggis to the summit only three hours and a quarter. I say "apparently," because the guide-book had already fooled us once,—about the distance from Allerheiligen to Oppenau,—and for aught I knew it might be getting ready to fool us again. We were only certain as to the altitudes,—we calculated to find out for ourselves how many hours it is from the bottom to the top. The summit is 6,000 feet above the sea, but only 4,500 feet above the lake. When we had walked half an hour, we were fairly into the swing and humor of the undertaking, so we cleared for action; that is to say, we got a boy whom we met to carry our alpenstocks and satchels and overcoats and things for us; that left us free for business.

I suppose we must have stopped oftener to stretch out on the grass in the shade and take a bit of a smoke than this boy was used to, for presently he asked if it had been our idea to hire him by the job, or by the year? We told him he could move along if he was in a hurry. He said he wasn't in such a very particular hurry, but he wanted to get to the top while he was young. We told him to clear out, then, and leave the things at the uppermost hotel and say we should be along presently. He said he would secure us a hotel if he could, but if they were all full he would ask them to build another one and hurry up and get the paint and plaster dry against we arrived. Still gently chaffing us he pushed ahead, up the trail, and soon disappeared. By six o'clock we were pretty high up in the air, and the view of lake and mountains had greatly grown in breadth and interest. We halted a while at a little public house, where we had bread and cheese and a quart or two of fresh milk, out on the porch, with the big panorama all before us,—and then moved on again.

Ten minutes afterward we met a hot, red-faced man plunging down the mountain, with mighty strides, swinging his alpenstock ahead of him and taking a grip on the ground with its iron point to support these big strides. He stopped, fanned himself with his hat, swabbed the perspiration from his face and neck with a red handkerchief, panted a moment or two, and asked how far it was to Wäggis. I said three hours. He looked surprised, and said,—

"Why, it seems as if I could toss a biscuit into the lake from here, it's so close by. Is that an inn, there?"

I said it was.

"Well," said he, "I can't stand another three hours, I've had enough for to-day; I'll take a bed there."

I asked,—"Are we nearly to the top?"

"Nearly to the *top!* Why, bless your soul, you haven't really started, yet."

I said we would put up at the inn, too. So we turned back and ordered a hot supper, and had quite a jolly evening of it with this Englishman.

The German landlady gave us neat rooms and nice beds, and when I and my agent turned in, it was with the resolution to be up early and make the utmost of our first Alpine sunrise. But of course we were dead tired, and slept like policemen; so when we awoke in the morning and ran to the window it was already too late, because it was half past eleven. It was a sharp disappointment. However, we ordered breakfast and told the landlady to call the Englishman, but she said he was already up and off at daybreak,—and swearing mad about something or other. We could not find out what the matter was. He had asked the landlady the altitude of her place above the level of the lake, and she told him fourteen hundred and ninety-five feet. That was all that was said; then he lost his temper. He said that between —————— fools and guide-books, a man could acquire ignorance enough in twenty-four hours in a country like this to last him a year. Harris believed our boy had been loading him up with misinformation; and this was probably the case, for his epithet described that boy to a dot.

We got under way about the turn of noon, and pulled out for the summit again, with a fresh and vigorous step. When we had gone about two hundred yards, and stopped to rest, I glanced to the left while I was lighting my pipe, and in the distance detected a long worm of black smoke crawling lazily up the steep mountain. Of course that was the locomotive. We propped ourselves on our elbows at once, to gaze, for we had never seen a mountain railway yet. Presently we could make out the train. It seemed incredible that that thing should creep straight up a sharp slant like the roof of a house,—but there it was, and it was doing that very miracle.

In the course of a couple hours we reached a fine breezy altitude where the little shepherd-huts had big stones all over their roofs to hold them down to the earth when the great storms rage. The country was wild and rocky about here, but there were plenty of trees, plenty of moss, and grass.

Away off on the opposite shore of the lake we could see some villages, and now for the first time we could observe the real difference between their proportions and those of the giant mountains at whose feet they slept. When one is in one of those villages it seems spacious, and its houses seem high and not out of proportion to the mountain that overhangs them—but from our altitude, what a change! The mountains were bigger and grander than ever, as they stood there thinking their solemn thoughts with their heads in the drifting clouds, but the villages at their feet,—when the painstaking eye could trace them up and find them,—were so reduced, so almost invisible, and lay so flat against the ground, that the exactest simile I can devise is to compare them to ant-deposits of granulated dirt over-shadowed by the huge bulk of a cathedral. The steamboats skimming along under the stupendous precipices were diminished by distance to the daintiest little toys, the sail-boats and row-boats to shallops proper for fairies that keep house in the cups of lilies and ride to court on the backs of bumble-bees.

Presently we came upon half a dozen sheep nibbling grass in the spray of a stream of clear water that sprang from a rock wall a hundred feet high, and all at once our ears were startled with a melodious "Lul . . . l. . . l. . . lul-lul-*la*hee-o-o-o!" pealing joyously from a near but invisible source, and recognized that we were hearing for the first time the famous Alpine *jodel* in its own native wilds. And we recognized, also, that it was that sort of quaint commingling of baritone and falsetto which at home we call "Tyrolese warbling."

The jodling (pronounced y*o*dling,—emphasis on the o,) continued, and was very pleasant and inspiriting to hear. Now the jodler appeared,—a shepherd boy of sixteen,—and in our gladness and gratitude we gave him a franc to jodel some more. So he jodeled, and we listened. We moved on, presently, and he generously jodeled us out of sight. After about fifteen minutes we came across another shepherd boy who was jodling, and gave him half a franc to keep it up. He also jodled us out of sight. After that, we found a jodler every ten minutes; we gave the first one eight cents, the second one six cents, the third one four, the fourth one a penny, contributed nothing to Nos. 5, 6, and 7, and during the remainder of the day hired the rest of the jodlers, at a franc apiece, not to jodel any more. There is somewhat too much of this jodling in the Alps.

About the middle of the afternoon we passed through a prodigious natural gateway called the Felsenthor, formed by two enormous upright rocks, with a third lying across the top. There was a very attractive little hotel close by, but our energies were not conquered yet, so we went on.

Three hours afterward we came to the railway track. It was planted straight up the mountain with the slant of a ladder that leans against a house, and it seemed to us that man would need good nerves who proposed to travel up it or down it either.

During the latter part of the afternoon we cooled our roasting interiors with ice-cold water from clear streams, the only really satisfying water we had tasted since we left home, for at the hotels on the continent they merely give you a tumbler of ice to soak your water in, and that only modifies its hotness, doesn't make it cold. Water can only be made cold enough for summer comfort by being prepared in a refrigerator or a closed ice-pitcher. Europeans say ice water impairs digestion. How do they know?—they never drink any.

At ten minutes past six we reached the Kaltbad station, where there is a spacious hotel with great verandas which command a majestic expanse of lake and mountain scenery. We were pretty well fagged out, now, but as we did not wish to miss the Alpine sunrise, we got through with our dinner as quickly as possible and hurried off to bed. It was unspeakably comfortable to stretch our weary limbs between the cool damp sheets. And how we did sleep!—for there is no opiate like Alpine pedestrianism.

In the morning we both awoke and leaped out of bed at the same instant and ran and stripped aside the window curtains; but we suffered a bitter disappointment again: it was already half past three in the afternoon.

We dressed sullenly and in ill spirits, each accusing the other of oversleeping. Harris said if we had brought the courier along, as we ought to have done, we should not have missed these sunrises. I said he knew very well that one of us would have had to sit up and wake the courier; and I added that we were having trouble enough to take care of ourselves, on this climb, without having to take care of a courier besides.

During breakfast our spirits came up a little, since we found by the guide-book that in the hotels on the summit the tourist is not left to trust to luck for his sunrise, but is roused betimes by a man who goes through the halls with a great Alpine horn, blowing blasts that would raise the dead. And there was another consoling thing: the guide-book said that up there on the summit the guests did not wait to dress much, but seized a red bed-blanket and sailed out arrayed like an Indian. This was good; this would be romantic; two hundred and fifty people grouped on the windy summit, with their hair flying and their red blankets flapping, in the solemn presence of the snowy ranges and the messenger splendors of the coming sun, would be a striking and memorable spectacle. So it was good luck, not ill luck, that we had missed those other sunrises.

We were informed by the guide-book that we were now 3,228 feet above the level of the lake,—therefore full two-thirds of our journey had been accomplished. We got away at a quarter past four, p.m.; a hundred yards above the hotel the railway divided; one track went straight up the steep hill, the other one turned square off to the right, with a very slight grade. We took the latter, and followed it more than a mile, turned a rocky corner and came in sight of a handsome new hotel. If we had gone on, we should have arrived at the summit, but Harris preferred to ask a lot of questions,—as usual, of a man who didn't know anything,—and he told us to go back and follow the other route. We did so. We could ill afford this loss of time.

We climbed, and climbed; and we kept on climbing; we reached about forty summits, but there was always another one just ahead. It came on to rain, and it rained in dead earnest. We were soaked through, and it was bitter cold. Next a smoky fog of clouds covered the whole region densely, and we took to the railway ties to keep from getting lost. Sometimes we slopped along in a narrow path on the left hand side of the track, but by and by when the fog blew aside a little and we saw that we were treading the rampart of a precipice and that our left elbows were projecting over a perfectly boundless and bottomless vacancy, we gasped, and jumped for the ties again.

The night shut down, dark and drizzly and cold. About eight in the evening the fog lifted and showed us a well worn path which led up a very steep rise to the left. We took it and as soon as we had got far enough from the railway to render the finding it again an impossibility, the fog shut down on us once more.

We were in a bleak unsheltered place, now, and had to trudge right along, in order to keep warm, though we rather expected to go over a precipice sooner or later. About nine o'clock we made an important discovery,—that we were not in any path. We groped around a while on our hands and knees, but could not find it; so we sat down in the mud and the wet scant grass to wait. We were terrified into this by being suddenly confronted with a vast body which showed itself vaguely for an instant and in the next instant was smothered in the fog again. It was really the hotel we were after, monstrously magnified by the fog, but we took it for the face of a precipice, and decided not to try to claw up it.

We sat there an hour, with chattering teeth and quivering bodies, and quarreled over all sorts of trifles, but gave most of our attention to abusing each other for the stupidity of deserting the railway track. We sat with our backs to that precipice, because what little wind there was came from that quarter. At some time or other the fog thinned a little; we did not know when, for we were facing the empty universe and the thinness could not show; but at last Harris happened to look around, and there stood a huge, dim, spectral hotel where the precipice had been. One could faintly discern the windows and chimneys, and a dull blur of lights. Our first emotion was deep, unutterable gratitude, our next was a foolish rage, born of the suspicion that possibly the hotel had been visible three-quarters of an hour while we sat there in those cold puddles quarreling.

Yes, it was the Rigi-Kulm hotel—the one that occupies the extreme summit, and whose remote little sparkle of lights we had often seen glinting high aloft among the stars from our balcony away down yonder in Lucerne. The crusty portier and the crusty clerks gave us the surly reception which their kind deal in in prosperous times, but by mollifying them with an extra display of obsequiousness and servility we finally got them to show us to the room which our boy had engaged for us.

We got into some dry clothing, and while our supper was preparing we loafed forsakenly through a couple of vast cavernous drawing rooms, one of which had a stove in it. This stove was in a corner, and densely walled around with people. We could not get near the fire, so we moved at large in the arctic spaces, among a multitude of people who sat silent, smileless, forlorn and shivering,—thinking what fools they were to come, perhaps. There were some Americans, and some Germans, but one could see that the great majority were English.

We lounged into an apartment where there was a great crowd, to see what was going on. It was a memento-magazine. The tourists were eagerly buying all sorts and styles of paper-cutters, marked "Souvenir of the Rigi," with handles made of the little curved horn of the ostensible chamois; there were all manner of wooden goblets and such things, similarly marked. I was going to buy a paper-cutter, but I believed I could remember the cold comfort of the Rigi-Kulm without it, so I smothered the impulse.

Supper warmed us, and we went immediately to bed,—but first, as Mr. Baedeker requests all tourists to call his attention to any errors which they may find in his guide-books, I dropped him a line to inform him that when he said the foot-journey from Wäggis to the summit was only three hours and a quarter, he missed it by just about three days. I had previously informed him of his mistake about the distance from Allerheiligen to Oppenau, and had also informed the Ordnance Department of the German government of the same error in the imperial maps. I will add, here, that I never got any answer to these letters, or any thanks from either of those sources; and what is still more discourteous, these corrections have not been made, either in the maps or the guide-books. But I will write again when I get time, for my letters may have miscarried.

We curled up in the clammy beds, and went to sleep without rocking. We were so sodden with fatigue that we never stirred nor turned over till the booming blasts of the Alpine horn aroused us. It may well be imagined that we did not lose any time. We snatched on a few odds and ends of clothing, cocooned ourselves in the proper red blankets, and plunged along the halls and out into the whistling wind bare-headed. We saw a tall wooden scaffolding on the very peak of the summit, a hundred yards away, and made for it. We rushed up the stairs to the top of this scaffolding, and stood there, above the vast outlying world, with hair flying and ruddy blankets waving and cracking in the fierce breeze.

"Fifteen minutes too late, at last!" said Harris, in a vexed voice. "The sun is clear above the horizon."

"No matter," I said, "it is a most magnificent spectacle, and we will see it do the rest of its rising, anyway."

In a moment we were deeply absorbed in the marvel before us, and dead to everything else. The great cloud-barred disk of the sun stood just above a limitless expanse of tossing white-caps,—so to speak,—a billowy chaos of massy mountain domes and peaks draped in imperishable snow, and flooded with an opaline glory of changing and dissolving splendors, whilst through rifts in a black cloud-bank above the sun, radiating lances of diamond dust shot to the zenith. The cloven valleys of the lower world swam in a tinted mist which veiled the ruggedness of their crags and ribs and ragged forests, and turned all the forbidding region into a soft and rich and sensuous paradise.

We could not speak. We could hardly breathe. We could only gaze in drunken ecstasy and drink in it. Presently Harris exclaimed,—"Why—— —nation, it's going *down!*"

Perfectly true. We had missed the *morning* horn-blow, and slept all day. This was stupefying. Harris said,—"Look here, the sun isn't the spectacle,—it's *us*,—stacked up here on top of this gallows, in these idiotic blankets, and two hundred and fifty well-dressed men and women down here gawking up at us and not caring a straw whether the sun rises or sets, as long as they've got such a ridiculous spectacle as this to set down in their memorandum-books. They seem to be laughing their ribs loose, and there's one girl there that appears to be going all to pieces. I never saw such a man as you before. I think you are the very last possibility in the way of an ass."

"What have *I* done?" I answered with heat.

"What have you done? You've got up at half past seven o'clock in the evening to see the sun rise, that's what you've done."

"And have you done any better, I'd like to know? I always used to get up with the lark, till I came under the petrifying influence of your turgid intellect."

"*You* used to get up with the lark,—O, no doubt,—you'll get up with the hangman one of these days. But you ought to be ashamed to be jawing here like this, in a red blanket, on a forty-foot scaffold on top of the Alps. And no end of people down here to boot; this isn't any place for an exhibition of temper."

And so the customary quarrel went on. When the sun was fairly down, we slipped back to the hotel in the charitable gloaming, and went to bed again. We had encountered the horn-blower on the way, and he had tried to collect compensation, not only for announcing the sunset, which we did see, but for the sunrise, which we had totally missed; but we said no, we only took our solar rations on the "European plan"—pay for what you get. He promised to make us hear his horn in the morning, if we were alive.

[Rigi-Kulm, Chapter 29]

He kept his word. We heard his horn and instantly got up. It was dark and cold and wretched. As I fumbled around for the matches, knocking things down with my quaking hands, I wished the sun would rise in the middle of the day, when it was warm and bright and cheerful, and one wasn't sleepy. We proceeded to dress by the gloom of a couple of sickly candles, but we could hardly button anything, our hands shook so. I thought of how many happy people there were in Europe, Asia and America, and everywhere, who were sleeping peacefully in their beds and did not have to get up and see the Rigi sunrise,—people who did not appreciate their advantage, as like as not, but would get up in the morning wanting more boons of Providence. While thinking these thoughts I yawned, in a rather ample way, and my upper teeth got hitched on a nail over the door, and whilst I was mounting a chair to free myself, Harris drew the window curtain, and said,—"O, this is luck! We shan't have to go out at all,—yonder are the mountains, in full view."

That was glad news, indeed. It made us cheerful right away. One could see the grand Alpine masses dimly outlined against the black firmament, and one or two faint stars blinking through rifts in the night. Fully clothed, and wrapped in blankets, we huddled ourselves up, by the window, with lighted pipes, and fell into chat, while we waited in exceeding comfort to see how an Alpine sunrise was going to look by candle light. By and by a delicate, spiritual sort of effulgence spread itself by imperceptible degrees over the loftiest altitudes of the snowy wastes,—but there the effort seemed to stop. I said, presently,—"There is a hitch about this sunrise somewhere. It doesn't seem to go. What do you reckon is the matter with it?"

"I don't know. It appears to hang fire somewhere. I never saw a sunrise act like that before. Can it be that the hotel is playing anything on us?"

"Of course not. The hotel merely has a property interest in the sun, it has nothing to do with the management of it. It is a precarious kind of property, too; a succession of total eclipses would probably ruin this tavern. Now what can be the matter with this sunrise?""

Harris jumped up and said,—"I've got it! I know what's the matter with it! We've been looking at the place where the sun *set* last night!"

"It is perfectly true! Why couldn't you have thought of that sooner?

Now we've lost another one! And all through your blundering. It was exactly like you to light a pipe and sit down to wait for the sun to rise in the west."

"It was exactly like me to find out the mistake, too. You never would have found it out. I find out all the mistakes."

"You make them all, too, else your most valuable faculty would be wasted on you. But don't stop to quarrel, now,—maybe we are not too late yet."

But we were. The sun was well up when we got to the exhibition ground.

On our way up we met the crowd returning—men and women dressed in all sorts of queer costumes, and exhibiting all degrees of cold and wretchedness in their gaits and countenances. A dozen still remained on the ground when we reached there, huddled together about the scaffold with their backs to the bitter wind. They had their red guide-books open at the diagram of the view, and were painfully picking out the several mountains and trying to impress their names and positions on their memories. It was one of the saddest sights I ever saw.

Two sides of this place were guarded by railings, to keep people from being blown over the precipices. The view, looking sheer down into the broad valley, eastward, from this great elevation,—almost a perpendicular mile,—was very quaint and curious. Counties, towns, hilly ribs and ridges, wide stretches of green meadow, great forest tracts, winding streams, a dozen blue lakes, a flock of busy steamboats—we saw all this little world in unique circumstantiality of detail—saw it just as the birds see it—and all reduced to the smallest of scales and as sharply worked out and finished as a steel engraving. The numerous toy villages, with tiny spires projecting out of them, were just as the children might have left them when done with play the day before; the forest tracts were diminished to cushions of moss; one or two big lakes were dwarfed to ponds, the smaller ones to puddles,—though they did not look like puddles, but like blue teardrops which had fallen and lodged in slight depressions, conformable to their shapes, among the moss-beds and the smooth levels of dainty green farm-land; the microscopic steamboats glided along, as in a city reservoir, taking a mighty time to cover the distance between ports which seemed only a yard apart; and the isthmus which separated two lakes looked as if one might stretch out on it and lie with both elbows in the water, yet we knew invisible wagons were toiling across it and finding the distance a tedious one. This beautiful miniature world had exactly the appearance of those "relief maps" which reproduce nature precisely, with the heights and depressions and other details graduated to a reduced scale, and with the rocks, trees, lakes, etc., colored after nature.

I believed we could walk down to Wäggis or Vitznau in a day, but I knew we could go down by rail in about an hour, so I chose the latter method. I wanted to see what it was like, anyway. The train came along about the middle of the forenoon, and an odd thing it was. The locomotive boiler stood on end, and it and the whole locomotive were tilted sharply backward. There were two passenger cars, roofed, but wide open all around. These cars were not tilted back, but the seats were; this enables the passenger to sit level while going down a steep incline.

There are three railway tracks; the central one is cogged; the "lantern wheel" of the engine grips its way along these cogs, and pulls the train up the hill or retards its motion on the down trip. About the same speed,— three miles an hour,—is maintained both ways. Whether going up or down, the locomotive is always at the lower end of the train. It pushes, in the one case, braces back in the other. The passenger rides backward, going up, and faces forward going down.

We got front seats, and while the train moved along about fifty yards on level ground, I was not the least frightened; but now it started abruptly down stairs, and I caught my breath. And I, like my neighbors, unconsciously held back all I could, and threw my weight to the rear, but of course that did no particular good. I had slidden down the balusters when I was a boy, and thought nothing of it, but to slide down the balusters in a railway train is a thing to make one's flesh creep. Sometimes we had as much as ten yards of almost level ground, and this gave us a few full breaths in comfort; but straightway we would turn a corner and see a long steep line of rails stretching down below us, and the comfort was at an end. One expected to see the locomotive pause, or slack up a little, and approach this plunge cautiously, but it did nothing of the kind; it went calmly on, and when it reached the jumping-off place it made a sudden bow, and went gliding smoothly down stairs, untroubled by the circumstances.

It was wildly exhilarating to slide along the edge of the precipices, after this grisly fashion, and look straight down upon that far-off valley which I was describing a while ago.

There was no level ground at the Kaltbad station; the railbed was as steep as a roof; I was curious to see how the stop was going to be managed. But it was very simple: the train came sliding down, and when it reached the right spot it just stopped—that was all there was "to it"—stopped on the steep incline, and when the exchange of passengers and baggage had been made, it moved off and went sliding down again. The train can be stopped anywhere, at a moment's notice.

There was one curious effect, which I need not take the trouble to describe,—because I can scissor a description of it out of the railway company's advertising pamphlet, and save my ink:

> On the whole tour, particularly at the Descent, we undergo an optical illusion which often seems to be incredible. All the shrubs, fir-trees, stables, houses, etc., seem to be bent in a slanting direction, as by an immense pressure of air. They are all standing awry, so much awry that the chalets and cottages of the peasants seem to be tumbling down. It is the consequence of the steep inclination of the line. Those who are seated in the carriage do not observe that they are going down a declivity of 20 to 25° (their seats being adapted to this course of proceeding and being bent down at their backs.) They mistake their carriage and its horizontal lines for a proper measure of the normal plain, and therefore all the objects outside which really are in a horizontal position, must show a disproportion of 20 to 25° declivity, in regard to the mountain.

By the time one reaches Kaltbad, he has acquired confidence in the railway, and he now ceases to try to ease the locomotive by holding back. Thenceforward he smokes his pipe in serenity, and gazes out upon the magnificent picture below and about him with unfettered enjoyment. There is nothing to interrupt the view or the breeze; it is like inspecting the world on the wing. However,—to be exact,—there is one place where the serenity lapses for a while: this is while one is crossing the Schnurrtobel Bridge, a frail structure which swings its gossamer frame down through the dizzy air, over a gorge, like a vagrant spider-strand.

One has no difficulty in remembering his sins while the train is creeping down this bridge; and he repents of them, too; though he sees, when he gets to Vitznau, that he need not have done it, the bridge was perfectly safe.

So ends the eventful trip which we made to the Rigi-Kulm to see an Alpine sunrise.

[Leukerbad, Switzerland, from Chapter 35]

At the table d'hote, we had this, for an incident. A very grave man,—in fact his gravity amounted to solemnity, and almost to austerity,—sat opposite us and he was "tight," but doing his best to appear sober. He took up a *corked* bottle of wine, tilted it over his glass a while, then set it out of the way, with a contented look, and went on with his dinner.

Presently he put his glass to his mouth, and of course found it empty. He looked puzzled, and glanced furtively and suspiciously out of the corner of his eye at a benignant and unconscious old lady who sat at his right. Shook his head, as much as to say, "No, she couldn't have done it." He tilted the corked bottle over his glass again, meantime searching around with his watery eye to see if anybody was watching him. He ate a few mouthfuls, raised his glass to his lips, and of course it was still empty. He bent an injured and accusing side gaze upon that unconscious old lady, which was a study to see. She went on eating and gave no sign. He took up his glass and his bottle, with a wise private nod of his head, and set them gravely on the left hand side of his plate,—poured himself another imaginary drink,—went to work with his knife and fork once more,—presently lifted his glass with good confidence, and found it empty, as usual.

This was almost a petrifying surprise. He straightened himself up in his chair and deliberately and sorrowfully inspected the busy old ladies at his elbows, first one and then the other. At last he softly pushed his plate away, set his glass directly in front of him, held on to it with his left hand, and proceeded to pour with his right. This time he observed that nothing came. He turned the bottle clear upside down; still nothing issued from it; a plaintive look came into his face, and he said, as if to himself, " *'ic! They've got it all!*" Then he set the bottle down, resignedly, and took the rest of his dinner dry.

[Zermatt and the Riffelberg, Chapter 37]

After I had finished my readings, I was no longer myself; I was tranced, uplifted, intoxicated, by the almost incredible perils and adventures I had been following my authors through, and the triumphs I had been sharing with them.* I sat silent some time, then turned to Harris and said,—"My mind is made up."

Something in my tone struck him; and when he glanced at my eye and read what was written there, his face paled perceptibly. He hesitated a moment, then said,—"Speak."

I answered, with perfect calmness,—"I WILL ASCEND THE RIF-FELBERG."

If I had shot my poor friend he could not have fallen from his chair more suddenly. If I had been his father he could not have pleaded harder to get me to give up my purpose. But I turned a deaf ear to all he said. When he perceived at last that nothing could alter my determination, he ceased to urge, and for a while the deep silence was broken only by his sobs. I sat in marble resolution, with my eyes fixed upon vacancy, for in spirit I was already wrestling with the perils of the mountains, and my friend sat gazing at me in adoring admiration through his tears. At last he threw himself upon me in a loving embrace and exclaimed in broken tones: "Your Harris will never desert you. We will die together!"

I cheered the noble fellow with praises, and soon his fears were forgotten and he was eager for the adventure. He wanted to summon the guides at once and leave at 2 in the morning, as he supposed the custom was; but I explained that nobody was looking, at that hour; and that the start in the dark was not usually made from the village but from the first night's resting place on the mountain side. I said we would leave the village at 3 or 4 p.m. on the morrow; meantime he could notify the guides, and also let the public know of the attempt which we proposed to make.

I went to bed, but not to sleep. No man can sleep when he is about to undertake one of these Alpine exploits. I tossed feverishly all night long, and was glad enough when I heard the clock strike half past eleven and knew it was time to get up for dinner. I rose, jaded and rusty, and went to the noon meal, where I found myself the centre of interest and curiosity; for the news was already abroad. It is not easy to eat calmly when you are a lion, but it is very pleasant, nevertheless.

* In Chapter 36, Twain refers to narratives by Edward Whymper and other Alpine adventurers.

As usual, at Zermatt, when a great ascent is about to be undertaken, everybody, native and foreign, laid aside his own projects and took up a good position to observe the start. The expedition consisted of 198 persons, including the mules; or 205, including the cows. As follows:

CHIEFS OF SERVICE.

Myself.
Mr. Harris.
17 Guides.
4 Surgeons.
1 Geologist.
1 Botanist.
3 Chaplains.
2 Draftsmen.
15 Barkeepers.
1 Latinist.

SUBORDINATES.

1 Veterinary Surgeon.
1 Butler.
12 Waiters.
1 Footman.
1 Barber.
1 Head Cook.
9 Assistants.
4 Pastry Cooks.
1 Confectionary Artist.

TRANSPORTATION, etc.

27 Porters.
44 Mules.
44 Muleteers.

3 Coarse Washers and Ironers.
1 Fine ditto.
7 Cows.
2 Milkers.

Total, 154 men, 51 animals. Grand Total, 205

RATIONS, etc.

16 Cases Hams.
2 Barrels Flour.
22 Barrels Whiskey.
1 Barrel Sugar.
1 Keg Lemons.
2,000 Cigars.
1 Barrel Pies.
1 Ton of Pemmican.
143 Pair Crutches.
2 Barrels Arnica.
1 Bale of Lint.
27 Kegs Paregoric.

APPARATUS.

25 Spring Mattrasses.
2 Hair ditto.
Bedding for same.
2 Mosquito Nets.
29 Tents.
Scientific Instruments.
97 Ice-axes.
5 Cases Dynamite.
7 Cans Nitro-glycerine.
22 40-foot Ladders.
2 Miles of Rope.
154 Umbrellas.

It was full four o'clock in the afternoon before my cavalcade was entirely ready. At that hour it began to move. In point of numbers and spectacular effect, it was the most imposing expedition that had ever marched from Zermatt.

I commanded the chief guide to arrange the men and animals in single file, twelve feet apart, and lash them all together on a strong rope. He objected that the first two miles was a dead level, with plenty of room, and that the rope was never used except in very dangerous places. But I would not listen to that. My reading had taught me that many serious accidents had happened in the Alps simply from not having the people tied up soon enough; I was not going to add one to the list. The guide then obeyed my order.

When the procession stood at ease, roped together, and ready to move, I never saw a finer sight. It was 3,122 feet long—over half a mile; every man but Harris and me was on foot, and had on his green veil and his blue goggles, and his white rag around his hat, and his coil of rope over one shoulder and under the other, and his ice-axe in his belt, and carried his alpenstock in his left hand, his umbrella (closed,) in his right, and his crutches slung at his back. The burdens of the pack mules and the horns of the cows, were decked with the Edelweiss and the Alpine rose.

I and my agent were the only persons mounted. We were in the post of danger in the extreme rear, and tied securely to five guides apiece. Our armor-bearers carried our ice-axes, alpenstocks and other implements for us. We were mounted upon very small donkeys, as a measure of safety; in time of peril we could straighten our legs and stand up, and let the donkey walk from under. Still, I cannot recommend this sort of animal,—at least for excursions of mere pleasure,—because his ears interrupt the view. I and my agent possessed the regulation mountaineering costumes, but concluded to leave them behind. Out of respect for the great numbers of tourists of both sexes who would be assembled in front of the hotels to see us pass, and also out of respect for the many tourists, whom we expected to encounter on our expedition, we decided to make the ascent in evening dress.

At 15 minutes past 4 I gave the command to move, and my subordinates passed it along the line. The great crowd in front of the Monte Rosa hotel parted in twain, with a cheer, as the procession approached; and as the head of it was filing by I gave the order, "Unlimber—make ready— HOIST!"—and with one impulse up went my half mile of umbrellas. It was a beautiful sight, and a total surprise to the spectators. Nothing like that had ever been seen in the Alps before. The applause it brought forth was deeply gratifying to me, and I rode by with my plug hat in my hand to testify my appreciation of it. It was the only testimony I could offer, for I was too full to speak.

We watered the caravan at the cold stream which rushes down a trough near the end of the village, and soon afterward left the haunts of civilization behind us. About half past 5 o'clock we arrived at a bridge which spans the Visp, and after throwing over a detachment to see if it was safe, the caravan crossed without accident. The way now led, by a gentle ascent, carpeted with fresh green grass, to the church of Winkelmatten. Without stopping to examine this edifice, I executed a flank movement to the right and crossed the bridge over the Findelenbach, after first testing its strength. Here I deployed to the right again, and presently entered an inviting stretch of meadow land which was unoccupied save by a couple of deserted huts toward its furthest extremity. These meadows offered an excellent camping place. We pitched our tents, supped, established a proper guard, recorded the events of the day, and then went to bed.

We rose at 2 in the morning and dressed by candlelight. It was a dismal and chilly business. A few stars were shining, but the general heavens were overcast, and the great shaft of the Matterhorn was draped in a sable pall of clouds. The chief guide advised a delay; he said he feared it was going to rain. We waited until nine o'clock, and then got away in tolerably clear weather.

Our course led up some terrific steeps, densely wooded with larches and cedars, and traversed by paths which the rains had guttered and which were obstructed by loose stones. To add to the danger and inconvenience, we were constantly meeting returning tourists on foot or horseback, and as constantly being crowded and battered by ascending tourists who were in a hurry and wanted to get by.

Our troubles thickened. About the middle of the afternoon the seventeen guides called a halt and held a consultation. After consulting an hour they said their first suspicion remained intact,—that is to say, they believed they were lost. I asked if they did not *know* it? No, they said, they *couldn't* absolutely know whether they were lost or not, because none of them had ever been in that part of the country before. They had a strong instinct that they were lost, but they had no proofs,—except that they did not know where they were. They had met no tourists for some time, and they considered that a suspicious sign.

Plainly we were in an ugly fix. The guides were naturally unwilling to go alone and seek a way out of the difficulty; so we all went together. For better security we moved slow and cautiously, for the forest was very dense. We did not move up the mountain, but around it, hoping to strike across the old trail. Toward nightfall, when we were about tired out, we came up against a rock as big as a cottage. This barrier took all the remaining spirit out of the men, and a panic of fear and despair ensued. They moaned and wept, and said they should never see their homes and their dear ones again. Then they began to upbraid me for bringing them upon this fatal expedition. Some even muttered threats against me.

Clearly it was no time to show weakness. So I made a speech in which I said that other Alp-climbers had been in as perilous a position as this, and yet by courage and perseverance had escaped. I promised to stand by them, I promised to rescue them. I closed by saying we had plenty of provisions to maintain us for quite a siege,—and did they suppose Zermatt would allow half a mile of men and mules to mysteriously disappear during any considerable time, right above their noses, and make no inquiries? No, Zermatt would send out searching-expeditions and we should be saved.

This speech had a great effect. The men pitched the tents with some little show of cheerfulness, and we were snugly under cover when the night shut down. I now reaped the reward of my wisdom in providing one article which is not mentioned in any book of Alpine adventure but this. I refer to the paregoric. But for that beneficent drug, not one of those men would have slept a moment during that fearful night. But for that gentle persuader they must have tossed, unsoothed, the night through; for the whisky was for me. Yes, they would have risen in the morning unfitted for their heavy task. As it was, everybody slept but my agent and me,—only we two and the barkeepers. I would not permit myself to sleep at such a time. I considered myself responsible for all those lives. I meant to be on hand and ready, in case of avalanches. I am aware now, that there were no avalanches up there, but I did not know it then.

We watched the weather all through that awful night, and kept an eye on the barometer, to be prepared for the least change. There was not the slightest change recorded by the instrument, during the whole time.

Words cannot describe the comfort that that friendly, hopeful, steadfast thing was to me in that season of trouble. It was a defective barometer, and had no hand but the stationary brass pointer, but I did not know that until afterward. If I should be in such a situation again, I should not wish for any barometer but that one.

All hands rose at 2 in the morning and took breakfast, and as soon as it was light we roped ourselves together and went at that rock. For some time we tried the hook-rope and other means of scaling it, but without success. That is without perfect success. The hook caught once, and Harris started up it hand over hand, but the hold broke and if there had not happened to be a chaplain sitting underneath at the time, Harris would certainly have been crippled. As it was, it was the chaplain. He took to his crutches, and I ordered the hook-rope to be laid aside. It was too dangerous an implement where so many people were standing around.

We were puzzled for a while; then somebody thought of the ladders. One of these was leaned against the rock, and the men went up it tied together in couples. Another ladder was sent up for use in descending. At the end of half an hour everybody was over, and that rock was conquered. We gave our first grand shout of triumph. But the joy was short-lived, for somebody asked how we were going to get the animals over.

This was a serious difficulty; in fact it was an impossibility. The courage of the men began to waver immediately; once more we were threatened with a panic. But when the danger was most imminent, we were saved in a mysterious way. A mule which had attracted attention from the beginning by its disposition to experiment, tried to eat a five-pound can of nitro-glycerin. This happened right along-side the rock. The explosion threw us all to the ground, and covered us with dirt and débris; it frightened us extremely, too, for the crash it made was deafening, and the violence of the shock made the ground tremble. However, we were grateful, for the rock was gone. Its place was occupied by a new cellar, about thirty feet across, by fifteen feet deep. The explosion was heard as far as Zermatt; and an hour and a half afterward, many citizens of that town were knocked down and quite seriously injured by descending portions of mule meat, frozen solid. This shows, better than any estimate in figures, how high the experimenter went.

We had nothing to do, now, but bridge the cellar and proceed on our way. With a cheer the men went at their work. I attended to the engineering, myself. I appointed a strong detail to cut down trees with ice-axes and trim them for piers to support the bridge. This was a slow business, for ice-axes are not good to cut wood with. I caused my piers to be firmly set up in ranks in the cellar, and upon them I laid six of my forty-foot ladders, side by side, and laid six more on top of them. Upon this bridge I caused a bed of boughs to be spread, and on top of the boughs a bed of earth six inches deep. I stretched ropes upon either side to serve as railings, and then my bridge was complete. A train of elephants could have crossed it in safety and comfort. By nightfall the caravan was on the other side and the ladders taken up.

Next morning we went on in good spirits for a while, though our way was slow and difficult, by reason of the steep and rocky nature of the ground and the thickness of the forest; but at last a dull despondency crept into the men's faces and it was apparent that not only they, but even the guides, were now convinced that we were lost. The fact that we still met no tourists was a circumstance that was but too significant. Another thing seemed to suggest that we were not only lost, but very badly lost: for there must surely be searching-parties on the road before this time, yet we had seen no sign of them.

Demoralization was spreading; something must be done, and done quickly, too. Fortunately, I am not unfertile in expedients. I contrived one now which commended itself to all, for it promised well. I took three-quarters of a mile of rope and fastened one end of it around the waist of a guide, and told him to go and find the road, whilst the caravan waited. I instructed him to guide himself back by the rope, in case of failure; in case of success, he was to give the rope a series of violent jerks, whereupon the Expedition would go to him at once. He departed, and in two minutes had disappeared among the trees. I payed out the rope myself, while everybody watched the crawling thing with eager eyes. The rope crept away quite slowly, at times, at other times with some briskness. Twice or thrice we seemed to get the signal, and a shout was just ready to break from the men's lips when they perceived it was a false alarm. But at last, when over half a mile of rope had slidden away, it stopped gliding and stood absolutely still,—one minute,—two minutes,—three,—while we held our breath and watched.

Was the guide resting? Was he scanning the country from some high point? Was he inquiring of a chance mountaineer? Stop,—had he fainted from excess of fatigue and anxiety?

This thought gave us a shock. I was in the very act of detailing an expedition to succor him, when the cord was assailed with a series of such frantic jerks that I could hardly keep hold of it. The huzza that went up, then, was good to hear. "Saved! saved!" was the word that rang out, all down the long rank of the caravan.

We rose up and started at once. We found the route to be good enough, for a while, but it began to grow difficult, by and by, and this feature steadily increased. When we judged we had gone half a mile, we momently expected to see the guide; but no, he was not visible anywhere; neither was he waiting, for the rope was still moving, consequently he was doing the same. This argued that he had not found the road, yet, but was marching to it with some peasant. There was nothing for us to do but plod along,—and this we did. At the end of three hours we were still plodding. This was not only mysterious, but exasperating. And very fatiguing, too; for we had tried hard, along at first, to catch up with the guide, but had only fagged ourselves, in vain; for although he was traveling slowly he was yet able to go faster than the hampered caravan over such ground.

At three in the afternoon we were nearly dead with exhaustion,—and still the rope was slowly gliding out. The murmurs against the guide had been growing steadily, and at last they were become loud and savage. A mutiny ensued. The men refused to proceed. They declared that we had been traveling over and over the same ground all day, in a kind of circle. They demanded that our end of the rope be made fast to a tree, so as to halt the guide until we could overtake him and kill him. This was not an unreasonable requirement, so I gave the order.

As soon as the rope was tied, the Expedition moved forward with that alacrity which the thirst for vengeance usually inspires. But after a tiresome march of almost half a mile, we came to a hill covered thick with a crumbly rubbish of stones, and so steep that no man of us all was now in a condition to climb it. Every attempt failed, and ended in crippling somebody. Within twenty minutes I had five men on crutches. Whenever a climber tried to assist himself by the rope, it yielded and let him tumble backward. The frequency of this result suggested an idea to me. I ordered the caravan to 'bout face and form in marching order; I then made the

tow-rope fast to the rear mule, and gave the command,—"Mark time—
by the right flank—forward—march!"

The procession began to move, to the impressive strains of a battle-
chant, and I said to myself, "Now, if the rope don't break I judge *this* will
fetch that guide into the camp." I watched the rope gliding down the hill,
and presently when I was all fixed for triumph I was confronted by a bitter disappointment: there was no guide tied to the rope, it was only a very
indignant old black ram. The fury of the baffled Expedition exceeded all
bounds. They even wanted to wreak their unreasoning vengeance on this
innocent dumb brute. But I stood between them and their prey, menaced
by a bristling wall of ice-axes and alpenstocks, and proclaimed that there
was but one road to this murder, and it was directly over my corpse. Even
as I spoke I saw that my doom was sealed, except a miracle supervened
to divert these madmen from their fell purpose. I see that sickening wall
of weapons now; I see that advancing host as I saw it then, I see the hate
in those cruel eyes; I remember how I drooped my head upon my breast,
I feel again the sudden earthquake shock in my rear, administered by the
very ram I was sacrificing myself to save, I hear once more the typhoon
of laughter that burst from the assaulting column as I clove it from van to
rear like a Sepoy shot from a Rodman gun.

I was saved. Yes, I was saved, and by the merciful instinct of ingrati-
tude which nature had planted in the breast of that treacherous beast. The
grace which eloquence had failed to work in those men's hearts, had been
wrought by a laugh. The ram was set free and my life was spared.

We lived to find out that that guide had deserted us as soon as he had
placed a half mile between himself and us. To avert suspicion, he had
judged it best that the line should continue to move; so he caught that
ram, and at the time that he was sitting on it making the rope fast to it, we
were imagining that he was lying in a swoon, overcome by fatigue and dis-
tress. When he allowed the ram to get up it fell to plunging around, trying to rid itself of the rope, and this was the signal which we had risen up
with glad shouts to obey. We had followed this ram round and round in a
circle all day—a thing which was proven by the discovery that we had
watered the Expedition seven times at one and the same spring in seven
hours. As expert a woodman as I am, I had somehow failed to notice this
until my attention was called to it by a hog. This hog was always wallow-
ing there, and as he was the only hog we saw, his frequent repetition, to-

gether with his unvarying similarity to himself, finally caused me to reflect that he must be the same hog, and this led me to the deduction that this must be the same spring, also,—which indeed it was.

I made a note of this curious thing, as showing in a striking manner the relative difference between glacial action and the action of the hog. It is now a well-established fact that glaciers move; I consider that my observations go to show, with equal conclusiveness, that a hog in a spring does not move. I shall be glad to receive the opinions of other observers upon this point.

To return, for an explanatory moment, to that guide, and then I shall be done with him. After leaving the ram tied to the rope, he had wandered at large a while, and then happened to run across a cow. Judging that a cow would naturally know more than a guide, he took her by the tail, and the result justified his judgment. She nibbled her leisurely way down hill till it was near milking-time, then she struck for home and towed him into Zermatt.

[The Riffelberg, Chapter 38]

We went into camp on that wild spot to which that ram had brought us. The men were greatly fatigued. Their conviction that we were lost was forgotten in the cheer of a good supper, and before the reaction had a chance to set in, I loaded them up with paregoric and put them to bed.

Next morning I was considering in my mind our desperate situation and trying to think of a remedy, when Harris came to me with a Baedeker map which showed conclusively that the mountain we were on was still in Switzerland,—yes, every part of it was in Switzerland. So we were not lost, after all. This was an immense relief; it lifted the weight of two such mountains from my breast. I immediately had the news disseminated and the map was exhibited. The effect was wonderful. As soon as the men saw with their own eyes that they knew where they were, and that it was only the summit that was lost and not themselves, they cheered up instantly and said with one accord, let the summit take care of itself, they were not interested in its troubles.

Our distresses being at an end, I now determined to rest the men in camp and give the scientific department of the Expedition a chance. First, I made a barometric observation, to get our altitude, but I could not perceive that there was any result. I knew, by my scientific reading, that either thermometers or barometers ought to be boiled, to make them accurate; I did not know which it was, so I boiled both. There was still no result; so I examined these instruments and discovered that they possessed radical blemishes: the barometer had no hand but the brass pointer and the ball of the thermometer was stuffed with tin foil. I might have boiled those things to rags, and never found out anything.

I hunted up another barometer; it was new and perfect. I boiled it half an hour in a pot of bean soup which the cooks were making. The result was unexpected: the instrument was not affected at all, but there was such a strong barometer taste to the soup that the head cook, who was a most conscientious person, changed its name in the bill of fare. The dish was so greatly liked by all, that I ordered the cook to have barometer soup every day. It was believed that the barometer might eventually be injured, but I did not care for that. I had demonstrated to my satisfaction that it could not tell how high a mountain was, therefore I had no real use for it. Changes of the weather I could take care of without it; I did not wish to know when the weather was going to be good, what I wanted to know was when it was going to be bad, and this I could find out from Harris's corns. Harris had had his corns tested and regulated at the government observatory in Heidelberg, and one could depend upon them with confidence. So I transferred the new barometer to the cooking department, to be used for the official mess. It was found that even a pretty fair article of soup could be made with the defective barometer; so I allowed that one to be transferred to the subordinate messes.

I next boiled the thermometer, and got a most excellent result; the mercury went up to about 200° Fahrenheit. In the opinion of the other scientists of the Expedition, this seemed to indicate that we had attained the extraordinary altitude of 200,000 feet above sea level. Science places the line of eternal snow at about 10,000 feet above sea level. There was no snow where we were, consequently it was proven that the eternal snow line ceases somewhere above the 10,000 foot level and does not begin any more. This was an interesting fact, and one which had not been observed by any observer before. It was as valuable as interesting, too, since it would open up the deserted summits of the highest Alps to population and agriculture. It was a proud thing to be where we were, yet it caused us a pang to reflect that but for that ram we might just as well have been 200,000 feet higher.

The success of my last experiment induced me to try an experiment with my photographic apparatus. I got it out, and boiled one of my cameras, but the thing was a failure: it made the wood swell up and burst, and I could not see that the lenses were any better than they were before.

I now concluded to boil a guide. It might improve him, it could not impair his usefulness. But I was not allowed to proceed. Guides have no feeling for science, and this one would not consent to be made uncomfortable in its interest.

In the midst of my scientific work, one of those needless accidents happened which are always occurring among the ignorant and thoughtless. A porter shot at a chamois and missed it and crippled the Latinist. This was not a serious matter to me, for a Latinist's duties are as well performed on crutches as otherwise,—but the fact remained that if the Latinist had not happened to be in the way a mule would have got that load. That would have been quite another matter, for when it comes down to a question of value there is a palpable difference between a Latinist and a mule. I could not depend on having a Latinist in the right place every time; so, to make things safe, I ordered that in the future the chamois must not be hunted within the limits of the camp with any other weapon than the forefinger.

My nerves had hardly grown quiet after this affair when they got another shake-up,—one which utterly unmanned me for a moment: a rumor swept suddenly through the camp that one of the barkeepers had fallen over a precipice!

However, it turned out that it was only a chaplain. I had laid in an extra force of chaplains, purposely to be prepared for emergencies like this, but by some unaccountable oversight had come away rather short-handed in the matter of barkeepers.

On the following morning we moved on, well refreshed and in good spirits. I remember this day with peculiar pleasure, because it saw our road restored to us. Yes, we found our road again, and in quite an extraordinary way. We had plodded along some two hours and a half, when we came up against a solid mass of rock about twenty feet high. I did not need to be instructed by a mule this time.—I was already beginning to know more than any mule in the Expedition.—I at once put in a blast of dynamite, and lifted that rock out of the way. But to my surprise and mortification, I found that there had been a chalet on top of it.

I picked up such members of the family as fell in my vicinity, and subordinates of my corps collected the rest. None of these poor people were injured, happily, but they were much annoyed. I explained to the head chaleteer just how the thing happened, and that I was only searching for the road, and would certainly have given him timely notice if I had known he was up there. I said I had meant no harm, and hoped I had not lowered myself in his estimation by raising him a few rods in the air. I said many other judicious things, and finally when I offered to rebuild his chalet, and pay for the breakages, and throw in the cellar, he was mollified and satisfied. He hadn't any cellar at all, before; he would not have as good a view, now, as formerly, but what he had lost in view he had gained in cellar, by exact measurement. He said there wasn't another hole like that in the mountains,—and he would have been right if the late mule had not tried to eat up the nitro-glycerin.

I put a hundred and sixteen men at work, and they rebuilt the chalet from its own debris in fifteen minutes. It was a good deal more picturesque than it was before, too. The man said we were now on the Feli-Stutz, above the Schwegmatt,—information which I was glad to get, since it gave us our position to a degree of particularity which we had not been accustomed to for a day or so. We also learned that we were standing at the foot of the Riffelberg proper, and that the initial chapter of our work was completed.

We had a fine view from here of the energetic Visp, as it makes its first plunge into the world from under a huge arch of solid ice, worn through the foot-wall of the great Gorner Glacier; and we could also see the Furggenbach, which is the outlet of the Furggen Glacier.

The mule-road to the summit of the Riffelberg passed right in front of the chalet, a circumstance which we almost immediately noticed, because a procession of tourists was filing along it pretty much all the time. {"Pretty much" may not be elegant English, but it is high time it was. There is no elegant word or phrase which means just what it means.—M.T.} The chaleteer's business consisted in furnishing refreshments to tourists. My blast had interrupted this trade for a few minutes, by breaking all the bottles on the place; but I gave the man a lot of whisky to sell for Alpine champaign, and a lot of vinegar which would answer for Rhine wine, consequently trade was soon as brisk as ever.

Leaving the Expedition outside to rest, I quartered myself in the chalet, with Harris, purposing to correct my journals and scientific observations before continuing the ascent. I had hardly begun my work when a tall, slender, vigorous American youth of about twenty-three, who was on his way down the mountain, entered and came toward me with that breezy self-complacency which is the adolescent's idea of the well bred ease of the man of the world. His hair was short and parted accurately in the middle, and he had all the look of an American person who would be likely to begin his signature with an initial, and spell his middle name out. He introduced himself, smiling a smirky smile borrowed from the courtiers of the stage, extended a fair-skinned talon, and whilst he gripped my hand in it he bent his body forward three times at the hips, as the stage-courtier does, and said in the airiest and most condescending and patronizing way,—I quote his exact language,—"Very glad to make your acquaintance, 'm sure; very glad indeed, assure you. I've read all your little efforts and greatly admired them, and when I heard you were here, I . . ."

I indicated a chair, and he sat down. This grandee was the grandson of an American of considerable note in his day, and not wholly forgotten yet,—a man who came so near being a great man that he was quite generally accounted one while he lived.

I slowly paced the floor, pondering scientific problems, and heard this conversation:

Grandson. First visit to Europe?

Harris. Mine? Yes.

G.S. (With a soft reminiscent sigh suggestive of by-gone joys that may be tasted in their freshness but once.) Ah, I know what it is to you. A first visit!—ah, the romance of it! I wish I could feel it again.

H. Yes, I find it exceeds all my dreams. It is enchantment. I go . . .

G.S. (With a dainty gesture of the hand signifying, "Spare me your callow enthusiasms, good friend.") Yes, *I* know, I know; you go to cathedrals, and exclaim; and you drag through league-long picture galleries and exclaim; and you stand here, and there, and yonder, upon historic ground, and continue to exclaim; and you are permeated with your first crude conceptions of Art, and are proud and happy. Ah, yes, proud and happy—that expresses it. Yes—yes, enjoy it—it is right,—it is an innocent revel.

H. And you? Don't you do these things now?

G.S. I! O, that is *very* good! My dear sir, when you are as old a traveler as I am, you will not ask such a question as that. *I* visit the regulation gallery, moon around the regulation cathedral, do the worn round of the regulation sights, *yet?*—Excuse me!

H. Well what *do* you do, then?

G.S. Do? I flit,—and flit,—for I am ever on the wing,—but I avoid the herd. To-day I am in Paris, to-morrow in Berlin, anon in Rome; but you would look for me in vain in the galleries of the Louvre or the common resorts of the gazers in those other capitals. If you would find me, you must look in the unvisited nooks and corners where others never think of going. One day you will find me making myself at home in some obscure peasant's cabin, another day you will find me in some forgotten castle worshiping some little gem of art which the careless eye has overlooked and which the unexperienced would despise; again you will find me a guest in the inner sanctuaries of palaces while the herd is content to get a hurried glimpse of the unused chambers by feeing a servant.

H. You are a *guest* in such places?

G.S. And a welcome one.

H. It is surprising. How does it come?

G.S. My grandfather's name is a passport to all the courts in Europe. I have only to utter that name and every door is open to me. I flit from court to court at my own free will and pleasure, and am always welcome. I am as much at home in the palaces of Europe as you are among your relatives. I know every titled person in Europe, I think. I have my pockets full of invitations all the time. I am under promise now, to go to Italy, where I am to be the guest of a succession of the noblest houses in the land. In Berlin my life is a continued round of gayety in the imperial palace. It is the same, wherever I go.

H. It must be very pleasant. But it must make Boston seem a little slow when you are at home.

G.S. Yes, of course it does. But I don't go home much. There's no life there—little to feed a man's higher nature. Boston's very narrow, you know. She doesn't know it, and you couldn't convince her of it—so I say nothing when I'm there: where's the use? Yes, Boston is very narrow, but she has such a good opinion of herself that she can't see it. A man who has traveled as much as I have, and seen as much of the world, sees it plain enough, but he can't cure it, you know, so the best way is to leave it and seek a sphere which is more in harmony with his tastes and culture. I run across there, once a year, perhaps, when I have nothing important on hand, but I'm very soon back again. I spend my time in Europe.

H. I see. You map out your plans and . . .

G.S. No, excuse me. I don't map out any plans. I simply follow the inclination of the day. I am limited by no ties, no requirements, I am not bound in any way. I am too old a traveler to hamper myself with deliberate purposes. I am simply a traveler—an inveterate traveler—a man of the world, in a word,—I can call myself by no other name. I do not say, "I am going here, or I am going there"— I say nothing at all, I only act. For instance, next week you may find me the guest of a grandee of Spain, or you may find me off for Venice, or flitting toward Dresden. I shall probably go to Egypt presently; friends will say to friends, "He is at the Nile cataracts"— and at that very moment they will be surprised to learn that I'm away off yonder in India somewhere. I am a constant surprise to people. They are always saying, "Yes, he was in Jerusalem when we heard of him last, but goodness knows where he is now."

Presently the Grandson rose to leave—discovered he had an appointment with some Emperor, perhaps. He did his graces over again: gripped me with one talon, at arm's length, pressed his hat against his stomach with the other, bent his body in the middle three times, murmuring,— "Pleasure, 'm sure; great pleasure, 'm sure. Wish you much success."

Then he removed his gracious presence. It is a great and solemn thing to have a grandfather.

I have not purposed to misrepresent this boy in any way, for what little indignation he excited in me soon passed and left nothing behind it but compassion. One cannot keep up a grudge against a vacuum. I have tried to repeat the lad's very words; if I have failed anywhere I have at least not failed to reproduce the marrow and meaning of what he said. He and the innocent chatterbox whom I met on the Swiss lake are the most unique and interesting specimens of Young America I came across during my foreign tramping. I have made honest portraits of them, not caricatures. The Grandson of twenty-three referred to himself five or six times as an "old traveler," and as many as three times, (with a serene complacency which was maddening,) as a "man of the world." There was something very delicious about his leaving Boston to her "narrowness," unreproved and uninstructed.

I formed the caravan in marching order, presently, and after riding down the line to see that it was properly roped together, gave the command to proceed. In a little while the road carried us to open, grassy land. We were above the troublesome forest, now, and had an uninterrupted view, straight before us, of our summit,—the summit of the Riffelberg.

We followed the mule road, a zigzag course, now to the right, now to the left, but always up, and always crowded and incommoded by going and coming files of reckless tourists who were never, in a single instance, tied together. I was obliged to exert the utmost care and caution, for in many places the road was not two yards wide, and often the lower side of it sloped away in slanting precipices eight and even nine feet deep. I had to encourage the men constantly, to keep them from giving way to their unmanly fears.

We might have made the summit before night, but for a delay caused by the loss of an umbrella. I was for allowing the umbrella to remain lost, but the men murmured, and with reason, for in this exposed region we stood in peculiar need of protection against avalanches; so I went into camp and detached a strong party to go after the missing article.

The difficulties of the next morning were severe, but our courage was high, for our goal was near. At noon we conquered the last impediment—we stood at last upon the summit, and without the loss of a single man except the mule that ate the glycerin. Our great achievement was achieved—the possibility of the impossible was demonstrated, and Harris and I walked proudly into the great dining-room of the Riffelberg Hotel and stood our alpenstocks up in the corner.

Yes, I had made the grand ascent; but it was a mistake to do it in evening dress. The plug hats were battered, the swallow-tails were fluttering rags, mud added no grace, the general effect was unpleasant and even disreputable.

There were about seventy-five tourists at the hotel,—mainly ladies and little children,—and they gave us an admiring welcome which paid us for all our privations and sufferings. The ascent had been made, and the names and dates now stand recorded on a stone monument there to prove it to all future tourists.

I boiled a thermometer and took an altitude, with a most curious result: *The summit was not as high as the point on the mountain side where I had taken the first altitude.* Suspecting that I had made an important discovery, I prepared to verify it. There happened to be a still higher summit (called the Gorner Grat,) above the hotel, and notwithstanding the fact that it overlooks a glacier from a dizzy height, and that the ascent is difficult and dangerous, I resolved to venture up there and boil a thermometer. So I sent a strong party, with some borrowed hoes, in charge of two chiefs of service, to dig a stairway in the soil all the way, and this I ascended, roped to the guides. This breezy height was the summit proper—so I accomplished even more than I had originally purposed to do. This fool-hardy exploit is recorded on another stone monument.

I boiled my thermometer, and sure enough, this spot, which purported to be 2,000 feet higher than the locality of the hotel, turned out to be 9,000 feet *lower.* Thus the fact was clearly demonstrated, that, *above a certain point, the higher a point seems to be, the lower it actually is.* Our ascent itself was a great achievement, but this contribution to science was an inconceivably greater matter.

Cavilers object that water boils at a lower and lower temperature the higher and higher you go, and hence the apparent anomaly. I answer that I do not base my theory upon what the boiling water does, but upon what a boiled thermometer says. You can't go behind the thermometer.

I had a magnificent view of Monte Rosa, and apparently all the rest of the Alpine world, from that high place. All the circling horizon was piled high with a mighty tumult of snowy crests. One might have imagined he saw before him the tented camps of a beleaguering host of Brobdignagians.

NOTE—I had the very unusual luck to catch one little momentary glimpse of the Matterhorn wholly unencumbered by clouds. I leveled my photographic apparatus at it without the loss of an instant, and should have got an elegant picture if my donkey had not interfered. It was my purpose to draw this photograph all by myself for my book, but was obliged to put the mountain part of it into the hands of the professional artist because I found I could not do landscape well.

6. "My Picture of the Matterhorn," from *A Tramp Abroad* (Hartford, CT: American Publishing Company, 1880).

But lonely, conspicuous, and superb, rose that wonderful upright wedge, the Matterhorn. Its precipitous sides were powdered over with snow, and the upper half hidden in thick clouds which now and then dissolved to cobweb films and gave brief glimpses of the imposing tower as through a veil. A little later the Matterhorn took to himself the semblance of a volcano; he was stripped naked to his apex—around this circled vast wreaths of white cloud which strung slowly out and streamed away slantwise toward the sun, a twenty-mile stretch of rolling and tumbling vapor, and looking just as if it were pouring out of a crater. Later again, one of the mountain's sides was clean and clear, and another side densely clothed from base to summit in thick smoke-like cloud which feathered off and blew around the shaft's sharp edge like the smoke around the corners of a burning building. The Matterhorn is always experimenting, and always gets up fine effects, too. In the sunset, when all the lower world is palled in gloom, it points toward heaven out of the pervading blackness like a finger of fire. In the sunrise—well, they say it is very fine in the sunrise.

Authorities agree that there is no such tremendous "lay-out" of snowy Alpine magnitude, grandeur and sublimity to be seen from any other accessible point as the tourist may see from the summit of the Riffelberg. Therefore, let the tourist rope himself up and go there; for I have shown that with nerve, caution, and judgment, the thing can be done.

I wish to add one remark, here,—in parentheses, so to speak,—suggested by the word "snowy," which I have just used. We have all seen hills and mountains and levels with snow on them, and so we think we know all the aspects and effects produced by snow. But indeed we do not, until we have seen the Alps. Possibly mass and distance add something,—at any rate, something *is* added. Among other noticeable things, there is a dazzling, intense whiteness about the distant Alpine snow, when the sun is on it, which one recognizes as peculiar, and not familiar to the eye. The snow which one is accustomed to has a tint to it,—painters usually give it a bluish cast,—but there is no perceptible tint to the distant Alpine snow when it is trying to look its whitest. As to the unimaginable splendor of it when the sun is blazing down on it,—well, it simply *is* unimaginable.

[Chamonix and Mont Blanc, Chapter 44]

After breakfast, that next morning in Chamonix, we went out in the yard and watched the gangs of excursioning tourists arriving and departing with their mules and guides and porters; then we took a look through the telescope at the snowy hump of Mont Blanc. It was brilliant with sunshine, and the vast smooth bulge seemed hardly five hundred yards away. With the naked eye we could dimly make out the house at the Pierre Pointue, which is located by the side of the great glacier, and is more than 3,000 feet above the level of the valley; but with the telescope we could see all its details. While I looked, a woman rode by the house on a mule, and I saw her with sharp distinctness; I could have described her dress. I saw her nod to the people of the house, and rein up her mule, and put her hand up to shield her eyes from the sun. I was not used to telescopes; in fact I never had looked through a good one before; it seemed incredible to me that this woman could be so far away. I was satisfied that I could see all these details with my naked eye; but when I tried it, that mule and those vivid people had wholly vanished, and the house itself was become small and vague. I tried the telescope again, and again everything was vivid. The strong black shadows of the mule and the woman were flung against the side of the house, and I saw the mule's silhouette wave its ears.

The telescopulist,—or the telescopulariat,—I do not know which is right,—said a party were making the grand ascent, and would come in sight on the remote upper heights, presently; so we waited to observe this performance.

Presently I had a superb idea. I wanted to stand with a party on the summit of Mont Blanc, merely to be able to say I had done it, and I believed the telescope could set me within seven feet of the uppermost man. The telescoper assured me that it could. I then asked him how much I owed him for as far as I had got? He said, one franc. I asked him how much it would cost to make the entire ascent? Three francs. I at once determined to make the entire ascent. But first I inquired if there was any danger? He said no,—not by telescope; said he had taken a great many parties to the summit, and never lost a man. I asked what he would charge to let my agent go with me, together with such guides and porters as might be necessary. He said he would let Harris go for two francs; and that unless we were unusually timid, he should consider guides and porters unnecessary; it was not customary to take them, when going by telescope, for they were rather an incumbrance than a help. He said that the party now on the mountain were approaching the most difficult part, and if we hurried we should overtake them within ten minutes, and could then join them and have the benefit of their guides and porters without their knowledge, and without expense to us.

I then said we would start immediately. I believe I said it calmly, though I was conscious of a shudder and of a paling cheek, in view of the nature of the exploit I was so unreflectingly engaging in. But the old dare-devil spirit was upon me, and I said that as I had committed myself I would not back down; I would ascend Mont Blanc if it cost me my life. I told the man to slant his machine in the proper direction and let us be off.

Harris was afraid and did not want to go, but I heartened him up and said I would hold his hand all the way; so he gave his consent, though he trembled a little at first. I took a last pathetic look upon the pleasant summer scene about me, then boldly put my eye to the glass and prepared to mount among the grim glaciers and the everlasting snows.

We took our way carefully and cautiously across the great Glacier des Bossons, over yawning and terrific crevices and amongst imposing crags and buttresses of ice which were fringed with icicles of gigantic proportions. The desert of ice that stretched far and wide about us was wild and desolate beyond description, and the perils which beset us were so great that at times I was minded to turn back. But I pulled my pluck together and pushed on.

We passed the glacier safely and began to mount the steeps beyond, with great celerity. When we were seven minutes out from the starting point, we reached an altitude where the scene took a new aspect; an apparently limitless continent of gleaming snow was tilted heavenward before our faces. As my eye followed that awful acclivity far away up into the remote skies, it seemed to me that all I had ever seen before of sublimity and magnitude was small and insignificant compared to this.

We rested a moment, and then began to mount with speed. Within three minutes we caught sight of the party ahead of us, and stopped to observe them. They were toiling up a long, slanting ridge of snow—twelve persons, roped together some fifteen feet apart, marching in single file, and strongly marked against the clear blue sky. One was a woman. We could see them lift their feet and put them down; we saw them swing their alpenstocks forward in unison, like so many pendulums, and then bear their weight upon them; we saw the lady wave her handkerchief. They dragged themselves upward in a worn and weary way, for they had been climbing steadily from the Grand Mulets, on the Glacier des Bossons, since three in the morning, and it was eleven, now. We saw them sink down in the snow and rest, and drink something from a bottle. After a while they moved on, and as they approached the final short dash of the home-stretch we closed up on them and joined them.

Presently we all stood together on the summit! What a view was spread out below! Away off under the northwestern horizon rolled the silent billows of the Farnese Oberland, their snowy crests glinting softly in the subdued lights of distance; in the north rose the giant form of the Wobblehorn, draped from peak to shoulder in sable thunder-clouds; beyond him, to the right, stretched the grand processional summits of the Cisalpine Cordillera, drowned in a sensuous haze; to the east loomed the colossal masses of the Yodelhorn, the Fuddelhorn and the Dinnerhorn, their cloudless summits flashing white and cold in the sun; beyond them shimmered the faint far line of the Ghauts of Jubbelpore and the Aiguilles des Alleghenies; in the south towered the smoking peak of Popocatapetl and the unapproachable altitudes of the peerless Scrabblehorn; in the west-south-west the stately range of the Himalayas lay dreaming in a purple gloom; and thence all around the curving horizon the eye roved over a troubled sea of sun-kissed Alps, and noted, here and there, the noble proportions and soaring domes of the Bottlehorn, and the Saddlehorn, and the Shovelhorn, and the Powderhorn, all bathed in the glory of noon and mottled with softly-gliding blots, the shadows flung from drifting clouds.

Overcome by the scene, we all raised a triumphant, tremendous shout, in unison. A startled man at my elbow said,—"Confound you, what do you yell like that, for, right here in the street?"

That brought me down to Chamonix, like a flirt. I gave that man some spiritual advice and disposed of him, and then paid the telescope man his full fee, and said that we were charmed with the trip and would remain down, and not re-ascend and require him to fetch us down by telescope. This pleased him very much, for of course we could have stepped back to the summit and put him to the trouble of bringing us home if we had wanted to.

I judged we could get diplomas, now, anyhow; so we went after them, but the Chief Guide put us off, with one pretext or another, during all the time we stayed in Chamonix, and we ended by never getting them at all. So much for his prejudice against people's nationality. However, we worried him enough to make him remember us and our ascent for some time. He even said, once, that he wished there was a lunatic asylum in Chamonix. This shows that he really had fears that we were going to drive him mad. It was what we intended to do, but lack of time defeated it.

I cannot venture to advise the reader one way or the other, as to ascending Mont Blanc. I say only this: if he is at all timid, the enjoyments of the trip will hardly make up for the hardships and sufferings he will have to endure. But if he has good nerve, youth, health, and a bold, firm will, and could leave his family comfortably provided for in case the worst happened, he would find the ascent a wonderful experience, and the view from the top a vision to dream about, and tell about, and recall with exultation all the days of his life.

While I do not advise such a person to attempt the ascent, I do not advise him against it. But if he elects to attempt it, let him be warily careful of two things: choose a calm clear day; and do not pay the telescope man in advance. There are dark stories of his getting advance-payers on the summit and then leaving them there to rot.

7. "The 'Baton Rouge,'" frontispiece from *Life on the Mississippi* (Boston: James R. Osgood and Company, 1883).

4

Life on the Mississippi (1883)

All of Mark Twain's longer works had a labored history behind them, but Mark Twain eventually wrote *Life on the Mississippi* (1883) in two sustained bursts of inspiration. Both of these efforts, however, were preceded by years of gestation. First of all Mark Twain had to find his way back to his piloting experiences as a source of potential literary material. It took him a surprisingly long time, for he made his name by recounting his travels to Hawaii, Europe, and the Holy Land, and even by rehearsing his life in the western desert region, before he belatedly discovered the fertile subject of the Mississippi River Valley where he had spent his youth and learned the science of river-piloting.

As early as 1866, Twain had in mind a plan to write a book of "about three hundred pages" concerning the Mississippi.[1] William Dean Howells as editor of the *Atlantic Monthly*, however, should get some of the credit for guiding him toward this core of his creative energies, not only for commissioning a series of reminiscences by Twain about his piloting days that appeared in 1875, but also for writing strong words of encouragement on November 23, 1874 after reading a manuscript for one of these installments: "The piece about the Mississippi is capital—it almost made the water in our ice-pitcher muddy as I read it."[2] Twain had vowed to his wife Olivia on November 27, 1871 that "when I come to write the Mississippi book, *then* look out! I will spend 2 months on the river & take notes, & I bet you I will make a standard work."[3] Despite his eagerness to tackle this project, it became an often deferred idea, partly because he had difficulty lining up a suitable traveling companion, until finally in the spring of 1882 he set off for St. Louis with his new publisher James R. Osgood and a male stenographer in tow.

Whereas the first part of what became the book titled *Life on the Mississippi*, episodes about his years as an apprentice pilot, had come to Twain rapidly and almost passionately, the remaining two-thirds of the book proved more difficult to produce. For one thing, his descent down the river turned into a depressing inventory of the demolition wrought upon the former glories of steamboating by the swift and invincible railroad network; even the shape of the river itself had been altered by intervening floods and now by levees under construction at various points. Although the sights and sounds of dawn aboard a steamboat were still the same as when Sam Clemens the cub pilot had been called for early morning watches, only a few of his former pilot-friends remained at the pilot wheel and electric lights were taking part of the danger and much of the mystery out of nighttime runs. However, the continued hazards of watercraft powered by steam were brought home when, only weeks after Twain left the river, a steamboat on which he had traveled, the *Gold Dust*, exploded, killing one pilot and injuring his brother. Twain had known these men earlier, had kidded with them during their recent days together, and would mention their subsequent accident mournfully in *Life on the Mississippi*.

Twain did endeavor to admire the trolley lines, street lights, and commercial progress he noted in towns along the river, but he also observed that the most commendable advances were reserved for the northern reaches of the river, which he explored on his trip back upriver from New Orleans. But even the statistics taken from local booster publications, his raillery with the river pilots, his nostalgic visit to New Orleans, and the return to his boyhood home in Hannibal were insufficient to fill all the necessary pages. As he wrote to William Dean Howells on October 3, 1882: "I went to work at nine o'clock yesterday morning, and went to bed an hour after midnight. Result of the day, (mainly stolen from books, tho' credit given,) 9500 words. . . . I have nothing more to borrow or steal; the rest must all be writing."[4] Twain was contrasting the impressions of early travelers like Mrs. Trollope, Charles Dickens, Harriet Martineau, and others with the orderly prosperity now often visible in the same cities or regions.

The chapters reprinted here describe Twain's return to the river in 1882 and sample his inimitable art of compression in language and situation.

They likewise show his abiding fondness for the piloting profession and his acknowledgment of its impact upon his life and authorship.

Notes

1. *Selected Mark Twain-Howells Letters, 1872–1910,* ed. Frederick Anderson, William M. Gibson, and Henry Nash Smith (Cambridge: Belknap/Harvard UP, 1967), 26, n. 1.

2. *Selected Mark Twain-Howells Letters,* 32.

3. *Mark Twain's Letters,* Volume 4, 1870–1871, ed. Victor Fischer and Michael B. Frank (Berkeley: U of California P, 1995), 499.

4. *Selected Mark Twain-Howells Letters,* 417.

From LIFE ON THE MISSISSIPPI

[St. Louis, Chapter 22]

After twenty-one years' absence, I felt a very strong desire to see the river again, and the steamboats, and such of the boys as might be left; so I resolved to go out there. I enlisted a poet for company, and a stenographer to "take him down," and started westward about the middle of April.

As I proposed to make notes, with a view to printing, I took some thought as to methods of procedure. I reflected that if I were recognized, on the river, I should not be as free to go and come, talk, inquire, and spy around, as I should be if unknown; I remembered that it was the custom of steamboatmen in the old times to load up the confiding stranger with the most picturesque and admirable lies, and put the sophisticated friend off with dull and ineffectual facts: so I concluded, that, from a business point of view, it would be an advantage to disguise our party with fictitious names. The idea was certainly good, but it bred infinite bother; for although Smith, Jones, and Johnson are easy names to remember when there is no occasion to remember them, it is next to impossible to recollect them when they are wanted. How do criminals manage to keep a brand-new *alias* in mind? This is a great mystery. I was innocent; and yet was seldom able to lay my hand on my new name when it was needed; and it seemed to me that if I had had a crime on my conscience to further confuse me, I could never have kept the name by me at all.

We left per Pennsylvania Railroad, at 8 A.M. April 18.

"*Evening.* Speaking of dress. Grace and picturesqueness drop gradually out of it as one travels away from New York."

I find that among my notes. It makes no difference which direction you take, the fact remains the same. Whether you move north, south, east, or west, no matter: you can get up in the morning and guess how far you have come, by noting what degree of grace and picturesqueness is by that time lacking in the costumes of the new passengers;—I do not mean of the women alone, but of both sexes. It may be that *carriage* is at the bottom of this thing; and I think it is; for there are plenty of ladies and gentlemen in the provincial cities whose garments are all made by the best tailors and dressmakers of New York; yet this has no perceptible effect upon the grand fact: the educated eye never mistakes those people for New-Yorkers. No, there is a godless grace, and snap, and style about a born and bred New-Yorker which mere clothing cannot effect.

"*April 19.* This morning, struck into the region of full goatees—sometimes accompanied by a mustache, but only occasionally."

It was odd to come upon this thick crop of an obsolete and uncomely fashion; it was like running suddenly across a forgotten acquaintance whom you had supposed dead for a generation. The goatee extends over a wide extent of country; and is accompanied by an iron-clad belief in Adam and the biblical history of creation, which has not suffered from the assaults of the scientists.

"*Afternoon.* At the railway stations the loafers carry *both* hands in their breeches pockets; it was observable, heretofore, that one hand was sometimes out of doors,—here, never. This is an important fact in geography."

If the loafers determined the character of a country, it would be still more important, of course.

"Heretofore, all along, the station-loafer has been often observed to scratch one shin with the other foot; here, these remains of activity are wanting. This has an ominous look."

By and by, we entered the tobacco-chewing region. Fifty years ago, the tobacco-chewing region covered the Union. It is greatly restricted now.

Next, boots began to appear. Not in strong force, however. Later—away down the Mississippi—they became the rule. They disappeared from other sections of the Union with the mud; no doubt they will disappear from the river villages, also, when proper pavements come in.

We reached St. Louis at ten o'clock at night. At the counter of the hotel I tendered a hurriedly-invented fictitious name, with a miserable attempt at careless ease. The clerk paused, and inspected me in the compassionate way in which one inspects a respectable person who is found in doubtful circumstances; then he said,—"It's all right; I know what sort of a room you want. Used to clerk at the St. James, in New York."

An unpromising beginning for a fraudulent career. We started to the supper room, and met two other men whom I had known elsewhere. How odd and unfair it is: wicked impostors go around lecturing under my *nom de guerre* and nobody suspects them; but when an honest man attempts an imposture, he is exposed at once.

One thing seemed plain: we must start down the river the next day, if people who could not be deceived were going to crop up at this rate: an unpalatable disappointment, for we had hoped to have a week in St. Louis. The Southern was a good hotel, and we could have had a comfortable time there. It is large, and well conducted, and its decorations do not make one cry, as do those of the vast Palmer House, in Chicago. True, the billiard-tables were of the Old Silurian Period, and the cues and balls of the Post-Pliocene; but there was refreshment in this, not discomfort; for there is rest and healing in the contemplation of antiquities.

The most notable absence observable in the billiard room, was the absence of the river man. If he was there he had taken in his sign, he was in disguise. I saw there none of the swell airs and graces, and ostentatious displays of money, and pompous squanderings of it, which used to distinguish the steamboat crowd from the dry-land crowd in the bygone days, in the thronged billiard-rooms of St. Louis. In those times, the principal saloons were always populous with river men; given fifty players present, thirty or thirty-five were likely to be from the river. But I suspected that the ranks were thin now, and the steamboatmen no longer an aristocracy. Why, in my time they used to call the "barkeep" Bill, or Joe, or Tom, and slap him on the shoulder; I watched for that. But none of these people did it. Manifestly a glory that once was had dissolved and vanished away in these twenty-one years.

When I went up to my room, I found there the young man called Rogers, crying. Rogers was not his name; neither was Jones, Brown, Dexter, Ferguson, Bascom, nor Thompson; but he answered to either of these that a body found handy in an emergency; or to any other name, in fact, if he perceived that you meant him. He said:—

"What is a person to do here when he wants a drink of water?—drink this slush?"

"Can't you drink it?"

"I could if I had some other water to wash it with."

Here was a thing which had not changed; a score of years had not affected this water's mulatto complexion in the least; a score of centuries would succeed no better, perhaps. It comes out of the turbulent, bank-caving Missouri, and every tumblerful of it holds nearly an acre of land in solution. I got this fact from the bishop of the diocese. If you will let your glass stand half an hour, you can separate the land from the water as easy as Genesis; and then you will find them both good: the one good to eat, the other good to drink. The land is very nourishing, the water is thoroughly wholesome. The one appeases hunger; the other, thirst. But the natives do not take them separately, but together, as nature mixed them. When they find an inch of mud in the bottom of a glass, they stir it up, and then take the draught as they would gruel. It is difficult for a stranger to get used to this batter, but once used to it he will prefer it to water. This is really the case. It is good for steamboating, and good to drink; but it is worthless for all other purposes, except baptizing.

Next morning, we drove around town in the rain. The city seemed but little changed. It *was* greatly changed, but it did not seem so; because in St. Louis, as in London and Pittsburgh, you can't persuade a new thing to look new; the coal smoke turns it into an antiquity the moment you take your hand off it. The place had just about doubled its size, since I was a resident of it, and was now become a city of 400,000 inhabitants; still, in the solid business parts, it looked about as it had looked formerly. Yet I am sure there is not as much smoke in St. Louis now as there used to be. The smoke used to bank itself in a dense billowy black canopy over the town, and hide the sky from view. This shelter is very much thinner now; still, there is a sufficiency of smoke there, I think. I heard no complaint.

However, on the outskirts changes were apparent enough; notably in dwelling-house architecture. The fine new homes are noble and beautiful and modern. They stand by themselves, too, with green lawns around them; whereas the dwellings of a former day are packed together in blocks, and are all of one pattern, with windows all alike, set in an arched frame-work of twisted stone; a sort of house which was handsome enough when it was rarer.

There was another change—the Forest Park. This was new to me. It is beautiful and very extensive, and has the excellent merit of having been made mainly by nature. There are other parks, and fine ones, notably Tower Grove and the Botanical Gardens; for St. Louis interested herself in such improvements at an earlier day than did the most of our cities.

The first time I ever saw St. Louis, I could have bought it for six million dollars, and it was the mistake of my life that I did not do it. It was bitter now to look abroad over this domed and steepled metropolis, this solid expanse of bricks and mortar stretching away on every hand into dim, measure-defying distances, and remember that I had allowed that opportunity to go by. Why I should have allowed it to go by seems, of course, foolish and inexplicable to-day, at a first glance; yet there were reasons at the time to justify this course.

A Scotchman, Hon. Charles Augustus Murray, writing some forty-five or fifty years ago, said: "The streets are narrow, ill paved and ill lighted." Those streets are narrow still, of course; many of them are ill paved yet; but the reproach of ill lighting cannot be repeated, now. The "Catholic New Church" was the only notable building then, and Mr. Murray was confidently called upon to admire it, with its "species of Grecian portico, surmounted by a kind of steeple, much too diminutive in its proportions, and surmounted by sundry ornaments" which the unimaginative Scotchman found himself "quite unable to describe;" and therefore was grateful when a German tourist helped him out with the exclamation: "By ———, they look exactly like bed-posts!" St. Louis is well equipped with stately and noble public buildings now, and the little church, which the people used to be so proud of, lost its importance a long time ago. Still, this would not surprise Mr. Murray, if he could come back; for he prophesied the coming greatness of St. Louis with strong confidence.

The further we drove in our inspection-tour, the more sensibly I realized how the city had grown since I had seen it last; changes in detail became steadily more apparent and frequent than at first, too: changes uniformly evidencing progress, energy, prosperity.

But the change of changes was on the "levee." This time, a departure from the rule. Half a dozen sound-asleep steamboats where I used to see a solid mile of wide-awake ones! This was melancholy, this was woeful. The absence of the pervading and jocund steamboatman from the billiard-saloon was explained. He was absent because he is no more. His occupation is gone, his power has passed away, he is absorbed into the common herd, he grinds at the mill, a shorn Samson and inconspicuous. Half a dozen lifeless steamboats, a mile of empty wharves, a negro fatigued with whiskey stretched asleep, in a wide and soundless vacancy, where the serried hosts of commerce used to contend! {Capt. Marryat, writing forty-five years ago, says: "St. Louis has 20,000 inhabitants. *The river abreast of the town is crowded with steamboats, lying in two or three tiers.*} Here was desolation, indeed.

> "The old, old sea, as one in tears,
> Comes murmuring, with foamy lips,
> And knocking at the vacant piers,
> Calls for his long-lost multitude of ships."

The towboat and the railroad had done their work, and done it well and completely. The mighty bridge, stretching along over our heads, had done its share in the slaughter and spoliation. Remains of former steamboatmen told me, with wan satisfaction, that the bridge doesn't pay. Still, it can be no sufficient compensation to a corpse, to know that the dynamite that laid him out was not of as good quality as it had been supposed to be.

The pavements along the river front were bad; the sidewalks were rather out of repair; there was a rich abundance of mud. All this was familiar and satisfying; but the ancient armies of drays, and struggling throngs of men, and mountains of freight, were gone; and Sabbath reigned in their stead. The immemorial mile of cheap foul doggeries remained, but business was dull with them; the multitudes of poison-swilling Irishmen had departed, and in their places were a few scattering handfuls of ragged negroes, some drinking, some drunk, some nodding, others asleep. St. Louis is a great and prosperous and advancing city; but the river-edge of it seems dead past resurrection.

Mississippi steamboating was born about 1812; at the end of thirty years, it had grown to mighty proportions; and in less than thirty more, it was dead! A strangely short life for so majestic a creature. Of course it is not absolutely dead; neither is a crippled octogenarian who could once jump twenty-two feet on level ground; but as contrasted with what it was in its prime vigor, Mississippi steamboating may be called dead.

It killed the old-fashioned keel-boating, by reducing the freight-trip to New Orleans to less than a week. The railroads have killed the steam-boat passenger traffic by doing in two or three days what the steamboats consumed a week in doing; and the towing-fleets have killed the through-freight traffic by dragging six or seven steamer-loads of stuff down the river at a time, at an expense so trivial that steamboat competition was out of the question.

Freight and passenger way-traffic remains to the steamers. This is in the hands—along the two thousand miles of river between St. Paul and New Orleans—of two or three close corporations well fortified with capi-tal; and by able and thoroughly business-like management and system, these make a sufficiency of money out of what is left of the once pro-digious steamboating industry. I suppose that St. Louis and New Or-leans have not suffered materially by the change, but alas for the wood-yard man!

He used to fringe the river all the way; his close-ranked merchandise stretched from the one city to the other, along the banks, and he sold un-countable cords of it every year for cash on the nail; but all the scattering boats that are left burn coal now, and the seldomest spectacle on the Mis-sissippi to-day is a wood-pile. Where now is the once wood-yard man?

[Down the river, Chapter 23]

My idea was, to tarry a while in every town between St. Louis and New Orleans. To do this, it would be necessary to go from place to place by the short packet lines. It was an easy plan to make, and would have been an easy one to follow, twenty years ago—but not now. There are wide inter-vals between boats, these days.

I wanted to begin with the interesting old French settlements of St. Genevieve and Kaskaskia, sixty miles below St. Louis. There was only one boat advertised for that section—a Grand Tower packet. Still, one boat was enough; so we went down to look at her. She was a venerable rack-heap, and a fraud to boot; for she was playing herself for personal property, whereas the good honest dirt was so thickly caked all over her that she was righteously taxable as real estate. There are places in New England where her hurricane deck would be worth a hundred and fifty dollars an acre. The soil on her forecastle was quite good—the new crop of wheat was already springing from the cracks in protected places. The companionway was of a dry sandy character, and would have been well suited for grapes, with a southern exposure and a little subsoiling. The soil of the boiler deck was thin and rocky, but good enough for grazing purposes. A colored boy was on watch here—nobody else visible. We gathered from him that this calm craft would go, as advertised, "if she got her trip;" if she didn't get it, she would wait for it.

"Has she got any of her trip?"

"Bless you, no, boss. She ain't unloadened, yit. She only come in dis mawnin'."

He was uncertain as to when she might get her trip, but thought it might be to-morrow or maybe next day. This would not answer at all; so we had to give up the novelty of sailing down the river on a farm. We had one more arrow in our quiver: a Vicksburg packet, the "Gold Dust," was to leave at 5 P.M. We took passage in her for Memphis, and gave up the idea of stopping off here and there, as being impracticable. She was neat, clean, and comfortable. We camped on the boiler deck, and bought some cheap literature to kill time with. The vender was a venerable Irishman with a benevolent face and a tongue that worked easily in the socket, and from him we learned that he had lived in St. Louis thirty-four years and had never been across the river during that period. Then he wandered into a very flowing lecture, filled with classic names and allusions, which was quite wonderful for fluency until the fact became rather apparent that this was not the first time, nor perhaps the fiftieth, that the speech had been delivered. He was a good deal of a character, and much better company than the sappy literature he was selling. A random remark, connecting Irishmen and beer, brought this nugget of information out of him:—

"They don't drink it, sir. They *can't* drink it, sir. Give an Irishman lager for a month, and he's a dead man. An Irishman is lined with copper, and the beer corrodes it. But whiskey polishes the copper and is the saving of him, sir."

At eight o'clock, promptly, we backed out and—crossed the river. As we crept toward the shore, in the thick darkness, a blinding glory of white electric light burst suddenly from our forecastle, and lit up the water and the warehouses as with a noon-day glare. Another big change, this,—no more flickering, smoky, pitch-dripping, ineffectual torch-baskets, now: their day is past. Next, instead of calling out a score of hands to man the stage, a couple of men and a hatful of steam lowered it from the derrick where it was suspended, launched it, deposited it in just the right spot, and the whole thing was over and done with before a mate in the olden time could have got his profanity-mill adjusted to begin the preparatory services. Why this new and simple method of handling the stages was not thought of when the first steamboat was built, is a mystery which helps one to realize what a dull-witted slug the average human being is.

We finally got away at two in the morning, and when I turned out at six, we were rounding to at a rocky point where there was an old stone warehouse—at any rate, the ruins of it; two or three decayed dwelling-houses were near by, in the shelter of the leafy hills; but there were no evidences of human or other animal life to be seen. I wondered if I had forgotten the river; for I had no recollection whatever of this place; the shape of the river, too, was unfamiliar; there was nothing in sight, anywhere, that I could remember ever having seen before. I was surprised, disappointed, and annoyed.

We put ashore a well-dressed lady and gentleman, and two well-dressed, lady-like young girls, together with sundry Russia-leather bags. A strange place for such folk! No carriage was waiting. The party moved off as if they had not expected any, and struck down a winding country road afoot.

But the mystery was explained when we got under way again, for these people were evidently bound for a large town which lay shut in behind a tow-head (*i.e.*, new island) a couple of miles below this landing. I couldn't remember that town; I couldn't place it, couldn't call its name. So I lost part of my temper. I suspected that it might be St. Genevieve—and so it proved to be. Observe what this eccentric river had been about: it had built up this huge useless tow-head directly in front of this town, cut off its river communications, fenced it away completely, and made a "country" town of it. It is a fine old place, too, and deserved a better fate. It was settled by the French, and is a relic of a time when one could travel from the mouths of the Mississippi to Quebec and be on French territory and under French rule all the way.

Presently I ascended to the hurricane deck and cast a longing glance toward the pilot-house.

[Down the river, from Chapter 30]

I had myself called with the four o'clock watch, mornings, for one cannot see too many summer sunrises on the Mississippi. They are enchanting. First, there is the eloquence of silence; for a deep hush broods everywhere. Next, there is the haunting sense of loneliness, isolation, remoteness from the worry and bustle of the world. The dawn creeps in stealthily; the solid walls of black forest soften to gray, and vast stretches of the river open up and reveal themselves; the water is glass-smooth, gives off spectral little wreaths of white mist, there is not the faintest breath of wind, nor stir of leaf; the tranquillity is profound and infinitely satisfying. Then a bird pipes up, another follows, and soon the pipings develop into a jubilant riot of music. You see none of the birds; you simply move through an atmosphere of song which seems to sing itself. When the light has become a little stronger, you have one of the fairest and softest pictures imaginable. You have the intense green of the massed and crowded foliage near by; you see it paling shade by shade in front of you; upon the next projecting cape, a mile off or more, the tint has lightened to the tender young green of spring; the cape beyond that one has almost lost color, and the furthest one, miles away under the horizon, sleeps upon the water a mere dim vapor, and hardly separable from the sky above it and about it. And all this stretch of river is a mirror, and you have the shadowy reflections of the leafage and the curving shores and the receding capes pictured in it. Well, that is all beautiful; soft and rich and beautiful; and when the sun gets well up, and distributes a pink flush here and a powder of gold yonder and a purple haze where it will yield the best effect, you grant that you have seen something that is worth remembering.

[Down the river, Chapter 34]

STACK ISLAND. I remembered Stack Island; also Lake Providence, Louisiana—which is the first distinctly Southern-looking town you come to, downward-bound; lies level and low, shade-trees hung with venerable gray beards of Spanish moss; "restful, pensive, Sunday aspect about the place," comments Uncle Mumford, with feeling—also with truth.[*]

A Mr. H. furnished some minor details of fact concerning this region which I would have hesitated to believe if I had not known him to be a

---

[*] Mumford, a fictional name, was the 1st mate on board the *Gold Dust*.

steamboat mate. He was a passenger of ours, a resident of Arkansas City, and bound to Vicksburg to join his boat, a little Sunflower packet. He was an austere man, and had the reputation of being singularly unworldly, for a river man. Among other things, he said that Arkansas had been injured and kept back by generations of exaggerations concerning the mosquitoes here. One may smile, said he, and turn the matter off as being a small thing; but when you come to look at the effects produced, in the way of discouragement of immigration, and diminished values of property, it was quite the opposite of a small thing, or thing in any wise to be coughed down or sneered at. These mosquitoes had been persistently represented as being formidable and lawless; whereas "the truth is, they are feeble, insignificant in size, diffident to a fault, sensitive"—and so on, and so on; you would have supposed he was talking about his family. But if he was soft on the Arkansas mosquitoes, he was hard enough on the mosquitoes of Lake Providence to make up for it—"those Lake Providence colossi," as he finely called them. He said that two of them could whip a dog, and that four of them could hold a man down; and except help come, they would kill him—"butcher him," as he expressed it. Referred in a sort of casual way—and yet significant way—to "the fact that the life policy in its simplest form is unknown in Lake Providence—they take out a mosquito policy besides." He told many remarkable things about those lawless insects. Among others, said he had seen them try to *vote*. Noticing that this statement seemed to be a good deal of a strain on us, he modified it a little: said he might have been mistaken, as to that particular, but knew he had seen them around the polls "canvassing."

There was another passenger—friend of H.'s—who backed up the harsh evidence against those mosquitoes, and detailed some stirring adventures which he had had with them. The stories were pretty sizable, merely pretty sizable; yet Mr. H. was continually interrupting with a cold, inexorable "Wait—knock off twenty-five per cent of that; now go on;" or, "Wait—you are getting that too strong; cut it down, cut it down—you get a leetle too much costumery on to your statements: always dress a fact in tights, never in an ulster;" or, "Pardon, once more: if you are going to load anything more on to that statement, you want to get a couple of lighters and tow the rest, because it's drawing all the water there is in the river already; stick to facts—just stick to the cold facts; what these gentlemen want for a book is the frozen truth—ain't that so, gentlemen?" He explained privately that it was necessary to watch this man all the time, and keep him within bounds; it would not do to neglect this precaution, as he, Mr. H., "knew to his sorrow." Said he, "I will not deceive you; he told me such a monstrous lie once, that it swelled my left ear up, and spread it so that I was actually not able to see out around it; it remained so for months, and people came miles to see me fan myself with it."

[Vicksburg, from Chapter 35]

The war history of Vicksburg has more about it to interest the general reader than that of any other of the river-towns. It is full of variety, full of incident, full of the picturesque. Vicksburg held out longer than any other important river-town, and saw warfare in all its phases, both land and water—the siege, the mine, the assault, the repulse, the bombardment, sickness, captivity, famine.

The most beautiful of all the national cemeteries is here. Over the great gateway is this inscription:—"HERE REST IN PEACE 16,600 WHO DIED FOR THEIR COUNTRY IN THE YEARS 1861 TO 1865."

The grounds are nobly situated; being very high and commanding a wide prospect of land and river. They are tastefully laid out in broad terraces, with winding roads and paths; and there is profuse adornment in the way of semi-tropical shrubs and flowers; and in one part is a piece of native wild-wood, left just as it grew, and, therefore, perfect in its charm. Everything about this cemetery suggests the hand of the national Government. The Government's work is always conspicuous for excellence, solidity, thoroughness, neatness. The Government does its work well in the first place, and then takes care of it.

By winding-roads—which were often cut to so great a depth between perpendicular walls that they were mere roofless tunnels—we drove out a mile or two and visited the monument which stands upon the scene of the surrender of Vicksburg to General Grant by General Pemberton. Its metal will preserve it from the hackings and chippings which so defaced its predecessor, which was of marble; but the brick foundations are crumbling, and it will tumble down by-and-by. It overlooks a picturesque region of wooded hills and ravines; and is not unpicturesque itself, being well smothered in flowering weeds. The battered remnant of the marble monument has been removed to the National Cemetery.

On the road, a quarter of a mile townward, an aged colored man showed us, with pride, an unexploded bomb-shell which has lain in his yard since the day it fell there during the siege.

"I was a-stannin' heah, an' de dog was a-stannin' heah; de dog he went for de shell, gwine to pick a fuss wid it; but I didn't; I says, 'Jes' make youseff at home heah; lay still whah you is, or bust up de place, jes' as you's a mind to, but *I*'s got business out in de woods, *I* has!'"

Vicksburg is a town of substantial business streets and pleasant residences; it commands the commerce of the Yazoo and Sunflower Rivers; is pushing railways in several directions, through rich agricultural regions, and has a promising future of prosperity and importance.

Apparently, nearly all the river towns, big and little, have made up their minds that they must look mainly to railroads for wealth and upbuilding, henceforth. They are acting upon this idea. The signs are, that the next twenty years will bring about some noteworthy changes in the Valley, in the direction of increased population and wealth, and in the intellectual advancement and the liberalizing of opinion which go naturally with these. And yet, if one may judge by the past, the river towns will manage to find and use a chance, here and there, to cripple and retard their progress. They kept themselves back in the days of steamboating supremacy, by a system of wharfage-dues so stupidly graded as to prohibit what may be called small *retail* traffic in freights and passengers. Boats were charged such heavy wharfage that they could not afford to land for one or two passengers or a light lot of freight. Instead of encouraging the bringing of trade to their doors, the towns diligently and effectively discouraged it. They could have had many boats and low rates; but their policy rendered few boats and high rates compulsory. It was a policy which extended— and extends—from New Orleans to St. Paul.

[Baton Rouge, from Chapter 40]

Baton Rouge was clothed in flowers, like a bride—no, much more so; like a greenhouse. For we were in the absolute South now—no modifications, no compromises, no half-way measures. The magnolia-trees in the Capitol grounds were lovely and fragrant, with their dense rich foliage and huge snow-ball blossoms. The scent of the flower is very sweet, but you want distance on it, because it is so powerful. They are not good bedroom blossoms—they might suffocate one in his sleep. We were certainly in the South at last; for here the sugar region begins, and the plantations—vast green levels, with sugar-mill and negro quarters clustered together in the middle distance—were in view. And there was a tropical sun overhead and a tropical swelter in the air.

And at this point, also, begins the pilot's paradise: a wide river hence to New Orleans, abundance of water from shore to shore, and no bars, snags, sawyers, or wrecks in his road.

Sir Walter Scott is probably responsible for the Capitol building; for it is not conceivable that this little sham castle would ever have been built if he had not run the people mad, a couple of generations ago, with his mediæval romances. The South has not yet recovered from the debilitating influence of his books. Admiration of his fantastic heroes and their grotesque "chivalry" doings and romantic juvenilities still survives here, in an atmosphere in which is already perceptible the wholesome and practical nineteenth-century smell of cotton-factories and locomotives; and traces of its inflated language and other windy humbuggeries survive along with it. It is pathetic enough, that a whitewashed castle, with turrets and things—materials all ungenuine within and without, pretending to be what they are not—should ever have been built in this otherwise honorable place; but it is much more pathetic to see this architectural falsehood undergoing restoration and perpetuation in our day, when it would have been so easy to let dynamite finish what a charitable fire began, and then devote this restoration-money to the building of something genuine.

Baton Rouge has no patent on imitation castles, however, and no monopoly of them. Here is a picture from the advertisement of the "Female Institute" of Columbia, Tennessee. The following remark is from the same advertisement:—"The Institute building has long been famed as a model of striking and beautiful architecture. Visitors are charmed with its resemblance to the old castles of song and story, with its towers, turreted walls, and ivy-mantled porches."

Keeping school in a castle is a romantic thing; as romantic as keeping hotel in a castle.

By itself the imitation castle is doubtless harmless, and well enough; but as a symbol and breeder and sustainer of maudlin Middle-Age romanticism here in the midst of the plainest and sturdiest and infinitely greatest and worthiest of all the centuries the world has seen, it is necessarily a hurtful thing and a mistake.

The approaches to New Orleans were familiar; general aspects were unchanged. When one goes flying through London along a railway propped
in the air on tall arches, he may inspect miles of upper bedrooms through
the open windows, but the lower half of the houses is under his level and
out of sight. Similarly, in high-river stage, in the New Orleans region, the
water is up to the top of the enclosing levee-rim, the flat country behind
it lies low—representing the bottom of a dish—and as the boat swims
along, high on the flood, one looks down upon the houses and into the
upper windows. There is nothing but that frail breastwork of earth between the people and destruction.

The old brick salt-warehouses clustered at the upper end of the city
looked as they had always looked; warehouses which had had a kind of
Aladdin's lamp experience, however, since I had seen them; for when the
war broke out the proprietor went to bed one night leaving them packed
with thousands of sacks of vulgar salt, worth a couple of dollars a sack,
and got up in the morning and found his mountain of salt turned into a
mountain of gold, so to speak, so suddenly and to so dizzy a height had
the war news sent up the price of the article.

The vast reach of plank wharves remained unchanged, and there were
as many ships as ever: but the long array of steamboats had vanished; not
altogether, of course, but not much of it was left.

The city itself had not changed—to the eye. It had greatly increased
in spread and population, but the look of the town was not altered. The
dust, waste-paper-littered, was still deep in the streets; the deep, trough-
like gutters alongside the curb-stones were still half full of reposeful water with a dusty surface; the sidewalks were still—in the sugar and bacon
region—encumbered by casks and barrels and hogsheads; the great blocks
of austerely plain commercial houses were as dusty-looking as ever.

Canal Street was finer, and more attractive and stirring than formerly, with
its drifting crowds of people, its several processions of hurrying street-
cars, and—toward evening—its broad second-story verandas crowded
with gentlemen and ladies clothed according to the latest mode.

Not that there is any "architecture" in Canal Street: to speak in broad,
general terms, there is no architecture in New Orleans, except in the
cemeteries. It seems a strange thing to say of a wealthy, far-seeing, and

energetic city of a quarter of a million inhabitants, but it is true. There is a huge granite U.S. Custom-house—costly enough, genuine enough, but as a decoration it is inferior to a gasometer. It looks like a state prison. But it was built before the war. Architecture in America may be said to have been born since the war. New Orleans, I believe, has had the good luck—and in a sense the bad luck—to have had no great fire in late years. It must be so. If the opposite had been the case, I think one would be able to tell the "burnt district" by the radical improvement in its architecture over the old forms. One can do this in Boston and Chicago. The "burnt district" of Boston was commonplace before the fire; but now there is no commercial district in any city in the world that can surpass it—or perhaps even rival it—in beauty, elegance, and tastefulness.

However, New Orleans has begun—just this moment, as one may say. When completed, the new Cotton Exchange will be a stately and beautiful building; massive, substantial, full of architectural graces; no shams or false pretenses or uglinesses about it anywhere. To the city, it will be worth many times its cost, for it will breed its species. What has been lacking hitherto, was a model to build toward; something to educate eye and taste; a *suggester,* so to speak.

The city is well outfitted with progressive men—thinking, sagacious, long-headed men. The contrast between the spirit of the city and the city's architecture is like the contrast between waking and sleep. Apparently there is a "boom" in everything but that one dead feature. The water in the gutters used to be stagnant and slimy, and a potent disease-breeder; but the gutters are flushed now, two or three times a day, by powerful machinery; in many of the gutters the water never stands still, but has a steady current. Other sanitary improvements have been made; and with such effect that New Orleans claims to be (during the long intervals between the occasional yellow-fever assaults) one of the healthiest cities in the Union. There's plenty of ice now for everybody, manufactured in the town. It is a driving place commercially, and has a great river, ocean, and railway business. At the date of our visit, it was the best lighted city in the Union, electrically speaking. The New Orleans electric lights were more numerous than those of New York, and very much better. One had this modified noonday not only in Canal and some neighboring chief streets, but all along a stretch of five miles of river frontage. There are good clubs in the city now—several of them but recently organized—and inviting modern-style pleasure resorts at West End and Spanish Fort. The telephone is everywhere. One of the most notable advances is in journalism. The newspapers, as I remember them, were not a striking feature. Now they are. Money is spent upon them with a free hand. They get the news, let it cost what it may. The editorial work is not hack-grinding, but literature. As an example of New Orleans journalistic achievement, it may be mentioned that the "Times-Democrat" of August 26, 1882, contained a report of the year's business of the towns of the Mississippi Valley, from New Orleans all the way to St. Paul—two thousand miles. That issue of the paper consisted of *forty* pages; seven columns to the page; two hundred and eighty columns in all; fifteen hundred words to the column; an aggregate of four hundred and twenty thousand words. That is to say, not much short of three times as many words as there are in this book. One may with sorrow contrast this with the architecture of New Orleans.

I have been speaking of public architecture only. The domestic article in New Orleans is reproachless, notwithstanding it remains as it always was. All the dwellings are of wood—in the American part of the town, I mean—and all have a comfortable look. Those in the wealthy quarter are spacious; painted snow-white usually, and generally have wide verandas, or double-verandas, supported by ornamental columns. These mansions stand in the centre of large grounds, and rise, garlanded with roses, out of the midst of swelling masses of shining green foliage and many-colored blossoms. No houses could well be in better harmony with their surroundings, or more pleasing to the eye, or more home-like and comfortable-looking.

One even becomes reconciled to the cistern presently; this is a mighty cask, painted green, and sometimes a couple of stories high, which is propped against the house-corner on stilts. There is a mansion-and-brewery suggestion about the combination which seems very incongruous at first. But the people cannot have wells, and so they take rain-water. Neither can they conveniently have cellars, or graves; {The Israelites are buried in graves—by permission, I take it, not requirement; but none else, except the destitute, who are buried at public expense. The graves are but three or four feet deep.} the town being built upon "made" ground; so they do without both, and few of the living complain, and none of the others.

[New Orleans, Chapter 44]

The old French part of New Orleans—anciently the Spanish part—bears
no resemblance to the American end of the city: the American end which
lies beyond the intervening brick business-centre. The houses are massed
in blocks; are austerely plain and dignified; uniform of pattern, with here
and there a departure from it with pleasant effect; all are plastered on the
outside, and nearly all have long, iron-railed verandas running along the
several stories. Their chief beauty is the deep, warm, varicolored stain
with which time and the weather have enriched the plaster. It harmonizes
with all the surroundings, and has as natural a look of belonging there as
has the flush upon sunset clouds. This charming decoration cannot be
successfully imitated; neither is it to be found elsewhere in America.

The iron railings are a specialty, also. The pattern is often exceedingly
light and dainty, and airy and graceful—with a large cipher or monogram
in the centre, a delicate cobweb of baffling, intricate forms, wrought in
steel. The ancient railings are hand-made, and are now comparatively rare
and proportionately valuable. They are become bric-a-brac.

The party had the privilege of idling through this ancient quarter of
New Orleans with the South's finest literary genius, the author of "the
Grandissimes." In him the South has found a masterly delineator of its
interior life and its history. In truth, I find by experience, that the un-
trained eye and vacant mind can inspect it, and learn of it and judge of it,
more clearly and profitably in his books than by personal contact with it.

With Mr. Cable along to see for you, and describe and explain and il-
luminate, a jog through that old quarter is a vivid pleasure. And you have
a vivid *sense* as of unseen or dimly seen things—vivid, and yet fitful and
darkling; you glimpse salient features, but lose the fine shades or catch
them imperfectly through the vision of the imagination: a case, as it were,
of an ignorant near-sighted stranger traversing the rim of wide vague ho-
rizons of Alps with an inspired and enlightened long-sighted native.

We visited the old St. Louis Hotel, now occupied by municipal offices.
There is nothing strikingly remarkable about it; but one can say of it as of
the Academy of Music in New York, that if a broom or a shovel has ever
been used in it there is no circumstantial evidence to back up the fact. It
is curious that cabbages and hay and things do not grow in the Academy

of Music; but no doubt it is on account of the interruption of the light by the benches, and the impossibility of hoeing the crop except in the aisles. The fact that the ushers grow their buttonhole-bouquets on the premises shows what might be done if they had the right kind of an agricultural head to the establishment.

We visited also the venerable Cathedral, and the pretty square in front of it; the one dim with religious light, the other brilliant with the worldly sort; and lovely with orange trees and blossomy shrubs; then we drove in the hot sun through the wilderness of houses and out on to the wide dead level beyond, where the villas are, and the water wheels to drain the town, and the commons populous with cows and children; passing by an old cemetery where we were told lie the ashes of an early pirate; but we took him on trust, and did not visit him. He was a pirate with a tremendous and sanguinary history; and as long as he preserved unspotted, in retirement, the dignity of his name and the grandeur of his ancient calling, homage and reverence were his from high and low; but when at last he descended into politics and became a paltry alderman, the public "shook" him, and turned aside and wept. When he died, they set up a monument over him; and little by little he has come into respect again; but it is respect for the pirate, not the alderman. To-day the loyal and generous remember only what he was, and charitably forget what he became.

Thence, we drove a few miles across a swamp, along a raised shell road, with a canal on one hand and a dense wood on the other; and here and there, in the distance, a ragged and angular-limbed and moss-bearded cypress, top standing out, clear cut against the sky, and as quaint of form as the apple-trees in Japanese pictures—such was our course and the surroundings of it. There was an occasional alligator swimming comfortably along in the canal, and an occasional picturesque colored person on the bank, flinging his statue-rigid reflection upon the still water and watching for a bite.

And by and by we reached the West End, a collection of hotels of the usual light summer-resort pattern, with broad verandas all around, and the waves of the wide and blue Lake Pontchartrain lapping the thresholds. We had dinner on a ground-veranda over the water—the chief dish the renowned fish called the pompano, delicious as the less criminal forms of sin.

Thousands of people come by rail and carriage to West End and to Spanish Fort every evening, and dine, listen to the bands, take strolls in the open air under the electric lights, go sailing on the lake, and entertain themselves in various and sundry other ways.

We had opportunities on other days and in other places to test the pompano. Notably, at an editorial dinner at one of the clubs in the city. He was in his last possible perfection there, and justified his fame. In his suite was a tall pyramid of scarlet cray-fish—large ones; as large as one's thumb; delicate, palatable, appetizing. Also devilled whitebait; also shrimps of choice quality; and a platter of small soft-shell crabs of a most superior breed. The other dishes were what one might get at Delmonico's, or Buckingham Palace; those I have spoken of can be had in similar perfection in New Orleans only, I suppose.

In the West and South they have a new institution,—the Broom Brigade. It is composed of young ladies who dress in a uniform costume, and go through the infantry drill, with broom in place of musket. It is a very pretty sight, on private view. When they perform on the stage of a theatre, in the blaze of colored fires, it must be a fine and fascinating spectacle. I saw them go through their complex manual with grace, spirit, and admirable precision. I saw them do everything which a human being can possibly do with a broom, except sweep. I did not see them sweep. But I know they could learn. What they have already learned proves that. And if they ever should learn, and should go on the war-path down Tchoupitoulas or some of those other streets around there, those thoroughfares would bear a greatly improved aspect in a very few minutes. But the girls themselves wouldn't; so nothing would be really gained, after all.

The drill was in the Washington Artillery building. In this building we saw many interesting relics of the war. Also a fine oil-painting representing Stonewall Jackson's last interview with General Lee. Both men are on horseback. Jackson has just ridden up, and is accosting Lee. The picture is very valuable, on account of the portraits, which are authentic. But, like many another historical picture, it means nothing without its label. And one label will fit it as well as another:—

First Interview between Lee and Jackson.
Last Interview between Lee and Jackson.
Jackson Introducing Himself to Lee.

Jackson Accepting Lee's Invitation to Dinner.
Jackson Declining Lee's Invitation to Dinner—with Thanks.
Jackson Apologizing for a Heavy Defeat.
Jackson Reporting a Great Victory.
Jackson Asking Lee for a Match.

It tells *one* story, and a sufficient one; for it says quite plainly and sat-isfactorily, "Here are Lee and Jackson together." The artist would have made it tell that this is Lee and Jackson's last interview if he could have done it. But he couldn't, for there wasn't any way to do it. A good legible label is usually worth, for information, a ton of significant attitude and expression in a historical picture. In Rome, people with fine sympathetic natures stand up and weep in front of the celebrated "Beatrice Cenci the Day before her Execution." It shows what a label can do. If they did not know the picture, they would inspect it unmoved, and say, "Young girl with hay fever; young girl with her head in a bag."

I found the half-forgotten Southern intonations and elisions as pleas-ing to my ear as they had formerly been. A Southerner talks music. At least it is music to me, but then I was born in the South. The educated Southerner has no use for an *r*, except at the beginning of a word. He says "honah," and "dinnah," and "Gove'nuh," and "befo' the waw," and so on. The words may lack charm to the eye, in print, but they have it to the ear. When did the *r* disappear from Southern speech, and how did it come to disappear? The custom of dropping it was not borrowed from the North, nor inherited from England. Many Southerners—most Southerners—put a *y* into occasional words that begin with the *k* sound. For instance, they say Mr. K'yahtah (Carter) and speak of playing k'yahds or of riding in the k'yahs. And they have the pleasant custom—long ago fallen into decay in the North—of frequently employing the respectful "Sir." Instead of the curt Yes, and the abrupt No, they say "Yes, Suh"; "No, Suh."

But there are some infelicities. Such as "like" for "as," and the addi-tion of an "at" where it isn't needed. I heard an educated gentleman say, "Like the flag-officer did." His cook or his butler would have said, "Like the flag-officer done." You hear gentlemen say, "Where have you been at?" And here is the aggravated form—heard a ragged street Arab say it to a comrade: "I was a-ask'n' Tom whah you was a-sett'n' at." The very elect carelessly say "will" when they mean "shall"; and many of them say, "I didn't go to do it," meaning "I didn't mean to do it." The Northern word "guess"—imported from England, where it used to be common, and now regarded by satirical Englishmen as a Yankee original—is but little used among Southerners. They say "reckon." They haven't any "doesn't" in their language; they say "don't" instead. The unpolished often use "went" for "gone." It is nearly as bad as the Northern "hadn't ought." This reminds me that a remark of a very peculiar nature was made here in my neighborhood (in the North) a few days ago: "He hadn't ought to have went." How is that? Isn't that a good deal of a triumph? One knows the orders combined in this half-breed's architecture without inquiring: one parent Northern, the other Southern. To-day I heard a school-mistress ask, "Where is John gone?" This form is so common—so nearly universal, in fact—that if she had used "whither" instead of "where," I think it would have sounded like an affectation.

We picked up one excellent word—a word worth traveling to New Orleans to get; a nice limber, expressive, handy word—"Lagniappe." They pronounce it lanny-*yap*. It is Spanish—so they said. We discovered it at the head of a column of odds and ends in the Picayune, the first day; heard twenty people use it the second; inquired what it meant the third; adopted it and got facility in swinging it the fourth. It has a restricted meaning, but I think the people spread it out a little when they choose. It is the equivalent of the thirteenth roll in a "baker's dozen." It is something thrown in, gratis, for good measure. The custom originated in the Spanish quarter of the city. When a child or a servant buys something in a shop—or even the mayor or the governor, for aught I know—he finishes the operation by saying—"Give me something for lagniappe."

The shopman always responds; gives the child a bit of licorice-root, gives the servant a cheap cigar or a spool of thread, gives the governor—I don't know what he gives the governor; support, likely.

When you are invited to drink,—and this does occur now and then in New Orleans,—and you say, "What, again?—no, I've had enough;" the other party says, "But just this one time more,—this is for lagniappe." When the beau perceives that he is stacking his compliments a trifle too high, and sees by the young lady's countenance that the edifice would have been better with the top compliment left off, he puts his "I beg pardon,—

no harm intended," into the briefer form of "Oh, that's for lagniappe." If the waiter in the restaurant stumbles and spills a gill of coffee down the back of your neck, he says "For lagniappe, sah," and gets you another cup without extra charge.

[Up the river, from Chapter 51]

We left for St. Louis in the "City of Baton Rouge," on a delightfully hot day, but with the main purpose of my visit but lamely accomplished. I had hoped to hunt up and talk with a hundred steamboatmen, but got so pleasantly involved in the social life of the town that I got nothing more than mere five-minute talks with a couple of dozen of the craft.

I was on the bench of the pilot-house when we backed out and "straightened up" for the start—the boat pausing for a "good ready," in the old-fashioned way, and the black smoke piling out of the chimneys equally in the old-fashioned way. Then we began to gather momentum, and presently were fairly under way and booming along. It was all as natural and familiar—and so were the shoreward sights—as if there had been no break in my river life. There was a "cub," and I judged that he would take the wheel now; and he did. Captain Bixby stepped into the pilot-house. Presently the cub closed up on the rank of steamships. He made me nervous, for he allowed too much water to show between our boat and the ships. I knew quite well what was going to happen, because I could date back in my own life and inspect the record. The captain looked on, during a silent half-minute, then took the wheel himself, and crowded the boat in, till she went scraping along within a hand-breadth of the ships. It was exactly the favor which he had done me, about a quarter of a century before, in that same spot, the first time I ever steamed out of the port of New Orleans. It was a very great and sincere pleasure to me to see the thing repeated—with somebody else as victim.

We made Natchez (three hundred miles) in twenty-two hours and a half,—much the swiftest passage I have ever made over that piece of water.

The next morning I came on with the four o'clock watch, and saw Ritchie successfully run half a dozen crossings in a fog, using for his guidance the marked chart devised and patented by Bixby and himself. This sufficiently evidenced the great value of the chart.

By and by, when the fog began to clear off, I noticed that the reflection of a tree in the smooth water of an overflowed bank, six hundred yards away, was stronger and blacker than the ghostly tree itself. The faint spectral trees, dimly glimpsed through the shredding fog, were very pretty things to see.

We had a heavy thunder-storm at Natchez, another at Vicksburg, and still another about fifty miles below Memphis. They had an old-fashioned energy which had long been unfamiliar to me. This third storm was accompanied by a raging wind. We tied up to the bank when we saw the tempest coming, and everybody left the pilot-house but me. The wind bent the young trees down, exposing the pale underside of the leaves; and gust after gust followed, in quick succession, thrashing the branches violently up and down, and to this side and that, and creating swift waves of alternating green and white according to the side of the leaf that was exposed, and these waves raced after each other as do their kind over a wind-tossed field of oats. No color that was visible anywhere was quite natural,—all tints were charged with a leaden tinge from the solid cloud-bank overhead. The river was leaden; all distances the same; and even the far-reaching ranks of combing white-caps were dully shaded by the dark, rich atmosphere through which their swarming legions marched. The thunder-peals were constant and deafening; explosion followed explosion with but inconsequential intervals between, and the reports grew steadily sharper and higher-keyed, and more trying to the ear; the lightning was as diligent as the thunder, and produced effects which enchanted the eye and sent electric ecstasies of mixed delight and apprehension shivering along every nerve in the body in unintermittent procession. The rain poured down in amazing volume; the ear-splitting thunder-peals broke nearer and nearer; the wind increased in fury and began to wrench off boughs and tree-tops and send them sailing away through space; the pilot-house fell to rocking and straining and cracking and surging, and I went down in the hold to see what time it was.

People boast a good deal about Alpine thunder-storms; but the storms which I have had the luck to see in the Alps were not the equals of some which I have seen in the Mississippi Valley. I may not have seen the Alps do their best, of course, and if they can beat the Mississippi, I don't wish to.

We took passage in one of the fast boats of the St. Louis and St. Paul Packet Company, and started up the river.

When I, as a boy, first saw the mouth of the Missouri River, it was twenty-two or twenty-three miles above St. Louis, according to the estimate of pilots; the wear and tear of the banks has moved it down eight miles since then; and the pilots say that within five years the river will cut through and move the mouth down five miles more, which will bring it within ten miles of St. Louis.

About nightfall we passed the large and flourishing town of Alton, Illinois; and before daylight next morning the town of Louisiana, Missouri, a sleepy village in my day, but a brisk railway centre now; however, all the towns out there are railway centres now. I could not clearly recognize the place. This seemed odd to me, for when I retired from the rebel army in '61 I retired upon Louisiana in good order; at least in good enough order for a person who had not yet learned how to retreat according to the rules of war, and had to trust to native genius. It seemed to me that for a first attempt at a retreat it was not badly done. I had done no advancing in all that campaign that was at all equal to it.

There was a railway bridge across the river here well sprinkled with glowing lights, and a very beautiful sight it was.

At seven in the morning we reached Hannibal, Missouri, where my boyhood was spent. I had had a glimpse of it fifteen years ago, and another glimpse six years earlier, but both were so brief that they hardly counted. The only notion of the town that remained in my mind was the memory of it as I had known it when I first quitted it twenty-nine years ago. That picture of it was still as clear and vivid to me as a photograph. I stepped ashore with the feeling of one who returns out of a dead-and-gone generation. I had a sort of realizing sense of what the Bastille prisoners must have felt when they used to come out and look upon Paris after years of captivity, and note how curiously the familiar and the strange were mixed together before them. I saw the new houses—saw them plainly enough—but they did not affect the older picture in my mind, for through their solid bricks and mortar I saw the vanished houses, which had formerly stood there, with perfect distinctness.

It was Sunday morning, and everybody was abed yet. So I passed through the vacant streets, still seeing the town as it was, and not as it is, and recognizing and metaphorically shaking hands with a hundred familiar objects which no longer exist; and finally climbed Holiday's Hill to get a comprehensive view. The whole town lay spread out below me then, and I could mark and fix every locality, every detail. Naturally, I was a good deal moved. I said, "Many of the people I once knew in this tranquil refuge of my childhood are now in heaven; some, I trust, are in the other place."

The things about me and before me made me feel like a boy again—convinced me that I was a boy again, and that I had simply been dreaming an unusually long dream; but my reflections spoiled all that; for they forced me to say, "I see fifty old houses down yonder, into each of which I could enter and find either a man or a woman who was a baby or unborn when I noticed those houses last, or a grandmother who was a plump young bride at that time."

From this vantage ground the extensive view up and down the river, and wide over the wooded expanses of Illinois, is very beautiful,—one of the most beautiful on the Mississippi, I think; which is a hazardous remark to make, for the eight hundred miles of river between St. Louis and St. Paul afford an unbroken succession of lovely pictures. It may be that my affection for the one in question biases my judgment in its favor; I cannot say as to that. No matter, it was satisfyingly beautiful to me, and it had this advantage over all the other friends whom I was about to greet again: it had suffered no change; it was as young and fresh and comely and gracious as ever it had been; whereas, the faces of the others would be old, and scarred with the campaigns of life, and marked with their griefs and defeats, and would give me no upliftings of spirit.

An old gentleman, out on an early morning walk, came along, and we discussed the weather, and then drifted into other matters. I could not remember his face. He said he had been living here twenty-eight years. So he had come after my time, and I had never seen him before. I asked him various questions; first about a mate of mine in Sunday school—what became of him?

"He graduated with honor in an Eastern college, wandered off into the world somewhere, succeeded at nothing, passed out of knowledge and memory years ago, and is supposed to have gone to the dogs."

"He was bright, and promised well when he was a boy."

"Yes, but the thing that happened is what became of it all."

I asked after another lad, altogether the brightest in our village school when I was a boy.

"He, too, was graduated with honors, from an Eastern college; but life whipped him in every battle, straight along, and he died in one of the Territories, years ago, a defeated man."

I asked after another of the bright boys.

"He is a success, always has been, always will be, I think."

I inquired after a young fellow who came to the town to study for one of the professions when I was a boy.

"He went at something else before he got through—went from medicine to law, or from law to medicine—then to some other new thing; went away for a year, came back with a young wife; fell to drinking, then to gambling behind the door; finally took his wife and two young children to her father's, and went off to Mexico; went from bad to worse, and finally died there, without a cent to buy a shroud, and without a friend to attend the funeral."

"Pity, for he was the best-natured, and most cheery and hopeful young fellow that ever was."

I named another boy.

"Oh, he is all right. Lives here yet; has a wife and children, and is prospering."

Same verdict concerning other boys.

I named three school-girls.

"The first two live here, are married and have children; the other is long ago dead—never married."

I named, with emotion, one of my early sweethearts.

"She is all right. Been married three times; buried two husbands, divorced from the third, and I hear she is getting ready to marry an old fellow out in Colorado somewhere. She's got children scattered around here and there, most everywheres."

The answer to several other inquiries was brief and simple,—

"Killed in the war."

I named another boy.

"Well, now, his case *is* curious! There wasn't a human being in this town but knew that that boy was a perfect chucklehead; perfect dummy;

just a stupid ass, as you may say. Everybody knew it, and everybody said it. Well, if that very boy isn't the first lawyer in the State of Missouri to-day, I'm a Democrat!"

"Is that so?"

"It's actually so. I'm telling you the truth."

"How do you account for it?"

"Account for it? There ain't any accounting for it, except that if you send a damned fool to St. Louis, and you don't tell them he's a damned fool *they'll* never find it out. There's one thing sure—if I had a damned fool I should know what to do with him: ship him to St. Louis—it's the noblest market in the world for that kind of property. Well, when you come to look at it all around, and chew at it and think it over, *don't* it just bang anything you ever heard of?"

"Well, yes, it does seem to. But don't you think maybe it was the Hannibal people who were mistaken about the boy, and not the St. Louis people?"

"Oh, nonsense! The people here have known him from the very cradle—they knew him a hundred times better than the St. Louis idiots *could* have known him. No, if you have got any damned fools that you want to realize on, take my advice—send them to St. Louis."

I mentioned a great number of people whom I had formerly known. Some were dead, some were gone away, some had prospered, some had come to naught; but as regarded a dozen or so of the lot, the answer was comforting:

"Prosperous—live here yet—town littered with their children."

I asked about Miss ——.

"Died in the insane asylum three or four years ago—never was out of it from the time she went in; and was always suffering, too; never got a shred of her mind back."

If he spoke the truth, here was a heavy tragedy, indeed. Thirty-six years in a mad-house, that some young fools might have some fun! I was a small boy, at the time; and I saw those giddy young ladies come tiptoeing into the room where Miss —— sat reading at midnight by a lamp. The girl at the head of the file wore a shroud and a doughface; she crept behind the victim, touched her on the shoulder, and she looked up and screamed, and then fell into convulsions. She did not recover from the fright, but went mad. In these days it seems incredible that people believed in ghosts so short a time ago. But they did.

After asking after such other folk as I could call to mind, I finally inquired about *myself:*

"Oh, he succeeded well enough—another case of damned fool. If they'd sent him to St. Louis, he'd have succeeded sooner."

It was with much satisfaction that I recognized the wisdom of having told this candid gentleman, in the beginning, that my name was Smith.

8. "Cab Substitute," from *Following the Equator* (Hartford, CT: American Publishing Company, 1897).

5

Following the Equator (1897)

Mark Twain concluded his travel-writing career in much the same way as he had begun it, weaving a narrative around a highly publicized journey with a specific itinerary. This farewell tour for America's most popular travel writer produced in *Following the Equator* his most conventionally structured travel book, a fitting bookend to his travel writings. At the same time, many critics have seen in its subdued humor and increasingly cynical outlook a personal revelation for Twain and a watershed for writers who had previously been ignoring or excusing the sinister aspects of imperialist colonialism.

In an ambitious effort to crawl out of financial bankruptcy, Twain departed in July 1895 from his wife's home town, Elmira, New York, and, accompanied by Olivia and their twenty-three-year-old daughter Clara, made an overland lecture trip along the northern border of the United States and then set sail in late August from Vancouver, British Columbia, bound for the South Seas. His main destinations were New Zealand, Australia, India, and South Africa. A year later he would reach England, thoroughly exhausted but with his spirits buoyed by the adoration he had received everywhere. Now he had to produce an account of the journey that would add to the receipts from his numerous lectures and help reduce his indebtedness. He nearly lost the struggle to write a halfway humorous book, as he explained to William Dean Howells in April 1899 after the volume was safely in print: "I wrote my last travel-book in hell; but I let on, the best I could, that it was an excursion through heaven. Some day I will read it, & if its lying cheerfulness fools me, then I shall believe it fooled the reader. How I did loathe that journey around the world!— except the sea-part & India."[1]

Without question Twain's final travel book represented a heroic endeavor in several respects. Journeys around the world by 1895 were no longer the fanciful imaginings of an author like Jules Verne, who had written about such a tour miraculously taking only eighty days. In Mark Twain's real-life version the journey required twelve months, but the feat none-theless remained a vast enterprise with the absolute certainty of tangled problems with routes, schedules, lodging, meals, and baggage. However, Twain counted on the essential novelty of the undertaking as one of the attention-getting aspects of his ambitious scheme. Added to that was the appeal of this being his "farewell" lecture tour. He also had the advan-tage of being photographed at various moments by one of the new Kodak portable cameras that would become so popular in the coming decades; his American lecture agent James B. Pond started him off on the cross-country portion of his trip by snapping pictures of Twain and his entou-rage at nearly every stop. Twain's courageous resolve showed through in his agreeing to the strain of the venture at sixty in the days when that was considered an advanced age. But this urgent need for substantial funds drove Twain to forgo the comforts of his family's Hartford home and their summer retreat, Quarry Farm in Elmira, New York, leave behind two of his daughters, Susy and Jean, and place himself at the mercy of the railroads, steamships, and carriages that would hurl himself, his wife, and his daughter into a lengthy orbit around the globe.

The actual composition of the travel book itself amounted to another act of supreme fortitude. The Clemenses' eldest daughter Susy died un-expectedly in the summer of 1896, after the travelers had reached London and were preparing to sail home, and Twain, with a heavy heart and self-recriminations, turned to his promised travel book as both a means of fi-nancial salvation and a form of grief therapy. Little wonder that the book is tinged with a new kind of biting irony.

In addition to concluding with this family tragedy, Twain's long jour-ney had exposed him to first-hand sights and sounds of the workings of colonialism, and his eyes were opened as never before to the amount of injustice and tyranny existing in the world as the twentieth century ap-proached. Even his awe at the grandeur and immensity of India could not blind him to the inequities he saw perpetrated there, and the history of the treatment of aboriginals in Australia and New Zealand nauseated him. European settlers warred against each other in South Africa, while African natives labored without any hope of ownership. He came back from this educational experience a changed man and a darker writer, and his daughter's death only added to his sense of rage at the futility of so much of humankind's idealistic assumptions and blind indifference.

This is not to say that Twain's sense of humor entirely forsook him as he recalled his trip and highlighted its incidents. The passages excerpted here offer evidence of his love of the satiric twist, the amusing jab, and the occasional joke on the author. *Following the Equator* deserves to be better known than it is, but apparently the subject matter—travel to foreign climes in a wide swath around the planet Earth—strikes many readers as daunting and presumably dated. Such skeptics are denying themselves part of the joy of knowing the complete Mark Twain.

Note

1. *Mark Twain-Howells Letters: The Correspondence of Samuel L. Clemens and William D. Howells, 1872–1910*, ed. Henry Nash Smith and William M. Gibson (Cambridge: Belknap/Harvard UP, 1960), 690.

From FOLLOWING THE EQUATOR

[Bombay, Chapter 38]

EVENING—*14th.* Sailed in the *Rosetta.* This is a poor old ship, and ought to be insured and sunk. As in the *Oceana,* just so here: everybody dresses for dinner; they make it a sort of pious duty. These fine and formal costumes are a rather conspicuous contrast to the poverty and shabbiness of the surroundings . . . . If you want a slice of a lime at four o'clock tea, you must sign an order on the bar. Limes cost 14 cents a barrel.

January 18th. We have been running up the Arabian Sea, lately. Closing up on Bombay now, and due to arrive this evening.

January 20th. Bombay! A bewitching place, a bewildering place, an enchanting place—the Arabian Nights come again! It is a vast city; contains about a million inhabitants. Natives, they are, with a slight sprinkling of white people—not enough to have the slightest modifying effect upon the massed dark complexion of the public. It is winter here, yet the weather is the divine weather of June, and the foliage is the fresh and heavenly foliage of June. There is a rank of noble great shade trees across the way from the hotel, and under them sit groups of picturesque natives of both sexes;

204 / Mark Twain on the Move

and the juggler in his turban is there with his snakes and his magic; and all day long the cabs and the multitudinous varieties of costumes flock by. It does not seem as if one could ever get tired of watching this moving show, this shining and shifting spectacle. . . . In the great bazar the pack and jam of natives was marvelous, the sea of rich-colored turbans and draperies an inspiring sight, and the quaint and showy Indian architecture was just the right setting for it. Toward sunset another show; this is the drive around the sea-shore to Malabar Point, where Lord Sandhurst, the Governor of the Bombay Presidency, lives. Parsee palaces all along the first part of the drive; and past them all the world is driving; the private carriages of wealthy Englishmen and natives of rank are manned by a driver and three footmen in stunning oriental liveries—two of these turbaned statues standing up behind, as fine as monuments. Sometimes even the public carriages have this superabundant crew, slightly modified—one to drive, one to sit by and see it done, and one to stand up behind and yell—yell when there is anybody in the way, and for practice when there isn't. It all helps to keep up the liveliness and augment the general sense of swiftness and energy and confusion and pow-wow.

In the region of Scandal Point—felicitous name—where there are handy rocks to sit on and a noble view of the sea on the one hand, and on the other the passing and repassing whirl and tumult of gay carriages, are great groups of comfortably-off Parsee women—perfect flower-beds of brilliant color, a fascinating spectacle. Tramp, tramp, tramping along the road, in singles, couples, groups, and gangs, you have the working-man and the working-woman—but not clothed like ours. Usually the man is a nobly-built great athlete, with not a rag on but his loin-handkerchief; his color a deep dark brown, his skin satin, his rounded muscles knobbing it as if it had eggs under it. Usually the woman is a slender and shapely creature, as erect as a lightning-rod, and she has but one thing on—a bright-colored piece of stuff which is wound about her head and her body down nearly half-way to her knees, and which clings like her own skin. Her legs and feet are bare, and so are her arms, except for her fanciful bunches of loose silver rings on her ankles and on her arms. She has jewelry bunched on the side of her nose also, and showy cluster-rings on her toes. When she undresses for bed she takes off her jewelry, I suppose. If she took off anything more she would catch cold. As a rule she has a large shiney brass water jar of graceful shape on her head, and one of her naked arms curves up and the hand holds it there. She is so straight, so erect, and she steps with such style, and such easy grace and dignity; and her curved arm and her brazen jar are such a help to the picture—indeed, our working-women cannot begin with her as a road-decoration.

It is all color, bewitching color, enchanting color—everywhere—all around—all the way around the curving great opaline bay clear to Government House, where the turbaned big native *chuprassies* stand grouped in state at the door in their robes of fiery red, and do most properly and stunningly finish up the splendid show and make it theatrically complete. I wish I were a chuprassy.

This is indeed India! the land of dreams and romance, of fabulous wealth and fabulous poverty, of splendor and rags, of palaces and hovels, of famine and pestilence, of genii and giants and Aladdin lamps, of tigers and elephants, the cobra and the jungle, the country of a hundred nations and a hundred tongues, of a thousand religions and two million gods, cradle of the human race, birthplace of human speech, mother of history, grandmother of legend, great-grandmother of tradition, whose yesterdays bear date with the mouldering antiquities of the rest of the nations—the one sole country under the sun that is endowed with an imperishable interest for alien prince and alien peasant, for lettered and ignorant, wise and fool, rich and poor, bond and free, the one land that *all* men desire to see, and having seen once, by even a glimpse, would not give that glimpse for the shows of all the rest of the globe combined.

Even now, after the lapse of a year, the delirium of those days in Bombay has not left me, and I hope never will. It was all new, no detail of it hackneyed. And India did not wait for morning, it began at the hotel—straight away. The lobbies and halls were full of turbaned, and fez'd and embroidered, cap'd, and barefooted, and cotton-clad dark natives, some of them rushing about, others at rest squatting, or sitting on the ground; some of them chattering with energy, others still and dreamy; in the dining-room every man's own private native servant standing behind his chair, and dressed for a part in the Arabian Nights.

Our rooms were high up, on the front. A white man—he was a burly German—went up with us, and brought three natives along to see to arranging things. About fourteen others followed in procession, with the hand-baggage; each carried an article—and only one; a bag, in some cases, in other cases less. One strong native carried my overcoat, another a parasol, another a box of cigars, another a novel, and the last man in the procession had no load but a fan. It was all done with earnestness and sincerity, there was not a smile in the procession from the head of it to the tail of it. Each man waited patiently, tranquilly, in no sort of hurry, till one of us found time to give him a copper, then he bent his head reverently, touched his forehead with his fingers, and went his way. They seemed a soft and gentle race, and there was something both winning and touching about their demeanor.

There was a vast glazed door which opened upon the balcony. It needed closing, or cleaning, or something, and a native got down on his knees and went to work at it. He seemed to be doing it well enough, but perhaps he wasn't, for the burly German put on a look that betrayed dissatisfaction, then without *explaining* what was wrong, gave the native a brisk cuff on the jaw and *then* told him where the defect was. It seemed such a shame to do that before us all. The native took it with meekness, saying nothing, and not showing in his face or manner any resentment. I had not seen the like of this for fifty years. It carried me back to my boyhood, and flashed upon me the forgotten fact that this was the *usual* way of explaining one's desires to a slave. I was able to remember that the method seemed right and natural to me in those days, I being born to it and unaware that elsewhere there were other methods; but I was also able to remember that those unresented cuffings made me sorry for the victim and ashamed for the punisher. My father was a refined and kindly gentleman, very grave, rather austere, of rigid probity, a sternly just and upright man, albeit he attended no church and never spoke of religious matters, and had no part nor lot in the pious joys of his Presbyterian family, nor ever seemed to suffer from this deprivation. He laid his hand upon me in punishment only twice in his life, and then not heavily; once for telling him a lie—which surprised me, and showed me how unsuspicious he was, for that was not my maiden effort. He punished me those two times only, and never any other member of the family at all; yet every now and then he cuffed our harmless slave boy, Lewis, for trifling little blunders and awkwardnesses. My father had passed his life among the slaves from his cradle up, and his cuffings proceeded from the custom of the time, not from his nature. When I was ten years old I saw a man fling a lump of iron-ore at a slave-man in anger, for merely doing something awkwardly—as if that were a crime. It bounded from the man's skull, and the man fell and never spoke again. He was dead in an hour. I knew the man had a right to kill his slave if he wanted to, and yet it seemed a pitiful thing and somehow wrong, though why wrong I was not deep enough to explain if I had been asked to do it. Nobody in the village approved of that murder, but of course no one said much about it.

It is curious—the space-annihilating power of thought. For just one second, all that goes to make the *me* in me was in a Missourian village, on the other side of the globe, vividly seeing again these forgotten pictures of fifty years ago, and wholly unconscious of all things but just those; and in the next second I was back in Bombay, and that kneeling native's smitten cheek was not done tingling yet! Back to boyhood—fifty years; back to age again, another fifty; and a flight equal to the circumference of the globe—all in two seconds by the watch!

Some natives—I don't remember how many—went into my bedroom, now, and put things to rights and arranged the mosquito-bar, and I went to bed to nurse my cough. It was about nine in the evening. What a state of things! For three hours the yelling and shouting of natives in the hall continued, along with the velvety patter of their swift bare feet—what a racket it was! They were yelling orders and messages down three flights. Why, in the matter of noise it amounted to a riot, an insurrection, a revolution. And then there were other noises mixed up with these and at intervals tremendously accenting them—roofs falling in, I judged, windows smashing, persons being murdered, crows squawking, and deriding, and cursing, canaries screeching, monkeys jabbering, macaws blaspheming, and every now and then fiendish bursts of laughter and explosions of dynamite. By midnight I had suffered all the different kinds of shocks there are, and knew that I could never more be disturbed by them, either isolated or in combination. Then came peace—stillness deep and solemn—and lasted till five.

Then it all broke loose again. And who re-started it? The Bird of Birds—the Indian crow. I came to know him well, by and by, and be infatuated with him. I suppose he is the hardest lot that wears feathers. Yes, and the cheerfulest, and the best satisfied with himself. He never arrived at what he is by any careless process, or any sudden one; he is a work of art, and "art is long"; he is the product of immemorial ages, and of deep calculation; one can't make a bird like that in a day. He has been re-incarnated more times than Shiva; and he has kept a sample of each incarnation, and

fused it into his constitution. In the course of his evolutionary promo-
tions, his sublime march toward ultimate perfection, he has been a gam-
bler, a low comedian, a dissolute priest, a fussy woman, a blackguard, a
scoffer, a liar, a thief, a spy, an informer, a trading politician, a swindler, a
professional hypocrite, a patriot for cash, a reformer, a lecturer, a lawyer,
a conspirator, a rebel, a royalist, a democrat, a practicer and propagator of
irreverence, a meddler, an intruder, a busybody, an infidel, and a wallower
in sin for the mere love of it. The strange result, the incredible result, of
this patient accumulation of all damnable traits is, that he does not know
what care is, he does not know what sorrow is, he does not know what re-
morse is, his life is one long thundering ecstasy of happiness, and he will
go to his death untroubled, knowing that he will soon turn up again as an
author or something, and be even more intolerably capable and comfortable than ever he was before.

In his straddling wide forward-step, and his springy sidewise series of
hops, and his impudent air, and his cunning way of canting his head to
one side upon occasion, he reminds one of the American blackbird. But
the sharp resemblances stop there. He is much bigger than the blackbird; and he lacks the blackbird's trim and slender and beautiful build
and shapely beak; and of course his sober garb of gray and rusty black is
a poor and humble thing compared with the splendid lustre of the blackbird's metallic sables and shifting and flashing bronze glories. The blackbird is a perfect gentleman, in deportment and attire, and is not noisy, I
believe, except when holding religious services and political conventions
in a tree; but this Indian sham Quaker is just a rowdy, and is always noisy
when awake—always chaffing, scolding, scoffing, laughing, ripping, and
cursing, and carrying on about something or other. I never saw such a bird
for delivering opinions. Nothing escapes him; he notices everything that
happens, and brings out his opinion about it, particularly if it is a matter that is none of his business. And it is never a mild opinion, but always
violent—violent and profane—the presence of ladies does not affect him.
His opinions are not the outcome of reflection, for he never thinks about
anything, but heaves out the opinion that is on top in his mind, and which
is often an opinion about some quite different thing and does not fit the
case. But that is his way; his main idea is to get out an opinion, and if he
stopped to think he would lose chances.

I suppose he has no enemies among men. The whites and Mohammedans never seemed to molest him; and the Hindoos, because of their religion, never take the life of any creature, but spare even the snakes and tigers and fleas and rats. If I sat on one end of the balcony, the crows would gather on the railing at the other end and talk about me; and edge closer, little by little, till I could almost reach them; and they would sit there, in the most unabashed way, and talk about my clothes, and my hair, and my complexion, and probable character and vocation and politics, and how I came to be in India, and what I had been doing, and how many days I had got for it, and how I had happened to go unhanged so long, and when would it probably come off, and might there be more of my sort where I came from, and when would *they* be hanged,—and so on, and so on, until I could not longer endure the embarrassment of it; then I would shoo them away, and they would circle around in the air a little while, laughing and deriding and mocking, and presently settle on the rail and do it all over again.

They were very sociable when there was anything to eat—oppressively so. With a little encouragement they would come in and light on the table and help me eat my breakfast; and once when I was in the other room and they found themselves alone, they carried off everything they could lift; and they were particular to choose things which they could make no use of after they got them. In India their number is beyond estimate, and their noise is in proportion. I suppose they cost the country more than the government does; yet that is not a light matter. Still, they pay; their company pays; it would sadden the land to take their cheerful voice out of it.

[Bombay, from Chapter 39]

You soon find your long-ago dreams of India rising in a sort of vague and luscious moonlight above the horizon-rim of your opaque consciousness, and softly lighting up a thousand forgotten details which were parts of a vision that had once been vivid to you when you were a boy, and steeped your spirit in tales of the East. The barbaric gorgeousnesses, for instance; and the princely titles, the sumptuous titles, the sounding titles,—how good they taste in the mouth! The Nizam of Hyderabad; the Maharajah of Travancore; the Nabob of Jubbelpore; the Begum of Bhopal; the Nawab of Mysore; the Ranee of Gulnare; the Ahkoond of Swat's; the Rao of Rohilkund; the Gaikwar of Baroda. Indeed, it is a country that runs richly to name. The great god Vishnu has 108—108 special ones—

108 peculiarly holy ones—names just for Sunday use only. I learned the whole of Vishnu's 108 by heart once, but they wouldn't stay; I don't remember any of them now but John W.

And the romances connected with those princely native houses—to this day they are always turning up, just as in the old, old times. They were sweating out a romance in an English court in Bombay a while before we were there. In this case a native prince, 16½ years old, who has been enjoying his titles and dignities and estates unmolested for fourteen years, is suddenly haled into court on the charge that he is rightfully no prince at all, but a pauper peasant; that the real prince died when two and one-half years old; that the death was concealed, and a peasant child smuggled into the royal cradle, and that this present incumbent was that smuggled substitute. This is the very material that so many oriental tales have been made of.

The case of that great prince, the Gaikwar of Baroda, is a reversal of the theme. When that throne fell vacant, no heir could be found for some time, but at last one was found in the person of a peasant child who was making mud pies in a village street, and having an innocent good time. But his pedigree was straight; he was the true prince, and he has reigned ever since, with none to dispute his right.

Lately there was another hunt for an heir to another princely house, and one was found who was circumstanced about as the Gaikwar had been. His fathers were traced back, in humble life, along a branch of the ancestral tree to the point where it joined the stem fourteen generations ago, and his heirship was thereby squarely established. The tracing was done by means of the records of one of the great Hindoo shrines, where princes on pilgrimage record their names and the date of their visit. This is to keep the prince's religious account straight, and his spiritual person safe; but the record has the added value of keeping the pedigree authentic, too.

When I think of Bombay now, at this distance of time, I seem to have a kaleidoscope at my eye; and I hear the clash of the glass bits as the splendid figures change, and fall apart, and flash into new forms, figure after figure, and with the birth of each new form I feel my skin crinkle and my nerve-web tingle with a new thrill of wonder and delight. These remembered pictures float past me in a sequence of contracts; following the same order always, and always whirling by and disappearing with the swiftness of a dream, leaving me with the sense that the actuality was the experience of an hour, at most, whereas it really covered days, I think.

[Bombay, from Chapter 41]

When we arrived at the bungalow, the large hall on the ground floor was already about full, and carriages were still flowing into the grounds. The company present made a fine show, an exhibition of human fireworks, so to speak, in the matters of costume and comminglings of brilliant color. The variety of form noticeable in the display of turbans was remarkable. We were told that the explanation of this was, that this Jain delegation was drawn from many parts of India, and that each man wore the turban that was in vogue in his own region. This diversity of turbans made a beautiful effect.

I could have wished to start a rival exhibition there, of Christian hats and clothes. I would have cleared one side of the room of its Indian splendors and repacked the space with Christians drawn from America, England, and the Colonies, dressed in the hats and habits of now, and of twenty and forty and fifty years ago. It would have been a hideous exhibition, a thoroughly devilish spectacle. Then there would have been the added disadvantage of the white complexion. It is not an unbearably unpleasant complexion when it keeps to itself, but when it comes into competition with masses of brown and black the fact is betrayed that it is endurable only because we are used to it. Nearly all black and brown skins are beautiful, but a beautiful white skin is rare. How rare, one may learn by walking down a street in Paris, New York, or London on a week-day—particularly an unfashionable street—and keeping count of the satisfactory complexions encountered in the course of a mile. Where dark complexions are massed, they make the whites look bleached-out, unwholesome, and sometimes frankly ghastly. I could notice this as a boy, down South in the slavery days before the war. The splendid black satin skin of the South African Zulus of Durban seemed to me to come very close to perfection. I can see those Zulus yet—'ricksha athletes waiting in front of the hotel for custom; handsome and intensely black creatures, moderately clothed in loose summer stuffs whose snowy whiteness made the black all the blacker by contrast. Keeping that group in my mind, I can compare those complexions with the white ones which are streaming past this London window now:

A lady. Complexion, new parchment.
Another lady. Complexion, old parchment.
Another. Pink and white, very fine.
Man. Grayish skin, with purple areas.
Man. Unwholesome fish-belly skin.
Girl. Sallow face, sprinkled with freckles.
Old woman. Face whitey-gray.
Young butcher. Face a general red flush.
Jaundiced man—mustard yellow.
Elderly lady. Colorless skin, with two conspicuous moles.
Elderly man—a drinker. Boiled-cauliflower nose in a flabby face veined
    with purple crinklings.
Healthy young gentleman. Fine fresh complexion.
Sick young man. His face a ghastly white.

No end of people whose skins are dull and characterless modifications of the tint which we miscall white. Some of these faces are pimply; some exhibit other signs of diseased blood; some show scars of a tint out of a harmony with the surrounding shades of color. The white man's complexion makes no concealments. It can't. It seemed to have been designed as a catch-all for everything that can damage it. Ladies have to paint it, and powder it, and cosmetic it, and diet it with arsenic, and enamel it, and be always enticing it, and persuading it, and pestering it, and fussing at it, to make it beautiful; and they do not succeed. But these efforts show what they think of the natural complexion, as distributed. As distributed it needs these helps. The complexion which they try to counterfeit is one which nature restricts to the few—to the very few. To ninety-nine persons she gives a bad complexion, to the hundredth a good one. The hundredth can keep it—how long? Ten years, perhaps.

The advantage is with the Zulu, I think. He starts with a beautiful complexion, and it will last him through. And as for the Indian brown—firm, smooth, blemishless, pleasant and restful to the eye, afraid of no color, harmonizing with all colors and adding a grace to them all—I think there is no sort of chance for the average white complexion against that rich and perfect tint.

To return to the bungalow. The most gorgeous costumes present were worn by some children. They seemed to blaze, so bright were the colors, and so brilliant the jewels strung over the rich materials. These children were professional nautch-dancers, and looked like girls, but they were boys. They got up by ones and twos and fours, and danced and sang to an accompaniment of weird music. Their posturings and gesturings were elaborate and graceful, but their voices were stringently raspy and unpleasant, and there was a good deal of monotony about the tune.

By and by there was a burst of shouts and cheers outside and the prince with his train entered in fine dramatic style. He was a stately man, he was ideally costumed, and fairly festooned with ropes of gems; some of the ropes were of pearls, some were of uncut great emeralds—emeralds renowned in Bombay for their quality and value. Their size was marvelous, and enticing to the eye, those rocks. A boy—a princeling—was with the prince, and he also was a radiant exhibition.

The ceremonies were not tedious. The prince strode to his throne with the port and majesty—and the sternness—of a Julius Caesar coming to receive and receipt for a back-country kingdom and have it over and get out, and no fooling. There was a throne for the young prince, too, and the two sat there, side by side, with their officers grouped at either hand and most accurately and creditably reproducing the pictures which one sees in the books—pictures which people in the prince's line of business have been furnishing ever since Solomon received the Queen of Sheba and showed her his things. The chief of the Jain delegation read his paper of congratulations, then pushed it into a beautifully engraved silver cylinder, which was delivered with ceremony into the prince's hands and at once delivered by him without ceremony into the hands of an officer. I will copy the address here. It is interesting, as showing what an Indian prince's subject may have opportunity to thank him for in these days of modern English rule, as contrasted with what his ancestor would have given them opportunity to thank him for a century and a half ago—the days of freedom unhampered by English interference. A century and a half ago an address of thanks could have been put into small space. It would have thanked the prince—

1. For not slaughtering too many of his people upon mere caprice;
2. For not stripping them bare by sudden and arbitrary tax levies, and bringing famine upon them;
3. For not upon empty pretext destroying the rich and seizing their property;
4. For not killing, blinding, imprisoning, or banishing the relatives of the royal house to protect the throne from possible plots;
5. For not betraying the subject secretly, for a bribe, into the hands of bands of professional Thugs, to be murdered and robbed in the prince's back lot.

Those were rather common princely industries in the old times, but they and some others of a harsh sort ceased long ago under English rule. Better industries have taken their place, as this Address from the Jain community will show:

"Your Highness,—We the undersigned members of the Jain community of Bombay have the pleasure to approach your Highness with the expression of our heartfelt congratulations on the recent conference on your Highness of the Knighthood of the Most Exalted Order of the Star of India. Ten years ago we had the pleasure and privilege of welcoming your Highness to this city under circumstances which have made a memorable epoch in the history of your State, for had it not been for a generous and reasonable spirit that your Highness displayed in the negotiations between the Palitana Durbar and the Jain community, the conciliatory spirit that animated our people could not have borne fruit. That was the first step in your Highness's administration, and it fitly elicited the praise of the Jain community, and of the Bombay Government. A decade of your Highness's administration, combined with the abilities, training, and acquirements that your Highness brought to bear upon it, has justly earned for your Highness the unique and honourable distinction—the Knighthood of the Most Exalted Order of the Star of India, which we understand your Highness is the first to enjoy among Chiefs of your Highness's rank and standing. And we assure your Highness that for this mark of honour that has been conferred on you by Her Most Gracious Majesty, the Queen-Empress, we feel no less proud than your Highness. Establishment of commercial factories, schools, hospitals, etc., by your Highness in your State has marked your Highness's career during these ten years, and we trust that your Highness will be spared to rule over your people with wisdom and foresight, and foster the many reforms that your Highness has been pleased to introduce in your State. We again offer your Highness our warmest felicitations for the honour that has been conferred on you. We beg to remain your Highness's obedient servants."

Factories, schools, hospitals, reforms. The prince propagates that kind of things in the modern times, and gets knighthood and guns for it.

After the address the prince responded with snap and brevity; spoke a moment with half a dozen guests in English, and with an official or two in a native tongue; then the garlands were distributed as usual, and the function ended.

[Allahabad, from Chapter 49]

I was up at dawn, the next morning. In India the tourist's servant does not sleep in a room in the hotel, but rolls himself up head and ears in his blanket and stretches himself on the veranda, across the front of his master's door, and spends the night there. I don't believe anybody's servant occupies a room. Apparently, the bungalow servants sleep on the veranda; it is roomy, and goes all around the house. I speak of men-servants; I saw none of the other sex. I think there are none, except child-nurses. I was up at dawn, and walked around the veranda, past the rows of sleepers. In front of one door a Hindoo servant was squatting, waiting for his master to call him. He had polished the yellow shoes and placed them by the door, and now he had nothing to do but wait. It was freezing cold, but there he was, as motionless as a sculptured image, and as patient. It troubled me. I wanted to say to him, "Don't crouch there like that and freeze; nobody requires it of you; stir around and get warm." But I hadn't the words. I thought of saying *jeldy jow*, but I couldn't remember what it meant, so I didn't say it. I knew another phrase, but it wouldn't come to my mind. I moved on, purposing to dismiss him from my thoughts, but his bare legs and bare feet kept him there. They kept drawing me back from the sunny side to a point whence I could see him. At the end of an hour he had not changed his attitude in the least degree. It was a curious and impressive exhibition of meekness and patience, or fortitude or indifference, I did not know which. But it worried me, and it was spoiling my morning. In fact, it spoiled two hours of it quite thoroughly. I quitted this vicinity, then, and left him to punish himself as much as he might want to. But up to that time the man had not changed his attitude a hair. He will always remain with me, I suppose; his figure never grows vague in my memory. Whenever I read of Indian resignation, Indian patience under wrongs, hardships, and misfortunes, he comes before me. He becomes a personi-fication, and stands for India in trouble. And for untold ages India in trouble has been pursued with the very remark which I was going to utter but didn't, because its meaning had slipped me: *Jeldy jow!* ("Come, shove along!") Why, it was the very thing.

In the early brightness we made a long drive out to the Fort. Part of the way was beautiful. It led under stately trees and through groups of native houses and by the usual village well, where the picturesque gangs are always flocking to and fro and laughing and chattering; and this time brawny men were deluging their bronze bodies with the limpid water, and making a refreshing and enticing show of it; enticing, for the sun was al-ready transacting business, firing India up for the day. There was plenty of this early bathing going on, for it was getting toward breakfast time, and with an unpurified body the Hindoo must not eat.

Then we struck into the hot plain, and found the roads crowded with pilgrims of both sexes, for one of the great religious fairs of India was be-ing held, just beyond the Fort, at the junction of the sacred rivers, the Ganges and the Jumna. Three sacred rivers, I should have said, for there is a subterranean one. Nobody has seen it, but that doesn't signify. The fact that it is there is enough. These pilgrims had come from all over India; some of them had been months on the way, plodding patiently along in the heat and dust, worn, poor, hungry, but supported and sustained by an unwavering faith and belief; they were supremely happy and content, now; their full and sufficient reward was at hand; they were going to be cleansed from every vestige of sin and corruption by these holy waters which make utterly pure whatsoever thing they touch, even the dead and rotten. It is wonderful, the power of a faith like that, that can make mul-titudes upon multitudes of the old and weak and the young and frail en-ter without hesitation or complaint upon such incredible journeys and endure the resultant miseries without repining. It is done in love, or it is done in fear; I do not know which it is. No matter what the impulse is, the act born of it is beyond imagination marvelous to our kind of people, the cold whites. There are choice great natures among us that could exhibit the equivalent of this prodigious self-sacrifice, but the rest of us know that we should not be equal to anything approaching it. Still, we all talk self-sacrifice, and this makes me hope that we are large enough to honor it in the Hindoo.

Two millions of natives arrive at this fair every year. How many start, and die on the road, from age and fatigue and disease and scanty nourishment, and how many die on the return, from the same causes, no one knows; but the tale is great, one may say enormous. Every twelfth year is held to be a year of peculiar grace; a greatly augmented volume of pilgrims results then. The twelfth year has held this distinction since the remotest times, it is said. It is said also that there is to be but one more twelfth year—for the Ganges. After that, that holiest of all sacred rivers will cease to be holy, and will be abandoned by the pilgrim for many centuries; how many, the wise men have not stated. At the end of that interval it will become holy again. Meantime, the data will be arranged by those people who have charge of all such matters, the great chief Brahmins. It will be like shutting down a mint. At a first glance it looks most unbrahminically uncommercial, but I am not disturbed, being soothed and tranquilized by their reputation. "Brer fox he lay low," as Uncle Remus says; and at the judicious time he will spring something on the Indian public which will show that he was not financially asleep when he took the Ganges out of the market.

Great numbers of the natives along the roads were bringing away holy water from the rivers. They would carry it far and wide in India and sell it. Tavernier, the French traveler (17th century), notes that Ganges water is often given at weddings, "each guest receiving a cup or two, according to the liberality of the host; sometimes 2,000 or 3,000 rupees' worth of it is consumed at a wedding."

The Fort is a huge old structure, and has had a large experience in religions. In its great court stands a monolith which was placed there more than 2,000 years ago to preach Budhism by its pious inscription; the Fort was built three centuries ago by a Mohammedan Emperor—a resanctification of the place in the interest of *that* religion. There is a Hindoo temple, too, with subterranean ramifications stocked with shrines and idols; and now the Fort belongs to the English, it contains a Christian Church. Insured in all the companies.

From the lofty ramparts one has a fine view of the sacred rivers. They join at that point—the pale blue Jumna, apparently clean and clear, and the muddy Ganges, dull yellow and not clean. On a long curved spit between the rivers, towns of tents were visible, with a multitude of fluttering pennons, and a mighty swarm of pilgrims. It was a troublesome place to get down to, and not a quiet place when you arrived; but it was interesting. There was a world of activity and turmoil and noise, partly religious, partly commercial; for the Mohammedans were there to curse and sell, and the Hindoos to buy and pray. It is a fair as well as a religious festival. Crowds were bathing, praying, and drinking the purifying waters, and many sick pilgrims had come long journeys in palanquins to be healed of their maladies by a bath; or if that might not be, then to die on the blessed banks and so make sure of heaven. There were fakeers in plenty, with their bodies dusted over with ashes and their long hair caked together with cow-dung; for the cow is holy and so is the rest of it; so holy that the good Hindoo peasant frescoes the walls of his hut with this refuse, and also constructs ornamental figures out of it for the gracing of his dirt floor. There were seated families, fearfully and wonderfully painted, who by attitude and grouping represented the families of certain great gods. There was a holy man who sat naked by the day and by the week on a cluster of iron spikes, and did not seem to mind it; and another holy man, who stood all day holding his withered arms motionless aloft, and was said to have been doing it for years. All of these performers have a cloth on the ground beside them for the reception of contributions, and even the poorest of the people give a trifle and hope that the sacrifice will be blessed to him. At last came a procession of naked holy people marching by and chanting, and I wrenched myself away.

[Lahore and Delhi, from Chapter 60]

We wandered contentedly around here and there in India; to Lahore, among other places, where the Lieutenant-Governor lent me an elephant. This hospitality stands out in my experiences in a stately isolation. It was a fine elephant, affable, gentlemanly, educated, and I was not afraid of it. I even rode it with confidence through the crowded lanes of the native city, where it scared all the horses out of their senses, and where children were always just escaping its feet. It took the middle of the road in a fine independent way, and left it to the world to get out of the way or take the consequences. I am used to being afraid of collisions when I ride or drive, but when one is on top of an elephant that feeling is absent. I could have ridden in comfort through a regiment of runaway teams. I could easily learn to prefer an elephant to any other vehicle, partly because of that immunity from collisions, and partly because of the fine view one has from up there, and partly because of the dignity one feels in that high place, and partly because one can look in at the windows and see what is going on privately among the family. The Lahore horses were used to elephants, but they were rapturously afraid of them just the same. It seemed curious. Perhaps the better they know the elephant the more they respect him in that peculiar way. In our own case we are not afraid of dynamite till we get acquainted with it.

We drifted as far as Rawal Pindi, away up on the Afghan frontier—I think it was the Afghan frontier, but it may have been Hertzegovina—it was around there somewhere—and down again to Delhi, to see the ancient architectural wonders there and in Old Delhi and not describe them, and also to see the scene of the illustrious assault, in the Mutiny days, when the British carried Delhi by storm, one of the marvels of history for impudent daring and immortal valor.

We had a refreshing rest, there in Delhi, in a great old mansion which possessed historical interest. It was built by a rich Englishman who had become orientalized—so much so that he had a zenana. But he was a broad-minded man, and remained so. To please his harem he built a mosque; to please himself he built an English church. That kind of a man will arrive, somewhere. In the Mutiny days the mansion was the British general's headquarters. It stands in a great garden—oriental fashion—and about it are many noble trees. The trees harbor monkeys; and they are monkeys of a watchful and enterprising sort, and not much troubled with fear. They invade the house whenever they get a chance, and carry off everything they don't want. One morning the master of the house was in his bath, and the window was open. Near it stood a pot of yellow paint and a brush. Some monkeys appeared in the window; to scare them away, the gentleman threw his sponge at them. They did not scare at all; they jumped into the room and threw yellow paint all over him from the brush, and drove him out; then they painted the walls and the floor and the tank and the windows and the furniture yellow, and were in the dressing-room painting that when help arrived and routed them.

Two of these creatures came into my room in the early morning, through a window whose shutters I had left open, and when I woke one of them was before the glass brushing his hair, and the other one had my note-book, and was reading a page of humorous notes and crying. I did not mind the one with the hair-brush, but the conduct of the other one hurt me; it hurts me yet. I threw something at him, and that was wrong, for my host had told me that the monkeys were best left alone. They threw everything at me that they could lift, and then went into the bathroom to get some more things, and I shut the door on them.

[Homeward Bound, from Conclusion]

We sailed on the 15th of July in the *Norman*, a beautiful ship, perfectly appointed. The voyage to England occupied a short fortnight, without a stop except at Madeira. A good and restful voyage for tired people, and there were several of us. I seemed to have been lecturing a thousand years, though it was only a twelvemonth, and a considerable number of the others were Reformers who were fagged out with their five months of seclusion in the Pretoria prison.*

Our trip around the earth ended at the Southampton pier, where we embarked thirteen months before. It seemed a fine and large thing to have accomplished—the circumnavigation of this great globe in that little time, and I was privately proud of it. For a moment. Then came one of those vanity-snubbing astronomical reports from the Observatory-people, whereby it appeared that another great body of light had lately flamed up in the remotenesses of space which was traveling at a gait which would enable it to do all that I had done in *a minute and a half.* Human pride is not worth while; there is always something lying in wait to take the wind out of it.

* Twain describes the Johannesburg Reformers and their cause in Chapter 66.

Selected Readings

Beidler, Philip D. "Realistic Style and the Problems of Context in *The Innocents Abroad." American Literature* 52 (1980): 33–49.

Berkove, Lawrence I. "Mark Twain: A Man for All Regions." *A Companion to the Regional Literatures of America.* Ed. Charles L. Crow. Maulden, MA: Blackwell, 2003. 496–512.

———. "No 'Mere Accidental Incidents': *Roughing It* as a Novel." *Mark Twain Annual* 1 (2003): 7–17.

———. "The Two Mark Twains as Tourists." *Literature and Tourism.* Ed. Mike Robinson, Hans Christian Andersen. London: Continuum, 2002. 191–207.

Brazil, John R. "Structure in Mark Twain's Art and Mind: *Life on the Mississippi." Mississippi Quarterly* 34 (1981): 91–112.

Bridgman, Richard. *Traveling in Mark Twain.* Berkeley: U of California P, 1987.

Brodwin, Stanley. "The Useful and Useless River: *Life on the Mississippi* Revisited." *Studies in American Humor* 2 (1976): 196–208.

Cardwell, Guy. "*Life on the Mississippi:* Vulgar Facts and Learned Errors." *ESQ* 29 (1973): 283–93.

A Companion to Mark Twain, ed. Peter Messent and Louis J. Budd. Oxford: Blackwell, 2005.

Cook, Nancy. "Finding His Mark: Twain's *The Innocents Abroad* as a Subscription Book." *Reading Books: Essays on the Material Text and Literature in America.* Ed. Michele Moylan and Lane Stiles. Amherst: U of Massachusetts P, 1996. 151–78.

Dolmestch, Carl. "*Our Famous Guest": Mark Twain in Vienna.* Athens: U of Georgia P, 1992.

Fiedler, Leslie A. "An American Abroad." *Partisan Review* 33 (1966): 77–91.

Florence, Don. *Persona and Humor in Mark Twain's Early Writings.* Columbia: U of Missouri P, 1995.

Frear, Walter Francis. *Mark Twain and Hawaii.* Chicago: Lakeside Press, 1947.

Ganzel, Dewey. *Mark Twain Abroad: The Cruise of the* Quaker City. Chicago: U of Chicago P, 1968.

Gunn, Drewey Wayne. "The Monomythic Structure of *Roughing It." American Literature* 61 (1989): 563–85.

Howe, Lawrence. Afterword. *Life on the Mississippi.* The Oxford Mark Twain. Ed. Shelley Fisher Fishkin. New York: Oxford UP, 1996. 1–18.

Kaplan, Amy. "Imperial Triangles: Mark Twain's Foreign Affairs." *Modern Fiction Studies* 43 (1997): 236–48.

Kaplan, Fred. Afterword. Following the Equator *and Anti-imperialist Essays*. The Oxford Mark Twain. Ed. Shelley Fisher Fishkin. New York: Oxford UP, 1996. 1–16.

Kruse, Horst H. *Mark Twain and* Life on the Mississippi. Amherst: U of Massachusetts P, 1982.

Leonard, James S. Afterword. *A Tramp Abroad*. The Oxford Mark Twain. Ed. Shelley Fisher Fishkin. New York: Oxford UP, 1996. 1–14.

Lowry, Richard S. "Framing the Authentic: The Modern Tourist and *The Innocents Abroad*." *New Orleans Review* 18 (1991): 18–28.

The Mark Twain Encyclopedia, ed. J. K. LeMaster and James D. Wilson. New York: Garland, 1993.

Mark Twain: The Complete Interviews. Ed. Gary Scharnhorst. Tuscaloosa: U of Alabama P, 2006.

McCarthy, Harold T. "Mark Twain's Pilgrim's Progress: *The Innocents Abroad*." *Arizona Quarterly* 26 (1970): 249–58.

McKee, John DeWitt. "*Roughing It* as Retrospective Reporting." *Western American Literature* 5 (1970): 113–19.

Melton, Jeffrey Alan. *Mark Twain, Travel Books, and Tourism*. Tuscaloosa: U of Alabama P, 2002.

Messent, Peter. "Tramps and Tourists: Europe in Mark Twain's *A Tramp Abroad*." *Yearbook of English Studies* 34 (2004): 128–54.

Michelson, Bruce. "Ever Such a Good Time: The Structure of Mark Twain's *Roughing It*." *Dutch Quarterly Review of Anglo-American Letters* 17 (1987): 182–99.

———. "Mark Twain the Tourist: The Form of *The Innocents Abroad*." *American Literature* 49 (1977): 385–98.

Obenzinger, Hilton. *American Palestine: Melville, Twain, and the Holy Land Mania*. Princeton: Princeton UP, 1999.

Overland with Mark Twain: James B. Pond's Photographs and Journal of the North American Lecture Tour of 1895. Ed. Alan Gribben and Nick Karanovich. Elmira, NY: Elmira College, Center for Mark Twain Studies, 1992.

Parsons, Coleman O. "Mark Twain: Traveler in South Africa." *Mississippi Quarterly* 29 (1975): 3–41.

Rassmussen, R. Kent. *Critical Companion to Mark Twain: A Literary Reference to His Life and Work*. 2 vols. New York: Facts on File, 2007.

Regan, Robert. "Mark Twain, 'the Doctor,' and a Guidebook by Dickens." *American Studies* 22 (1981): 35–55.

———. "The Reprobate Elect in *The Innocents Abroad*." *American Literature* 54 (1982): 240–57.

Robinson, Forrest G. "Patterns of Consciousness in *The Innocents Abroad*." *American Literature* 58 (1986): 46–63.

———. "'Seeing the Elephant': Some Perspectives on Mark Twain's *Roughing It*." *American Studies* 21 (1980): 43–64.

Rogers, Franklin R. "The Road to Reality: Burlesque Travel Literature and Mark

Twain's *Roughing It.*" *Literature as Mode of Travel.* Ed. Warner G. Rice. New York: New York Public Library, 1963. 85–98.

Shillingsburg, Miriam Jones. *At Home Abroad: Mark Twain in Australasia.* Jackson: UP of Mississippi, 1988.

Sloane, David E. E. Afterword. *The Innocents Abroad.* The Oxford Mark Twain. Ed. Shelley Fisher Fishkin. New York: Oxford UP, 1996. 1–18.

Steinbrink, Jeffrey. *Getting to be Mark Twain.* Berkeley: U of California P, 1991.

———. "Why the Innocents Went Abroad: Mark Twain and American Tourism in the Late Nineteenth Century." *American Literary Realism* 16 (1983): 278–86.

Walker, Franklin D. *Irreverent Pilgrims: Melville, Browne, and Mark Twain in the Holy Land.* Seattle: U of Washington P, 1974.

Wonham, Henry B. Afterword. *Roughing It.* The Oxford Mark Twain. Ed. Shelley Fisher Fishkin. New York: Oxford UP, 1996. 1–17.

Yothers, Brian. *The Romance of the Holy Land in American Travel Writing, 1790–1876.* Burlington, VT: Ashgate, 2007.

Ziff, Larzer. *Return Passages: Great American Travel Writing, 1780–1910.* New Haven: Yale UP, 2000.

Index

Aboriginals, Australia, 202
Aboriginals, New Zealand, 202
Abraham, biblical, 61
Academy of Music, New York City, 188–89
Achilles, 38
Acropolis, The, 38–41, 43
Adam, biblical, 57, 59, 172
Adam, tomb of, 58
Afghan frontier, 219
Agamemnon, 38
Aladdin, 205
Alkali desert, 85–87
Allahabad, India, 215–17
Alligators, in New Orleans, 189
Alpine horn, 136, 138–40
Alpine scenery, 124, 131, 141, 162–64, 166–67
Alpine sunrises, 133, 135–36, 138–41
Alta California, 1, 111
Alton, Illinois, 195
American flag, 14
American Publishing Company, 1
Arabian Nights, 205
Archbishop of Paris, 12–13
Architecture, American, 186
Architecture, New Orleans, 187–88
Architecture, Southern, 184
Areopagus, Greek, 44
Aristotle, 44
Arkansas, state of, 48–49
Arthur, King, 117
Art lessons, 112–13, 115–17, 162
Asnieres, 14
Athens, Greece, 36, 38–47

Atlantic Monthly, 169
Attica, Greece, 46
Azores, 10, 12

Baalam's ass, 51
Baedeker, Karl, 138, 154
Baldwin I, 60
Balloon voyages, 92
Barber shop, 9–10
Bastille, The, 8, 195
Bathing, Hindu, 216
Baton Rouge, Louisiana, 183–84
Beer, 178
Beirut, 51
Bemis, George, 71
Berlichingen, Gotz von, 115–17, 123
Bethesda, 53
Billiards, 10–11, 99, 173, 176
Birch, Dr., 45
Bixby, Horace, 193
Blondin, 14–15
Bois de Boulogne, 16–17
Bombay, India, 203–215
Bombay, praise for, 205
Boots, 172
Borrowing, literary, 170
Boston, 159–61
Boy, hired, 132–33, 137
Boyhood, in Hannibal, 195–99, 206–07
Braggarts, 6–7
Brahmins, 217
Broom Brigades, 190
Browne, Charles Farrar, 68

Bucksheesh, 53
Buffalo, 69
Bunker Hill Monument, 62
Burns, Robert, 16
Byron, George Gordon, 23

Cable, George Washington, 188
Caesar, Gaius Julius, 30, 213
California climate, 96–98
California flowers, 97–98
California scenery, 94–95
California seasons, 95–96
Calvary, Hill of, 54, 59–60, 62–63
Camels, appetite of, 78–79
Cameras, Kodak, 202
Campfires, 77–78, 89, 93
Can-can dance, 15–16
Canova, Antonio, 23
Card games, 92
Carracci, 18
Carson City, Nevada, 68, 70, 94
Cathedral of Notre Dame, 11–13
Cats, 52–53, 99
Cemeteries, New Orleans, 185, 187, 189
Cenci, Beatrice, 191
Center of the world, 57–58
Centipedes, 101
Chambermaid, labors, 120–121
Chamois, 156
Chamonix, 164, 167
Christ, 17–18
Christ, flagellation of, 55
Christ, mercy of, 50–51, 63
Christian martyrs, 29, 31–32
Church of the Holy Sepulchre, The, 53–54, 56–57, 60–63
City of Baton Rouge, 193
City of Refuge, 103–04
Civil War, American, 67, 182–83, 190–91, 195
Clemens, Clara, 112, 201
Clemens, Jane Lampton, 2
Clemens, Jean, 202
Clemens, John Marshall, 206
Clemens, Olivia Langdon, 112, 169, 201
Clemens, Orion, 67–70
Clemens, Susy, 112; death of, 202–03

Cleopatra, 19
Coffee, 8, 47, 49–50
Coliseum, Roman, 28–32
Colonialism, 202, 206–07,213–16, 219
Columbia, Tennessee, 184
Columbus, Christopher, 33–35
Column of July, 8
Colussus of Rhodes, 37
"Come, Gentle Trembler" (poem), 176
Connecticut, state of, 49
Constantine, Emperor, 54, 59
Constantinople, 38, 47–50, 52
Cotton Exchange, New Orleans, 186
Crows, Indian, 207–09
Crucifixion, The, 53–55, 58–63
Crusades, Christian, 56
Cub pilots, 193

Damascus, 50
Dan, 14
Davis, Jefferson, 21
Dawn, on Mississippi River, 180
Delhi, India, 219
Delmonico's, New York City, 190
Demosthenes, 44
Derby, George Horatio, 98
Desert travel, rigors of, 51, 85–87
Diamond Head, 98
Dickens, Charles, 67, 170
Dietz, 113
Dijon, France, 6
Diogenes, 38, 44
Donner Lake, 98
Doughface, 198
Dress, Christian, 211
Dress, Indian, 211
Drunk man in hotel, 144
Dynamite, 156, 184, 219

Edelweiss, 147
Egypt, 63–65
Egyptian mummy, 35, 89
Electric lights, 186, 190, 195
Elephants, Indian, 218–19
Elmira, New York, 201–02
English colonialism, 213–15, 219

Englishman, misdirected, 132–33
Esau, biblical, 82
Euclid, 44
European guides, 32

Ferguson, guide, 6, 13–14, 17, 35
Fishing, 92
Flag, American, 14
Fools, and St. Louis, 198–99
Forest fire, 93–94
Forest Park, St. Louis, 175
Foscari, Giacopo, 23
France, country of, 3–6
Frankfurt, 112
French barbers, 9–10
French language, 8
French pronunciations, 22–23
French Revolution, 12

Gaikwar of Baroda, 210
Ganges River, 216–18
Garden of Eden, 47, 100
Genesis, Book of, 174
Genoa, Italy, 33
German Conversation-Grammar, 125, 129
German hotelkeeper, 205–07
German language, 112, 114
Germany, scenery, 119–22
Ghosts, 199
Gibraltar, 10
Glacier Garden, 123
Glaciers, 154, 157
Gladiators, Roman, 31–32
Goatees, 172
Godfrey of Bouillon, 56, 60
Gold Dust, 170, 178–80
Golgotha, 58, 63
Gondolas, 21
Goodman, Joseph T., 68
Grand Hotel du Louvre, 11
Grandissimes, The, 188
Grandson of a near-great man, 158–61
Granita, 21
Grant, Ulysses S., 182
Griffin, George, 112
Grimes, 56

Guide books, 42; untrustworthy, 138
Guides, European, 13–14, 17, 32–36
Gulliver's Travels, 77, 162

Hacks, 7–8
Haemmerling, 113, 115
Hamburg, 112
Hannibal, Missouri, 195–99, 206–07
Harem, Indian, 219
Harris, Joe Chandler, 217
Harris, Mr., 113–14, 119, 135–41, 145–47,150, 154–
    55, 157, 161, 165
Hartford, Connecticut, 202
Harvard University, 126, 129
Hawaiian flowers, 99–100
Hawaiian fruits, 101
Hawaiian Islands, 98–109
Hawaiian people, physical appearance, 99–100
Hay, Rosina, 112
Heidelberg, Germany, 112, 117, 119
Heidelberg Castle, 113–14
Heilbronn, Germany, 113–14, 116–18
Helena, Saint, 54, 59–62
Hell, vision of, 106
Hercules, god, 42
Herodotus, 44
Herzegovina, 219
Hindu pilgrims, 216–18
Holiday's Hill, 195
Holsatia, 112, 125
Holy Sepulchre, Church of, 60–61
Holy Sepulchre, The, 53–54, 56–57, 62–63
Honaunau ruins, 101, 103–05
Honolulu, Hawaii, 99
Horatius Cocles, 29
Horses, mistreatment of, 50–52
Howells, William Dean, 169–70, 201
Human pride, 220
Humor, sense of, 203

Ice water, 135
Iliad, 37
Illinois, state of, 196
Immaculate Conception, 20, 28
Incognito, 171, 173, 199
India, admiration for, 201, 205

India, climate, 203
India, native peoples' dress, 204–05, 211, 213
"Innocents at Home," 67
Inquisition, 29–30
Insane woman, 198–99
Intoxicated man in hotel, 144
Irishman, characterized, 178
Israel, 106

Jackrabbits, 76
Jackson, Stonewall, 190–91
Jain prince, 213–15
Jardin Mabille, 14
Jerusalem, 52–53, 55–60
Jewelry, 8–9
Jews, cemeteries of, 187
Johannesburg Reformers, 220
John the Baptist, 21
Joseph of Aramathea, 54
Josephus, Flavius, 87
Journalism, New Orleans, 187
Judas Iscariot, 17
Jumna River, 216–17

Kaleidoscopes, 210
Kansas, state of, 72
Kau, Hawaii, 105
Kearney, Nebraska, 85
Kilauea, volcano, 105–09

Lagniappe, 192–93
Lahore, India, 218–19
Lake Providence, Louisiana, 180–81
Laocoon, The, 30
Last Supper, The, 17–20
Latin language, 146, 156
Lecture tour, 201
Lee, Robert E., 190–91
Leonardo da Vinci, 17–18
Levees, New Orleans, 185
Lightning, 107
Lightning-rod, 97
Lion of Lucerne, 123, 131
Loafers, 100, 172
London, Jack, 68
Lot, biblical, 61
Louisiana, Missouri, 195

Louis Napoleon, 6
Louvre, 8, 16, 159
Lucerne, Lake, 123
Lucerne, village of, 131
Lyons, France, 7

Madeira, 220
Madonna, 20
Magnolia trees, 183
Marryat, Frederick, 176
Mars Hill, Greece, 44, 46
Martineau, Harriet, 170
Mary Magdalen, 54, 61–63
Marysville, Kansas, 76
Massachusetts, state of, 107
Mathews, Charles James, 20
Matterhorn, The, 148, 162–63
Maximilian, Ferdinand, Joseph, 59
Melchizedek (Melchisedech), 60–61
Memory, 64
Memphis, Tennessee, 178
Messina, Italy, 37
Meteors, speed of, 220
Milan, Italy, 17–18, 20–21
Minerva, goddess, 42
Mississippi River, scenery of, 196
Missouri River, 69–70, 195
Monkeys, 207, 219–20
Mont Blanc, 164–67
Monte Rosa, 162
Moonlight, 39, 42–45, 209
Morgue of Paris, 13–14
Mosque of Omar, 52
Mosquitoes, 101, 181, 207
Mountain railway, 133, 135, 142–44
Mueller, 113
Mumford, Uncle, 180
Munich, 112
Murillo, Bartolome Esteban, 20
Murray, Charles Augustus, 175
Muslims, Indian, 218
Mutiny, Indian, 219

Names, Americans convert to French, 22–23
Napoleon, Louis, 6, 23
Narghili, 48–49
Natchez, Mississippi, 193

Native Americans, 69

Neckar River, 113, 115, 117–22

Nevada Territory, 67, 69, 87

New England seasons, 95

New Orleans, Louisiana, 185–93

New Orleans Picayune, 192

New York style, 172

Niagara Falls, 27

Nicodemus, 54

Nitroglycerin, 150, 161

Norman, 220

North Platte River, 85

Oakland, California, 96

Oceana, 203

Old masters, 24–26

Old traveler, 158–61

Old Travelers, 6–7

Oracle, The, 37

Osgood, James R., 169

Otto, Emil, 125, 129

Outrigger canoes, 101–02

Paintings, historical, 190–91

Paintings of martyrs, 24–26

Palestine, 59

Palma Giovanne, 24

Palmer House, Chicago, 173

Pantheon, 30–31

Paris, France, 8–17, 112

Paris Salon of 1879, 117

Parthenon, The, 38, 41–46

Paul, St., 44–45

Pele, goddess, 109

Pemberton, John Clifford, 182

Pesaro, Giovanni, 23

Peter, St., 30

Phidias, 43–44

Phocion, 44

Phoenix, John, 98

Pilate, Pontius, 59

Pilgrims, Hindu, 216–18

Piloting, river, 67, 170, 193

Pindar, 44

Piraeus, Greece, 38–39, 45–46

Pirate, New Orleans, 189

Pistol, 70–71, 76, 80

Plague, 23

Plato, 38, 44

Platte River, 85

Pompano, 189–90

Pond, James B., 202

Pontchartrain, Lake, 189

Porsena, Lars, 29

Praxiteles, 43–44

Prime, William C., 56, 61

Prince, Jain, 213–15

Pyramids, Egyptian, 104

Pythagoras, 44

Quaker City, 1–2, 36, 67; passengers' quarrels, 51

Quarry Farm, Elmira, 202

Racial complexions, 211–13

Rafts, 117–22

Railroads, 4–7; growth of, 170, 176–77, 195

Railway stations, 172

Raphael, 18

Rawal pindi, Pakistan, 219

Read, Thomas Buchanan, 176. *See also* "Come, Gentle Trembler"

Reign of Terror, 12

Remus, 29

Remus, Uncle, 217

Retreating, military, 195

Rhine River, 113

Rhone Glacier, 123

Richard I, the Lion-Hearted, 56

Riffelberg, 145, 164

Riffelberg expedition, 145–49, 151–57, 161–62

Riffelberg Hotel, 61, 162

Rigi-Kulm, 124, 126–27, 131–32, 137–38, 140

Ritchie, Mr., 193

River piloting, 67, 170

Rogers, Mr., 173

Rome, Italy, 191

Rome, Italy, 26–32, 35–36, 112, 191

Romulus, 29

Rosetta, 203

Rubens, Peter Paul, 16, 18

Russian Czar, 17

Sabbath, observance of, 50–51

Sacramento, California, 97–98

Saewulf, 60

Sagebrush, 77–79

Sahara Desert, 85

Saladin, 56

Salt Lake City, 85

Samson, biblical, 82, 176

Sandhurst, Lord, 204

Sandwich Islands, 21, 98–109

San Francisco Daily Alta California, 1

San Francisco, California, 69, 96, 99

Santa Maria dei Frari (church), 23–24

Saone, France, 7

Schiller, Johann Christoph Friedrich von, 128

Schloss Hotel, 118

Schumann, 113

Scorpions, 100–101

Scott, Sir Walter, 184

Scylla and Charybdis, 37

Sea, poem, 176. *See* Read, Thomas Buchanan

Sea voyages, love of, 201

Sens, France, 7

Servants, in India, 215–16

Shakespeare, William, 25

Sheba, Queen of, 213

Shell road, New Orleans, 189

Shiva (Siva), Hindu god, 207

Slavery, American, 206–07

Smoking, 4, 5, 11, 71, 75, 79, 84, 89, 91–92, 132

Socrates, 41, 44

Sodom and Gomorrah, 37, 82

Solomon, King, 56, 213

Solomon's Temple, 28

South African natives, 202

Southampton, England, 220

Southern Hotel, St. Louis, 173

Southern medievalism, 184

Southern speech, 191–92

Space travel, 220

Spaulding, Clara, 112

Spectacles, German, 122–23

Sphinx, The, 63–65, 73

Stagecoach drivers, status of, 80–82

Stage coaches, 4

Stagecoach station meals, 83–84

Stagecoach travel, 67–85

St. Bartholomew's Massacre, 12

St. Dimas, 59

Steamboating, decline of, 173, 175–77, 183, 185

Steamboat travel, 69–70, 121–22

St. Genevieve, Missouri, 179

St. Helena, 54, 59–62

St. James Hotel, New York, 173

St. Jerome, paintings of, 25

St. Joseph, Missouri, 70

St. Louis, Missouri, 69, 173–76,195, 198

St. Louis Hotel, New Orleans, 188

St. Mark, Great Square of, 21

St. Mark, paintings of, 25

St. Matthew, paintings of, 25

St. Paul, 44–45

St. Peter, Church of, 26–30

Stromboli, 36

St. Sebastian, paintings of, 25

Sunflower River, 183

Sunrises, on Mississippi River, 180

Surfing, 102–03

Swift, Jonathan, 77, 162

Swimming, 121

Syria, 50–60, 78

Tahoe, Lake, 87–94

Talkative tourist, 125–31

Tall tales, 181–82

Tamarinds, 101

Tam O'Shanter, 16

Tancred, 56

Tarantulas, 101

Tavernier, Jean Baptiste, 217

Telephone, 187

Telescope, 164–67

Tell, William, 129

Tent Life in the Holy Land, 61

Theseus, Temple of, 44

Thunderstorms, Alpine, 194

Thunderstorms, on Mississippi River, 194

Tintoretto (Jacopo Robusti), 24

Titian Vecelli, 23–25

Titles, Indian, 209

Tobacco-chewing, 172

Tomb of the Saviour, 61–62

Tourists, idiocy of, 22

Tower of Hippicus, 52

Travel, rigors of, 202
Trollope, Frances, 170
Troy, city of, 38
Tuileries, 12
Turkish bath, 47–50
Turkish coffee, 47, 49–50
Turner, Joseph Mallord William, 113
Twichell, Joseph, 112

Uncle Remus, 217

Vandals, American, 64–65, 128
Vatican museums, 35
Venice, Italy, 21–24, 26, 112
Verne, Jules, 202
Vesuvius, allusion to, 48
Vesuvius, Mount, 105
Vicksburg, Mississippi, 182–83
Vinci, Leonardo da, 17–18
Virgin Mary, 20, 25, 53–54, 61–63
Vishnu, Hindu god, 209–10
Vogel, 113

Waggis, 131–32, 138, 142
Ward, Artemus, 68
Warner, Charles Dudley, 111

Warren, Joseph, 62
Washington, George, 21
Washington Artillery Building, 190
Water, in St. Louis, 174
Whiskey, 178
Whymper, Edward, 145
Wimpfen, 115
Wind River Mountains, 4
Wines, 6, 8, 11
Wines, Rhine, 123
Woman passenger, talkative, 72–73
Women, work of, 120
Woodyards, river, 177

Xenophon, 44
Xerxes, 41–42

Yazoo River, 183
Yellow fever, 186
Yodeling, 134–35
Young American tourist, 125–31, 158–61
Yuma, Arizona, 98

Zermatt, Switzerland, 146–47, 149–50, 154
Zeuxis (painter), 44
Zulu, appearance of, 212